NEXT STOP

An Autistic Son Grows Up

GLEN FINLAND

BERKLEY BOOKS
New York

THE BERKLEY PUBLISHING GROUP
Published by the Penguin Group
Penguin Group (USA) Inc.
375 Hudson Street, New York, New York 10014, USA

USA / Canada / UK / Ireland / Australia / New Zealand / India / South Africa / China

Penguin Books Ltd., Registered Offices: 80 Strand, London WC2R 0RL, England
For more information about the Penguin Group, visit penguin.com.

Berkley trade paperback ISBN: 978-0-425-26103-3

The Library of Congress has catalogued the Amy Einhorn books hardcover edition as follows:

Finland, Glen.
Next stop: a son with autism grows up / Glen Finland.
p. cm.
ISBN: 978-0-399-15860-5
1. Finland, Glen.   2. Parents of autistic children—United States—biography.
3. Autistic children—Family relationships.   4. Mothers and sons.   I. Title.
RJ506.A9 F56 2012
618.92—858820092

PUBLISHING HISTORY
Amy Einhorn Books / G. P. Putnam's Sons hardcover edition / March 2012
Berkley trade paperback edition / April 2013

PRINTED IN THE UNITED STATES OF AMERICA

10 9 8 7 6 5 4 3 2 1

Text design by Meighan Cavanaugh.

Penguin is committed to publishing works of quality and integrity.
In that spirit, we are proud to offer this book to our readers;
however, the story, the experiences, and the words
are the author's alone.

ALWAYS LEARNING   PEARSON

To Bruce, for reminding me to laugh

YOU ARE HERE

One of the best things in life is to have someone tell you a story.

Stories matter because they bring human faces out of the shadows. Faces that belong to the quiet ones among us like my son, David, a grown man who is tall, dark, and autistic. Although David is quite normal in appearance—handsome, even—a profound unknowability surrounds him. In another era someone like him might have been hidden away from society, an unheard spirit, his story left untold. Now, I am only a mother with memories that are steadily gathering dust. But I can tell you stories.

First, it's important to know that a story about autism isn't a story about a single child. It is a story about an entire family. Looking back over the last quarter century spent raising our three sons, I realize that my husband and I stumbled along in the dark, looking for answers, isolated by the sheer mystery of what autism is and what it can do to a family. So this is not a story about what we think we know but rather what we don't know. It is a story about a little boy who identifies wild birds high in the trees by their songs, a walled-off adolescent whose ancient grandmother teaches him to drive her car, and a reclusive teenager who runs at night through rain and snow in search of something only he can see. These are snapshots in time, grounded in a mother's perpetually tested hope. But what will happen when this boy becomes a man?

When I began this book, I thought it would be about letting go of David as he matured into an adult. But, hardwired to protect him, I had missed the deeper story. That one is about accepting parts of a young man I will never fully understand, then stepping out of his way to let him make his own choices. When the son who has never said "I love you, Mom" calls me to say he's spotted a red-winged blackbird swooping over the Potomac, and that a flood of water is roaring over the river rocks, his calling means, simply, he knows he is loved. It's an even exchange.

And yet this is still not the story I sat down to write. Watching a child with the deck stacked against him become a man has made me into an accidental noticer. This opened a door for many strangers to creep into these pages. They are easy to miss sitting alone in the theater, hovering uncertainly at the bottom of an escalator, or spotting birds along the edge of the river. Here among others are the legless woman, the upbeat busboy, and the naked man in his combat boots. Though their faces remain in the shadows, they have always been present among us, just unaccounted for.

Using both heart and mind to describe the evidence, I have dug hard to find the truth about life with David. Quite often it isn't pretty, but it is what is remembered. Still, I do not fear harsh judgment from the members of my unique tribe, the hundreds of thousands of families with autistic sons and daughters—the first generation to have come of age in the Age of Autism—who know not to expect a fairy-tale ending.

While mawkish TV shows and movies focus on beautiful, hazy-eyed toddlers and quirky adolescents who fit in somewhere along the spectrum, our very real autistic sons and daughters have grown into flesh-and-blood adults with matter-of-fact needs to be met in the communities they live in. We families get that instead of seeing autistic adults as targets for therapy, we must commit to a society in which they have equal access to jobs and the skills to succeed with the support and legal rights they deserve. But we also get that expecting empathy for those who *lack* it is a tough sell.

And this is why families must bear witness to their sons' and daughters' potential. Although there is still no known cause or cure for what huddles under the broad umbrella of autism, I believe other healing agents will come out of the telling of our stories. After all, we families live the reality that the researchers are digging ever deeper to comprehend. While we may not understand it, we get it.

So, let's tell our stories—and laugh, and cry, and bang our heads on the table if we must—but let's tell them true.

Here, then, coming to you from the edge of the Potomac River, is the story of one of the quiet ones and the family that loves him.

You know, everybody's ignorant, just on different subjects.

—WILL ROGERS

NEXT STOP

DOORS OPENING

We had spent the tail end of that summer riding the Metro—my son David and I—not so much going anywhere, just riding from stop to stop. Counting the look-alike stations between Clarendon and Metro Center, hugging the right side of the escalator to switch to the Red Line, then coming up for air in the river of humanity that is midday Chinatown in Washington, D.C.

So it goes, when your handsome twenty-one-year-old is a rangy six-footer with a sexy five o'clock shadow and the mind of a good-natured adolescent. Pervasive developmental delays cause their own set of problems, and David's is a kind of exuberance that reveals itself by his swinging an imaginary baseball bat whenever he's really happy. Feet squared, wrists piled up high on his right shoulder, and *swoosh!* The impulse reflects an open innocence that's way too friendly when it comes to strangers. At Eighth and F, NW, when a homeless man asks him for change, David pulls out his wallet and says, "Okay, how much?"

But if he could learn to ride the Metro, my husband and I believed, then he could travel to a job site; and when he locked down that job, he could pay his rent. With a job and an apartment, he would have a real life. And who knows? Maybe even find somebody other than his dad and me to love him well into the future. It was a goal we could all agree on. David swung his imaginary bat whenever we talked about it.

So at the end of the summer David and I got cozy with all the different Metro routes. We visited the zoo and met the guy who scrubs the elephants' backs. We surfaced in Chinatown, where David walked around with a starry-eyed look on his face because of "the pretty Korean girls." One morning, we hopped off at the Smithsonian for him to run to the Lincoln Memorial while I waited on a bench in a light downpour. David had a passion for running. Ever since he was a child, he could run like a deer, and in high school he had run cross-country. At the Arlington National Cemetery station, we followed the path to Section 60, where we sat beside a nineteen-year-old marine's grave and talked about the war in Iraq. David would like to be a soldier, and he wasn't interested in my political musings. Instead he wondered if the soldiers had lived a good life before they died. Another day, we raced up the escalators toward the wrong train and ended up in Shady Grove, then doubled back and rode home the long way. We didn't have anywhere we had to be that afternoon. No worries.

It stayed that way until the August evening when David

told me he was ready to go it alone. We both knew this was coming; it was, in fact, exactly what we'd been working toward. I just hadn't realized he'd be ready sooner than I was.

David, my third son, was born in 1987. He was a failure-to-thrive baby who spit up half his birth weight during his first months before doctors diagnosed reflux and mild cerebral palsy. He did not walk until he was three and a half. At age five, a neurologist concluded his developmental delays were attributable to a combination of autism and static encephalopathy, a brain pause that impairs intelligence, like a circuit misfire in the brain. Imagine driving through the mountains, hitting static on the radio, and suddenly losing the music. Sometimes David loses the music.

But by the time he turned seven, every doctor we saw offered us a different diagnosis. A specialist tagged on a mean mix of ADHD, obsessive-compulsive disorder, and Tourette's syndrome, a neurological disorder of involuntary and repetitive motor and vocal tics. The tics include eye blinking, head or shoulder jerking, facial grimacing, and, in David's case, snorting sounds often combined with an upper body twist, a hop, and a punch to his own mouth. Just watching this child sleep could wear me out.

By age fifteen, David had grown tall, with high cheekbones, and so thin I could count every notch along his spine. His twisting body kept him busy corralling the tics that jerked him around and sometimes burst out of his throat without warning. Once, during a National Theatre matinee of *Cats*, his tics nearly got us tossed out of our third-row seats. The usher said David was distracting the cats.

Even with the difficulty in conveying his thoughts, David made it clear he wanted to be included in the mainstream activities at his public high school—and not just the special education program. But teenagers have their own hierarchy, and even the most accepting ones play by their peers' social rules. The mascot syndrome revealed itself in well-intentioned pats and theatrical hugs from passing acquaintances in the halls, but the phone never rang for him at home. In 2005, he would turn eighteen. There had never been any hope of college or SAT tests. What would happen after high school?

The school psychologist recommended a relatively new approach: an expensive two-year basic skills program. The downside was its far-away location in Fort Lauderdale, Florida. However, it had a residential component geared toward independent living and targeting task completion, money management, and social skills for developmentally disabled young adults. So, after two decades of navigating our county's murky special education system and investigating expensive drug therapy and psychiatric care, in 2006 my husband, Bruce, and I enrolled David in the program, adjacent to a sprawling community college campus in south Florida.

David was all for it. "This is my college—right, Mom?" he asked.

It was as close as it would ever get. David has always operated under a different reality, his functioning compromised by both his cognitive limitations and his fine motor weaknesses. Standing in line with me at our neighborhood grocery store where he had worked for a brief time as a courtesy clerk, he jerked his head like a pogo stick and proudly told the cashier that he was going off to college in Florida. This was the same woman who had him fired for staring off into the distance and not taking care of a cleanup in the aisles. "Really," she said, rolling her eyes. Then she handed me my change.

In the morning Bruce comes into the kitchen, sniffing and circling me like an old dog. He picks me up and, hip joints protesting, I wrap my legs around his waist. "Kiss me like you mean it," he says, and I peck him on his neck, his jaw, then land a wet one on his mouth. At that moment, an unshaven and blurry-eyed David pads in wearing a T-shirt, shorts, and one sock; he opens the fridge and stares in. Bruce drops me onto my feet. "Oh-kaay, then," he says in a tight voice. "Coffee?"

What kind of middle-aged parents don't look forward to the time their adult children are able to live on their own? With David's two older brothers, Max and Eric, grown and out of the house, the prospect of becoming real empty nesters gleamed in the near future for Bruce and me. Still, I struggled with David's risky move into an apartment a thousand miles from home. After decades of being my intellectually disabled son's advocate, how could I just shut off my dependency on his dependency on me?

That was not how my husband saw it. "I just want some time alone together," he said, his eyes lighting up, "before we get old and floppy."

So Bruce began what was to be a summer of early prepara-
tion. He doled out instructions to David on how to open
canned goods, boil water for pasta, shave himself, cut his toenails, do his laundry, and send an e-mail. It was hard work for
David, but for Bruce, who is not known for his patience, it
was excruciating. If David got bored, he would just walk away
from the boiling water. If he got frustrated, he would drop the
razor mid-shave, leaving a ring of white cream around his
jaw, and go chase the cat.

"Like pushing wet cotton," Bruce said, but he kept David at
it. Still, sometimes Bruce's rat-a-tat style and multistep directions would backfire. Like the lesson on sandwich making.

"With this skill, David, pretty soon, you can get a job making sandwiches in a deli. But," Bruce would warn, "you have to
wash your hands first." Smiling now. Upbeat. Then, "No. Not
like that. You have to use soap. No. You have to get in there and
really scrub. No. Not like that. Come on, David, really scrub!"

Pushing this boy beyond his limits resulted in crumbs
everywhere, a huge glob of mayonnaise on the top of David's
shoe, no trace of a sandwich, and Bruce shouting, "Finish the
job! You wanna live here with Mom and me forever?" Which
was my cue to walk in and growl, "Leave him alone! You're
giving him too many directions at once!" And while Bruce
and I faced off, David opened and closed his fists, as if he
could shut us both up with the fragile strength of his hands.
Then he drifted off into another room to play with the cat.
Lesson over.

Still, when August came around and it was time for David
to make the move to Florida, Bruce pronounced David ready.

Ready for the chance to succeed or fail on his own. "He wants out," Bruce assured me. "He wants his own place, his own life. Let him go. What could happen?"

Tugging a U-Haul trailer on the long drive from northern Virginia, we crossed into Florida. On a road trip, you can't ask for a better traveling companion than David—if being on the lookout for police cars is your thing. "Look quick, Mom—Homeland Security vehicle," "K-9 officer coming up from behind," and "Duval County Sheriff's car!" David has always liked cops because he believes they're the good guys, and he loves cars because they're fast.

Well, honey, welcome to Florida. South Florida drivers take off from red lights like they're shot out of a cannon, catching pedestrians halfway across the intersection, then saluting them with the finger for making them wait.

This is where we had chosen to leave our son.

At the orientation, I looked around the room at an exhausted group of parents and recognized in all of us the effects of decades of steady advocacy: the fatigue, the frustration, and the anxiety attached to avoiding a missed step for your special needs adult child. None of the couples seemed to be touching; in fact, we looked like a room full of shock victims. There would be no trophies here for our kids, no cheery crossing of the finish line accompanied by a Best Buddy and a flashbulb. Instead, the director insisted *now* was the time to take off the training wheels: "Let the kids feel empowered by their new living situation. Allow them to make mistakes—because they will—and then let them become the problem solver."

David and about one hundred students would now be scattered throughout a large public apartment complex, where they would microwave their own meals and be expected to make it to their vocational training classes on time every day. Adult resident advisers lived within the complex, but this was not a 24/7 managed system. There would be no bed checks here. We bought David his first cell phone and, for weeks prior to the move, the three of us recited those digits—along with his Social Security number—out loud throughout the day.

David's first e-mail home read: *hey i was just wondering how i can get hot water for my oatmeal if i eat it. Because the sink water dosent work.*

"At least he figured out the Internet," Bruce said.

He rarely called home, so we made a deal that we would phone him every other night around dinnertime, just to check in. Those calls never lasted longer than a minute: he was "fine," his classes were "fine," the nice roommate he had failed to bond with was "fine," and all David ever asked was, "How's the cat?" Our real info came from calls we initiated to the program's counselors and therapists. It seemed he had found his way to his classes, but he was living off boxed cereal. The vocational counselor set him up with an unpaid afternoon job in the deli section of the grocery store near his apartment. That guaranteed him at least one hoagie sandwich a day.

During weekends at the independent living program, the

students were left mostly on their own. Drawing on a happy childhood memory of a kind Pentagon Police officer who gave him a few rides in his cruiser, David had gotten into a routine of dropping by the nearby Broward County police station to take cell phone photos of the parked squad cars. It wasn't too long before he was escorted off the property for peering too closely. So he returned to his apartment, got on the Internet, and discovered websites of police cars for virtually every city in Florida. He'd print out the photos on Monday mornings at his school and bring them back to his bedroom to stick on his wall. When Halloween rolled around, he decided to dress up as a cop. He walked seven blocks to a uniform warehouse and bought himself a black POLICE T-shirt and a riot helmet with a face mask. When the big night came he set out to patrol his apartment complex grounds, cautioning the trick-or-treaters to "Be careful!" and to "Watch out for cars!" The sight of a tall, thin fellow in blue jeans and a riot helmet apparently spooked several parents. Soon enough, management was called in to usher David back inside his apartment with a no-nonsense warning about impersonating an officer.

With David in Florida, Bruce and I were suddenly liberated. Gone was David's habit of unclasping our fingers to separate us anytime he saw us holding hands in public. Absent that tension, a simple, quiet rhythm crept back into our relationship. It felt solid, familiar, and promising. Coming home from our jobs to an orderly house, dinner became a beautiful event for us. Bruce, the better cook, revived his favorite recipes, stopping nightly at the market to shop for fresh produce. I'd hop up on the cool granite counter, sip a glass of wine, and toss the salad while we talked about our day. Sometimes, after dinner, we would dance. It began in the kitchen and, even on cold nights in coats and gloves, we'd open the doors and slow-dance ourselves outside under the trees.

For the first time in twenty-five years, we didn't have to manage someone else's life hour by hour. Somehow, my husband's clear-eyed approach had unchained me from the tyranny of being the good parent. I did not feel guilty, but the new freedom struck me as flirting with danger, like driving down a dark country road with the headlights off. Two days in a row might pass between phone calls from David. Maybe this was the most we could expect from the commitment we'd made to his new life. For the first time in two decades we had time to kill.

On a lazy Saturday in April, one that looked like a hard rain coming, Bruce and I picked our favorite things to do together. We spent the morning wandering around Eastern Market, a sprawling open-air marketplace in our old Capitol Hill neighborhood. The air there is scented with patchouli, fresh flowers, and cut-to-taste cucumbers. Inside the market's red-brick center, barbecued chickens turn on a spit and Jack, a dairyman in a white jacket, tempts customers with slivers of cheddar from a three-foot-wide cheese wheel. We bought bosomy green peppers and a clump of fresh basil. We haggled over a quirky painting of the market with Fred, a tattooed artist. Fred's painting captured the feel of the place with its eclectic mix of people, flowers, and food. It would be perfect for my kitchen and I ended up taking it home.

We left the market and followed the Georgetown trolley tracks toward the Book Hill library. We climbed a hundred steps to the flower garden and sat under my umbrella in the misty drizzle. Suddenly the skies opened up, drilling us with fat bullets of rain. We raced around to the front of the 180-year-old library and entered through heavy wooden doors.

The library smelled the way libraries used to smell, some perfect mixture of tree pulp and cool anticipation. We found the fiction section and played an old game: Walk down any aisle, grab an armful of books, and meet at the window seat. There we opened to page one of each book and, taking turns, read the first few sentences out loud. That was the game: Rate the book by its opening lines—hook or no hook? Today's hands-down favorite was N. Scott Momaday's *The Way to Rainy Mountain*: "A single knoll rises out of the plain in Oklahoma, north and west of the Wichita Range. . . . The hardest weather in the world is there."

I looked out the window across the damp lawn and saw the rain had slowed. Our day's hardest weather had passed and it was time to move on.

Monday, as I was hanging up the marketplace painting in my kitchen, I heard the news. Over the weekend, closed for business and without a single witness, both the marketplace and—on the opposite side of town—the library had caught fire and burned. Electrical fires had resulted from ancient wiring, and no one was to blame in either case. Charred books soaked to the spine were now strewn across Book Hill's trampled garden. There was nothing left of Jack the dairy-man's cheese wheel at Eastern Market. It was good to have the tattooed artist's painting to hold in my hands.

Now I looked around my kitchen at the family photographs I'd selected over the years for hanging—some good memories, some bad. Over there, my three little boys stand at attention in sailor caps. Beside that, in a Popsicle frame, David, the young-est, sleeps sprawled out on the kitchen floor, his head on the belly of a good dog. In another, my middle boy, Eric, grins, graduation cap askew, a cigar stuck in his teeth. And in the corner, looking into the lens with the cold and condemning eyes of an inaccessible young man, my firstborn, Max, shovels snow from our stoop.

Those three young faces have changed and scattered in new directions, the years having vanished behind them, with Max working his way through law school now and Eric study-ing music in Boston. It was fine to have their earlier like-nesses there to hold on to that morning and to remember all of it without keeping score, because the hardest weather has passed, and it was time to move on.

The phone call came in to our home on a late spring after-noon, just before nightfall. It was nine months into David's program stay. I hopped off the treadmill and leaned against the basement wall, the one I'd helped the boys' paint with their signature red, black, and purple handprints in 1995. I remember joking that we'd always have their fingerprints handy if they didn't show up for dinner some night.

"Mom." David sounded excited. "Guess where I am?"

"Don't know, sweetie. Where?"

"The Everglades."

My throat closed up tight as David explained that a man named "Nelson from the Internet" was driving him into the Everglades. They'd met up at the drugstore.

"Put Nelson on the phone, David."

There was some background rumbling before David came back on the line. "He says he doesn't speak English."

"David. Get out of the car. Now."

"I'm on the highway, Mom."

"Nelson!" I roared through the phone to this stranger a thousand miles away. "Bring my son back this minute. I'm calling the police now!"

"Okay, okay, okay," said the voice in the background.

I kept David on the line: "What does the big green road sign say now? What color is Nelson's car?"

I took notes while Bruce called in details to the Broward County police. There was an employee named Nelson at the drugstore near David's apartment and the police ran a security check on him. Nothing turned up. No laws had been broken and, after all, David was legally an adult. The police told us there was nothing to do but wait. Forty-five agonizing minutes later—keeping David on the line—I heard a car door open and close—"Good-bye"—and a single set of footsteps slapping up the stairs. I counted them. A key turned in a door and David spoke into the phone, "I'm home, Mom."

To him, it was just another adventure. For us, it was more missing pieces to the forever puzzling life of our son.

———

Much of Florida utterly delighted David. Eight-inch Jesus liz-
ards with a predilection for running on water scampered
about on their hind legs, arms open wide. Green parrots whistled at him from the tops of palm trees. David has always loved
birds, and those crazy parrots really cracked him up. The
months passed quickly, but the highlight of his two years in
Florida came toward the end after he scored a volunteer job at
the Abandoned Pet Rescue shelter in a run-down strip mall off
Ninth Avenue. There, a loudmouthed "guard parrot" named
Bueno screeched at visitors like a club bouncer. Six-toed kittens leapt onto aluminum bookshelves stacked with cat food
and kitty litter. Feral felines the size of bobcats slept in open
desk drawers. Thirty to forty caged dogs barked in wild des-
peration whenever David opened the doors to clean their
quarters. His job was feeder and scoop-up man and, along
with his grooming chores, he loved the work. He stayed
focused and finished the jobs he was given, gently brushing
the cats in his free time. He did so well, one day he called
home with big news.

"The shelter lady offered me a job. She wants to pay me,
Mom."

The school confirmed it and our hopes skyrocketed. I
called his big brothers and squealed, "David has a job!" For
two weeks we dreamed of him on his own: a steady income,
the bus route he'd need to master, the prospect of his own set
of friends, how often we'd get down there to visit . . . Bruce
called the county vocational training counselor to nail down

the salary schedule so that we could begin to make a budget plan, but received only vague promises of a callback. When the call finally came, it was dispiriting:

"Somebody jumped the gun here," said the counselor. "The shelter would hire David *if* they had the extra money. But there is no extra money. And there is no job."

And so, after two years of living on his own and with no prospects for another job, the adventure had come to an end. And now David was headed home to start over.

It took a few weeks for us all to get used to each other, but David was back home, and the cat was sleeping in the bend of his knee again. The first thing we did was to put his name on the county's group housing list for people with intellectual disabilities, gamely landing at the end of the line with a three-year waiting period.

David was twenty-one now, had grown another inch taller, and needed to be reminded to shave every day. However, I sensed a welcome new level of curiosity in him about his future. Lately, instead of surfing the Internet for photos of police cars, he'd been searching for job openings at local animal shelters.

He and I spent his first few weeks home reversing the avalanche of paperwork that involves updating Supplemental Security Income (SSI), Medicaid, and the Department of Rehabilitation information whenever a recipient changes his address.

We stood on line again at the crowded SSI office to push

his benefits as high as legally possible. During the long wait, I couldn't help but notice the silent young woman in a wheelchair in front of us. Her legs were cut off at the knees, and her face was disfigured. What stuck out in my mind was that she appeared to be all alone.

Four hours and a lost day's work later, our mound of paperwork was completed. Stepping out of the SSI office into the sunshine, David let loose a day's worth of pent-up tics by setting his feet shoulder width apart and swinging his imaginary baseball bat over and over again. Just happy to be out in the fresh air and free to tic away, free of all the social workers talking over his head to his mother about what "he" planned to do with the rest of his life.

On the ride home, the haunting image of the legless woman returned to me. I looked over at David and said, "Dave, do you realize what a lucky guy you are to have someone love you enough to go through what we just did today?"

"Yeah," he said, pausing a beat in his traffic watching. "Who?"

With David's paperwork tackled, it was time to continue the Metro lessons. The hope was still that someday the subway would transport him to a job, an apartment, and even a social life all his own. Of course, David had ridden the Metro since childhood, staring out the window into the darkness on city trips to the zoo, my fingers circling his bony wrist like a handcuff. Things were different now: starting over as an adult, it was all about the journey, but not in the bromidic

Hallmark sense. We were actively going nowhere, working out how to get there and back via the city's underground tunnels. On a good day, if all went as planned, we'd stay down here in this cave studying the routes, calculating the fares. We'd never come up for fresh air, never see daylight, never hear a car honk; we just hoped to make the loop out and back again without a glitch, imprinting the pattern in David's memory. The first time on our mission, I told David, "Watch carefully." I bought the farecards and helped him feed them into the turnstile slot, cupping his fingers as he bent the ticket every which way. I traced our route on the wall map, and he followed me down onto the train's platform. There we stood with our toes on the yellow line and peered over the edge at the tracks. We pressed to the side while riders got off, then he followed me onto the train. Once inside, he sat staring out the window in a daze, just as he'd done when he was five. We were moving along at a good pace, but something was wrong: David looked like a puppet set aside between shows, dull and lifeless. It dawned on me that this wasn't liberating for him, and it wasn't educational; this was following. David needed to be the one holding the strings.

The next morning found us back on the train, studying the maps of the city. Maps are everywhere you look inside the Metro, and David loves maps. Especially ones that tell him: *You Are Here.*

It's actually quite hard to get lost on the Metro, but somehow I had done it again. I didn't realize it until we climbed out of the underground to surface in the morning bustle and stir of Judiciary Square.

"I thought you'd like to see what's aboveground here, David." As I spoke, he stared at my mouth, not my eyes, most likely missing the facial cues that might alert him to the snow job I was giving him. But with David, nothing is ever exactly what it seems.

"You got us lost again, didn't you, Mom."

We turned around and headed back down into the station. At the fare gate, David inserted his Metro card and passed easily through the turnstile. I stuck my card in, too, but it spit right out with a little digital alert that said *Add fare*.

David and I were now separated by the turnstile in the pushiness of rush hour.

"Dave, stay right where you are," I said. "I've got to put more money on my farecard. Back in a sec."

The line at the farecard machine stood six deep. I fumbled around in my bag for my wallet. A dollar bill and four quarters. Yeah, that should do it. I looked back over my shoulder to gesture to David to be patient—and he was gone. Vanished. I raced over to the turnstile and pushed against it, straining to pick him out of the crowd.

The stationmaster appeared at my side. "Ma'am, you can't get in without a farecard."

"But my kid's gone ahead of me. You gotta let me in."

"How old is he?" asked the guard, a middle-aged black guy with bushy gray eyebrows.

"Twenty-one, but . . ."

His concern transformed into a scoff. "Ma'am," he said, hiking up his pants, "you can't get in without a farecard."

"My boy doesn't know where he's going. I've got to get to him."

The stationmaster shook his head.

"Sir. My son is autistic."

The man looked at me with a blank expression.

"He's, he's . . ." *Ah, damn.* How do you explain the cognitive buckshot of autism in the time it takes a child to disappear? With each second stealing David further away, I had no choice. I resorted to the shortcut word that everybody knows. It was the wrong word, a throwaway word, but it meant something and was the only word that could get me what I needed right now. And that was David. With my conscience shrieking, *Wrong! Wrong! Wrong!* I looked into the stationmaster's eyes and said, "My son is retarded. You have to let me go find him."

"Tell me his name," said the guard. "I'll make an announcement over the PA system."

"See, that's just it. He'd never pay attention to a stranger's voice—only *my* voice. *Please . . .*"

The guard took my elbow and led me to his kiosk. He reached through a window, pressed a button, and withdrew a microphone. "Make it short," he said, holding the mic up to my face. "Tell him to return to the fare gate."

I leaned toward the mic and an enormous voice I didn't recognize jumped out of my throat. "David, it's Mom," I said. "Come back to the fare gate."

The words quivered and, still holding the mic to my mouth, the stationmaster said, "One more time."

"Come back, David. Come back to where you started."

This time the words flew over the crowded train platforms and ricocheted off the steel rails. Disregarded by most commuters, they were plain enough to grab one young man's attention, wherever he'd gotten to.

And then he was there. Undamaged and unconcerned. "Hey, Mom" was all he had to say. There was nothing for me to do but to shake it off and get back on the train.

The stationmaster approached us and handed me something: a pocket map of the Metro system. "Just in case your mother gets lost again," he said to David. Then he keyed open the fare gate and, with the gentlest shoulder pat, eased me through.

DON'T ASK, DON'T TELL

First the note of impatience in the father's voice as he cautions his son to slow the grocery cart down in the dog food aisle. The maybe-seven-year-old looks just like his dad in a T-shirt and shorts, but he moves with an awkward, unfocused gait.

"Nolan!" the dad shouts. "Stop right there and look at me. Look at Dad. Nolan!" Too late—*bang!* Staring down at his flip-flops, Nolan has bumped his empty cart into mine. No damage done, but I pick up on the faraway look in the child's eyes and the sound of fatigue in his dad's pleading, "Nolan! Look at Dad, Nolan!"

"No worries," I say to the father, winking at Nolan and giving them both a big, goofy smile. Nolan doesn't smile back at me, but I can see he's paying attention now, and as I push on down the aisle I recognize that look on Nolan's face and I sense the helplessness in the father's voice.

I remember other trips to the grocery store that went awry. I remember the condescending looks from others when I would repeat myself endlessly to get my David to move away from wherever he had gotten himself stuck. And I remember the raised eyebrows that insinuated I tiptoed around a kid I had lost control of. What they couldn't have known was that we parents have learned to adjust because we understand that our kids cannot. So right now I want to tell Nolan's dad that it's okay for his boy to tap his cart into mine because I could see Nolan had been enjoying watching his flip-flops slide across the cool, clean floor. I want to tell Nolan's dad that he's doing a good job today, taking his son on an errand, just the two of them, maybe giving Mom a rare break. But I say nothing.

Even though my autism radar has kicked in full force, being David's mother has taught me this: with the spectrum diverging so widely, when you've met one autistic kid, well, you've met *one* autistic kid. It would have been completely presumptuous of me, a stranger, to make a quick and tidy diagnosis of Nolan's abilities, because each person with autism is genetically unique, with his or her own version of the developmental disorder.

So it's eyes down now. Maybe a lifted slant to the corners of my mouth at the most. And I don't dare tell Nolan's dad that "I've got a grown-up Nolan at home and, believe me, you're doing a good job, Dad." Instead I bite my tongue and zip around the corner to the lightbulb display.

Still, I wanted so badly to pat the guy on the back, offer a little solidarity on the silent battlefront, and encourage him to hope his hard work will pay off down the road. But I do not cross that privacy line. And this is how autism works to isolate us further as parents: it creates its own sort of secret society for the families who are in it for life, in constant search of any place where the right to be a different sort of human is honored.

Meanwhile, back in the lightbulb section, I find the familiar in an unexpected place once again. Here comes Nolan, bearing down on me with his grocery cart, only this time he's staring at me with a big smile on his face. *Bang!* And there is one less lightbulb in the world. His stressed-out dad follows close behind him with his palms turned up. Then he recognizes me as the dog-food-aisle lady and we both laugh.

"Look out, Dad," I let myself tell him, remembering all of it like it was yesterday. "The fun is just beginning—"

1987

"What a good baby," strangers in line at the grocery store would often comment. They did not know my third son was a silent child. He had never shown interest in the mobile above his crib. There had been no peekaboo playfulness, and he did not respond to a smiling face. He rarely cried. There seemed to be so little of life in him.

With his translucent skull and a tiny little heart that beat against his rib cage in rhythmic lifts, he was as fragile as a baby bird. I thought I knew a lot about baby boys from raising his two older brothers, but this child had me stumped. Our first hint of trouble came at four months after a bout of pneumonia when a pediatric specialist detected a mild form of cerebral palsy in David's floppy body.

"Early intervention treatment is key, and there is reason to be hopeful," the specialist told us, casually cradling her own fisted right hand in her lap. The doctor's nonchalant attitude about her own disability encouraged me to trust her when she warned us that sudden noises or coarse fabrics might disturb our son. I remember thinking, *She gets it.*

Soon, peculiar words like "apraxia," "tactile defensiveness," and "limited spatial awareness" crept into our kitchen table conversations, and at nine months old David began biweekly sensory integration sessions at the local cerebral palsy center. There, a therapist took my droopy little boy out of my arms and plopped him into a mesh swing that hung from the ceiling. I was reluctant to let him go. "Step back," she assured me, "he'll be all right on his own." Then she wound the swing up tight and released it, free-spinning him inside. As his world spun by I watched his eyes open with a first ever hint of interest. "See?" she insisted. "He likes it. Let him go."

Next up, the balance beam. In a bright yellow room, mothers of all ages, races, and socioeconomic classes sat in a circle where we balanced our soft babies on cylindrical leather bolsters. The goal was for the baby to lift his head up with his own strength. I could look around the room and see one- or two-year-old children much more severely disabled than my own son, some who would never speak or walk alone—but the ones I worried the most about were the silent babies who were handled roughly or spoken to harshly by their exhausted, confused young mothers. That was where I first learned the unwritten rule so many of us mothers of special needs children adhere to: Don't ask, don't tell. In this room few of us spoke to anyone other than the therapist, because the feeling was unmistakable: *Uh-uh, sister. I've got all I can handle right here; don't ask me to share your burden.* This struck me as wildly unsympathetic, because helping each other is something women in a community have always done: we bond by telling our secrets, sharing our stories, then showing each other a little compassion.

But not here. Perhaps it was all for the better, because for many of us the sessions came to an abrupt halt once our medical insurers refused to cover them. In the late eighties, cognitive behavioral therapy to reduce anxiety in autistic children was still considered experimental. Many pediatricians endorsed it for children like David who were diagnosed on the autism spectrum with the mouthful known as pervasive developmental disorders not otherwise specified (PDD-NOS). Not knowing much about autism, I focused on the word "developmental," figuring it would be something David would grow out of. Like colic.

When the cutoff notice from our insurance company arrived, I kept David at home and let his two older brothers play airplane with him for free. One at a time his brothers Max and Eric raced between the kitchen and the living room holding their baby brother over their heads, breathlessly eager for a giggle or wide eyes.

"How come he just sits there?" asked six-year-old Max, panting from all the zooming around the house. David's lack of happy baby traits had stumped us all.

NOW, WHERE DID THAT COME FROM?

The term "mad as a hatter" is believed to have originated in seventeenth-century England to shed light on the neurological damage suffered by craftsmen who used quicksilver—mercury—to cure felt hats. First, a slight tremor would develop in their hands, quickly spreading to the eyelids, lips, and tongue. Gradually, victims suffered uncontrollable muscular tremors and twitching limbs known as "hatter's shakes." The shakes brought with them a high level of irritability, insomnia, and extreme shyness, perhaps because the victim's disordered movements caused people to stare at them.

Four hundred years later, mercury came under suspicion again for its use as a preservative in children's vaccines. A large public outcry erupted from many parents convinced of a mercury tie-in to the wide-ranging neurological disorders associated with autism, including Tourette's "twitching limbs," speech delays, and attention deficit disorder. For the record, David and his brothers were part of the millions of children who received their MMR and DPT vaccinations in the 1980s, a decade before the FDA investigation began. Yet studies have concluded that mercury is not the culprit and the vaccines are safe for children.

It seems to me that current research has revealed more about what we *don't* know about autism than what we do. Now many specialists are looking backward, stirring up a family's collective memory for clues to its behavioral past. But a genetic trail, where family secrets zigzag into the past and squirm out of the tight places, is only the beginning of that journey.

1941

My husband's father grew up using his hands to get by. Not woodworking like his Russian immigrant father before him, but street fighting to stay aboveground in the turbulence of the Chelsea ghetto just outside of Boston. Strong and sturdy, with a misbehaving cowlick in his black hair, Morris David was rough-edged but sharp, soaking in his education between rumbles. Early on in his career he discovered the one real skill he owned: he could sell anything. Scratching to make a living, the first thing he sold was a set of hot tires out of the trunk of a stolen car.

In December of '41, America was at war and the Army Air

Corps suited Morris David because he knew his way around engines. He met his bride at a USO dance; Dorothy married him fast before he shipped out, and she began a lifetime of waiting for him to come back. After the war the young couple settled in a seaside village of modest saltbox homes. Morris David began traveling up and down the New England coastline in his yellow Cadillac, hawking a trendy new product that promised a cheap way to make old houses look fresh: aluminum siding. Within a span of five years, the kid from Chelsea was making real money. But he found himself with a bit of a problem: an unconventional wife who hadn't made it through high school, plus three rowdy boys who crimped his style by calling him "Pop."

Pop's idea of a family vacation was a nonstop road trip to Miami on a fistful of bennies, the three boys bouncing around the backseat like popcorn. Along about 1956, Pop left for a road trip all by himself and didn't come back. It didn't take Dorothy long to figure out he wasn't going to. A nervous woman whose hands were never quite still, Dorothy packed up her three little boys and went looking. She tracked him down in Atlanta via an old army buddy. There, Dorothy set herself and the boys up in the faded Briarcliff Hotel on Ponce De Leon Avenue.

Permanently on the road now, Pop visited his family sporadically, sending them just enough money to get by. It was Dorothy who provided the boys their moral compass, ferrying them to Hebrew school and afternoon sports between her two jobs. At a chic ladies' spa she arranged fashion magazines and attached an automatic quiver belt to the clotted-cream fat on the clients' thighs. But at night she came alive, moonlighting as a mystery shopper in downtown Atlanta's elegant department stores, where she annoyed store employees with irrational requests, then ranked them on their customer service. After an evening of detective work, she would slip into a quiet little bistro and treat herself to a cup of tea and a dainty crepe served on a white tablecloth where the service was good. A respectable tipper, at the end of the meal she'd gather her shopping bags and head on home to her boys with a light heart and a purse full of silverware.

Somewhere on the other side of town, our all-female household was a quiet one, operating under a stiff tent of privacy and good manners. Every night we sat down to dinner with our TV trays balanced on our laps to watch *The Huntley-Brinkley Report*. Button-downed restraint marked my mother's people—practical Welsh who survived the Depression by simply going leaner. Yet there was occasional liveliness in the house because my mother played the piano easy as breathin'. Her love of music and books took her through college, then on to the Columbia University School of Social Work. When the war came along, she quit New York for a job with the Atlanta Red Cross and married a gentle soul named John. In their gang of a boy and three little girls, I was the family's caboose.

In the single photograph I have of the two of them, my mother, a no-nonsense woman without a dose of sentimentality, sports a pair of snappy white gloves against a Mamie

Eisenhower navy cloth coat. She is confident, stylish and tall, nearly as tall as my father in his boxy blue suit. His left thumb tamps down the Flying Dutchman tobacco in the bowl of his mahogany pipe. His right hand sits on her hip and the smile on his generous face says, *Hey, isn't she something?*

But the men just didn't seem to last very long in our house. In 1961, a drunk driver sideswiped my father's Volvo, rocketing the humpbacked little car into a concrete wall at sixty miles an hour. My dad left my mother with a wink of a nickname that couldn't have been wronger, a perfect misnomer that stuck. He called her Sug, short for Sugar, pronounced *Shug*.

There was never a Mother or a Mom in our house, there was only Sug. A strong lady who could climb a tree and hack off the dead bough without any help, she rebuffed a show of affection with a philosophy of self-control and a pat on the arm. She never mentioned our father but kept his mahogany pipe in a shallow drawer on top of her dresser. For years afterward, when one of us sisters opened it to borrow her pearls, the scent of his pipe tobacco brought him back into the room.

It wasn't too much later, around 1963, when I watched from the hallway as my nineteen-year old brother Mac slung a green duffel bag across his thin shoulders, tilted his enlisted man's cap low, and kissed Sug good-bye. I spun the globe to locate his destination on the opposite side of the world.

Sug worked overtime most nights now, rushing home to throw together a dry dinner of meatballs and peas for us three sisters. But on lazy Sundays, our plates were full of garlicky succotash, fresh collard greens, and homemade biscuits— gifts from the women who gathered at our house for dinner. Never-married Aunt Lynda, a film booker for United Artists who talked on the phone to people in Hollywood, always brought a gallon jug of Mogen David, thumping it down in the middle of the table. As we ate, she told us movie star stories. She had seen both Elvis and Liberace up close, and Liberace, she said, wore high heels. I stared across the starched white tablecloth for the effect of this tidbit on my two grandmothers—stiff Florence, who disapproved of my half-full wineglass, and Depression-era generous Dearie, who passed around more biscuits. Yet there was no reaction at all. In a house full of females, men may have been the missing parts here, but the women seemed at ease without them.

One Sunday, we sisters learned that our grandmothers would be staying with us for a month while Sug went to the hospital to have cancer removed from her breasts. Overnight, Florence and then Dearie moved into our lives, ready to do what they could.

Ten days later, Sug came home from the hospital. I was relieved to see her standing there in the foyer, pale with a done-in smile on her face. My sister Cathy and I hung back, afraid to touch our mother, but Betsy, the oldest, took Sug's gaunt arm and helped her into her four-poster bed where she slept on her back straight through till morning.

The first time I saw Sug step out of the shower, her new body startled me. The thin red scars on her scooped-out chest could have been shoulder blades. This would take some getting used to. But in a simple act of tenderness, Betsy flipped through the dusty Betty Crocker cookbook on the top of the fridge and taught herself to cook. Tall, skinny Cathy cleaned the house with a regulated vengeance, fuming at my kicked-off sandals and rolling the vacuum cleaner over my bare toes. Chased out of the house, I looked around the garage and discovered what sparked the red and black battery clamps under the hood of Sug's unreliable Country Sedan. And in time, without any fuss, Sug healed. She just got up one morning and went back to work.

She worked downtown as the Red Cross liaison for families of servicemen stationed across Southeast Asia. That Christmas she set up a reel-to-reel tape recorder in her office so they could send voice messages to their soldiers. Endless varieties of "I love you, sweetheart" and "Come home soon, hon"—nothing fancy. One Friday night she loaded the tape deck into our old station wagon and brought it home. Nineteen sixty-five's master tape included a recording for her own son, a radio specialist now on his second tour of duty, laying communication lines somewhere along the DMZ.

In our little living room, Sug pressed the record button and held the mic in close for Betsy's somber reading of "The Road Not Taken." Next up on the piano, Cathy hammered out a Chopin rondo with the precision of a sewing machine. The slick brown tape ticked on while we three rolled up the braided rug to expose the wood floor for my tap dance number. With a smear of red lipstick, a bowler hat, and a cane, I clacked away to "Sentimental Journey," the 45 circling the heavy tone arm of

Betsy's portable record player. Beneath the piano, our lame collie Bob jangled his collar, scratching after a flea.

Half a world away, Mac would hear the tags clink and,
more than anything else, ache to hold the old dog. But like
most young soldiers, he wasn't much of a letter writer when it
came to keeping up with little sisters.

New Year's came and went with no response to our pro-
duction. January, then February too. Sug listened for Mr. Zell
the postman on the front porch and we all pretended it was
the bills she was racing to grab out of his hands. Nothing was
said because we were loath to break the no-whining code at
our house.

In March, Sug left the Red Cross to start a new career
working with the special ed students at my high school, the
ones we called the Retards. Half teacher, half social worker,
she gave top billing to the kids zoning out in the back of the
class, flapping their arms. She phoned around to gas stations
and grocery stores scouting out part-time jobs for her students, giving them driving lessons in her station wagon after
school.

I ignored the Retards in the hallway the same way my
friends did. But I couldn't help knowing each one of them.
Sug had me grade their papers two nights a week while she
worked a second job, teaching English to Vietnamese refu-
gees. Those were the ones we called Boat People. My friends
and I had a special name for everybody but ourselves.

That winter and spring passed slowly at our house. With
no men left, it felt clean, empty, and too quiet. One night,

washing the supper dishes, I looked through the window and spotted my mother in the backyard. She stood in the night shade of the old collie's persimmon tree, an empty egg carton at her feet. She wore a shirtwaist dress and an apron with big, loose pockets. I watched her reach down into one of the pockets and withdraw a small white egg. With bull's-eye accuracy in her windup, Sug exploded the egg against the back of the garage. Then she did it again and again, until there were no more eggs left to throw. When she finished, she stared straight ahead at her mark, breathing hard. I decided she'd gone a little crazy that night—not dog-barking mad, but still. . . .

It was overcast and chilly by the time she got home from work the next afternoon—no rain yet. She shoved open the heavy front door and looked around the neat living room. The quiet of the house without Mac's cavernous shoes tossed here and there always took some getting used to.

After another silent dinner, the big peacock spread its wings across our black-and-white TV and Chet Huntley's face popped up like God. I settled in next to my mother on the sofa, but we only half listened. Instead, we clung to our nightly ritual, scouring the camouflaged features of American boys flickering across the screen for the face we knew by heart. Sug leaned in closer to the television set, tilting her head to focus on the soldiers' vacant eyes as they clambered into the helicopter without looking back. Night after night Chet talked about Hanoi and Khe Sanh, but those frightened faces, those were the stories that mattered most to us. While Chet reported the rising numbers of U.S. troops deployed, we searched for just one face, the one with the lopsided grin and the chin dimple just like mine that let people know we were family.

The thought of Mac's goofy smile set off a little jerk in my shoulders, because it wasn't only my brother's face I imagined being swept away by the war. It was all of their faces. Happy-go-lucky boys I had smoked cigarettes with, boys I had straddled on the swings at night in the park, boys I had told to "Stop it. Now."

I wheezed out a choking sound. Sug shut off the TV, collapsing Chet Huntley's old punching bag of a face into a single white pinpoint. She took a step toward me but stopped herself. Instead she headed straight into the kitchen and opened the fridge. She fumbled around inside, not showing her face for a little while, then her hands came away filled with eggs. She eased them into her pockets and brushed by my shoulder.

"C'mon," she said. "Follow me."

It had begun to sprinkle. Fat drops of rain slid off the leaves of the persimmon tree. Stepping out onto the back porch, Sug grabbed a worn sweater from the door hook and threw it over her shoulders. I raced to catch up with her long strides.

As we walked, I could hear the eggs knocking together in my mother's pockets. The *tock-tock*ing made me worry something might break. Sug stopped at the back of the wooden garage, about twenty feet from the columns of egg stains that held fast to the boards, undiluted by a season's rain. She reached into her apron pocket and passed me three eggs. A dozen eggs cost sixty-eight cents that year and my mother was not the sort of woman to throw money away.

Sug stared hard at the yellowed bull's-eye she'd formed there after the drunk sideswiped my father's little Volvo. Newer, brighter stains had accumulated throughout Mac's first tour of duty. Sug was breathing hard now and I realized I had never seen her cry. Then she looked over at me and spoke in a raspy whisper that made my throat tighten and scared me plenty. "Put your trouble inside the egg." She tapped the little egg in my hand and stepped back.

I zeroed in on the center of the target. Then I did exactly what she told me to do. I squeezed my worries inside the egg and flat-out threw. The first throw sailed in a wild loopy arc and disappeared into the weeds.

For my second throw, I dug my toe into the moist earth like I'd seen her do. My windup triggered a real haymaker but it hit wide of the mark. I looked down at the lone egg left and back over my shoulder at the kitchen light stretching across the night yard. Then, from somewhere deep in the memory of my bones, I began to hear my brother's voice. Faint at first.

Squirl! Hey, Squirt! The voice grew stronger, tumbling out of the shadows of the persimmon tree that had always been home plate, and then he was there. Not all of him, but his teasing face, with its outsized, toothy grin and the deep dimple in the chin, just like mine. *Hey, Squirt. You throw like a girl—*

Gripping my last egg, I twisted my left foot into the little mound of dirt and leaned forward to eyeball the center of the target. I railed back and uncoiled a loose-limbed *thwack!* that exploded like a landmine. The inside of the egg oozed down the wall like slow tears, clinging to the old stains. Breathing

hard, I stared straight ahead at my mark, unaware of the drizzle that had turned into a steady rain.

In late April, Mr. Zell hand-delivered a letter in a thin blue
envelope. Mac had written home to say he was fine and that
the tape reel had arrived in good shape. He said he and his
bunkmates had listened to it and then passed it on to the next
tent, but that's where he lost track of it. Said those guys
must've handed it over to the next tent, and then the next,
and from then on, it became known as the "listen to this and
try not to cry" tape.

Mac said he'd meant to write home about that.

IT TAKES TWO, BABY

The squeal of the Metro brakes jostles me out of my daydream. An unseen conductor's voice calls out "Farragut West. This is the Blue Line" and, swinging in place on the low-hanging strap, David perks up. Two more stops until the Air and Space Museum on the National Mall. On this humid summer day, it's a sure thing Washington's busiest footpath will be knotted with fanny-packed tourists. But the crowds don't seem to bother David. We're still fine-tuning various Metro routes, but more and more I sense David pulling away from my direction. He is making up his own mind about where he wants the train to take him. Stop by stop.

This afternoon he stands across the aisle from my seat and down a few rows, his attention riveted on something over my shoulder. I crane my neck to see what has captured him so. Oh, there it is. In the last row of the train a young couple is coming awfully close to doing it, the two of them so wrapped up in each other I can't tell where one begins and the other ends.

"Hey, Dave? How 'bout we . . . get off here, okay?"

"Not our stop, Mom." He's focused. This will be a fare to remember.

I turn back in my seat and see reflected in the glass another of Metro's lessons for David: chemistry. What we have here is a working example of the multilayered neuroscience responsible for social bonding. All around us, an unwritten code of silence between Metro passengers conceals the unspoken things that human beings must recognize for ourselves. The yearning and long glances and unsuppressed emotions—all powerful parts of the human experience involved in promoting reproduction. The train is the perfect petri dish to test a variety of mating signals between fresh specimens.

So I do not scoff at the young couple back there doing it. No, their physical attraction is the natural order of things, their brains' throbbing neurotransmitters pumping out enough dopamine to spur them on to the next level. Desire may be chemistry and neuroscience, but it isn't that complicated—for most of us. The longing, the sheer want-to, is inborn and not the sort of thing you need your mother around to make happen. Oh, I wish this couple a lifetime of craving it. A lifetime of flushed cheeks and quickened pulses and delicious kisses.

So take a good long look, David. Imagine how fine it would be to want to share your life with another person. Imagine how it might feel to care about what someone else thinks and wants and tastes like. Look closely at tenderness. Yearn for it.

1974

John Updike called marriage a clash between two dysfunctional families. My first collision with Bruce took place over a clattering AP news wire. It was at one of those 10,000-watt radio stations where the DJ sits in the soundproof booth getting high at the top of the hour while some wahoo lights a match to the edge of your on-air script. In between the Joplin and Hendrix discs, Bruce ran the sports desk and I read the drive-time news.

Smart, passionate, and refreshingly blunt, Bruce was one of those complicated types who could keep several ideas spinning in his head at the same time. Unafraid to take a risk, his flexibility brought him success because he could seamlessly switch tracks to chase down a new lead. He just needed someone else to drive him there, since he got lost easy. Itching to be his own boss, he soon made good on his plan to move to Washington, D.C., and start up an independent news service covering Capitol Hill. Two years later I would join him at this growing new company, where we worked together as reporters for years. With my nitpicking attention to detail and his ability to see the bigger picture, we seemed well matched.

At age thirty, we married. We were on our way to being all set.

1983

"I don't babysit, so don't ask." It was my mother-in-law's immediate reaction to the news of the two-months-premature birth of our first son. Equal parts kindness and quirky contradictions, it was also Dorothy who held my hand as a phalanx of nurses tended to Baby Max like a hothouse flower under glass. Five weeks later we brought him home dressed in doll's clothes, tiny but growing stronger by the minute. Three years later a second son was born. We named him Eric, the yin to Max's yang. Eric was a pint-size acrobat who sailed out into the world celebrating himself with a high-arcing spray of golden pee. There they were: two healthy boys spaced neatly apart.

Max, always and always my second heart, was a thoughtful, serious child with sky blue eyes and thick dark hair. A boy who so loved to be read to, I called him the Book Swallower. Only three, he would hold a picture book in his lap and "read" aloud, mouthing the words from memory with the same emphasis I had put on them, pausing a stiff beat to lick his finger before turning the page. Baby Eric, on the other hand, was a rolling sort of baby. He rolled from room to room like a loose football. Some babies do this. I'd put him down surrounded by pillows in the middle of a bed, look away, and he'd be gone. One day he rolled out of his crib and across the hall to the top of the stairs, then slid down the thirteen steps on the belly of his cotton onesie, feetfirst and giggling. In next to no time Eric became the kind of toddler a frenzied mother has to put a leash on and hopes no one will notice.

Two children, two hands. A full house. With two boys to navigate, my husband and I were happy but pie-eyed from the fatigue caused by little feet. We soon learned what all parents come to know: a single child folds into a couple's routine smooth enough, but every child after that leaves you playing catch-up. And you never do.

On a Saturday night when Eric was not quite a year old, Bruce needed to drop a package off downtown. A neighbor offered to babysit the boys so I could go along for the ride. On weekends the city's business district empties out like a ghost town. For the first time in weeks—or was it months?—we found ourselves completely alone. In a dark alley.

"I've got a great idea . . ." Bruce adjusted the rearview mirror and turned to me.

A third child often comes to families unbidden and unexpected. I was a sensible thirty-five-year-old mother of two the night I conceived between the child seats in the back of our car. I knew I was pregnant again by the next morning; I knew it the way a woman knows what time it is in the middle of the night without looking at a clock. Motherhood teaches you that. It had also taught me I couldn't handle another kid.

Although my boys always went to sleep between clean sheets, well hugged with their teeth brushed, perhaps I was one of those women who didn't feel what she was supposed to about children. After all, my emotional template had been a breadwinning single mother, a well-meaning but unskilled cook with little time for housekeeping. Her four latchkey kids had thrived without any overeager parental clapping—no big deal. When Sug stepped through the back door after a long day's work, the message was clear: *Pitch in. Do your part.* We did.

By now, staying home with children had begun to feel like I wasn't doing my part. Here I had put in my mom duty and was right on schedule to return to work. But pregnant for a third time meant the slow days would start up all over again. Dulled by the tedium of child care, my belly would grow round, my breasts pendulous, and, harnessed across the back by one kid while dragging the other by the hand, I'd plod along like a tranquilized bear. Yes, I knew what lay ahead.

Over the next few weeks, anxiety fractured my sleep. In a noxious recurring dream, I sloshed barefoot through a field of baby shit under a threatening sky. The foul-smelling sludge squeezed in between my toes, covered my ankles, and crawled up my knees. I held the hem of my thin white nightgown and watched it sop up the diaper stew before the slow-motion ooze rattled me awake.

Better women carry on, no doubt, but I knew what I had to do. I made an appointment at a women's clinic, but the receptionist said I had to wait a week. If they'd let me come in the same day, I wouldn't be telling this story now.

It's peculiar how many secrets we are able to keep from those who know us best. As the days ticked by, my predicament was getting harder to hold back. Lying in the dark next to my husband, I stared at the digital clock beside the bed.

"Bruce," I said, my voice loud in the silent room. "I don't want to have another baby."

No answer. I poked him in the back with a pointy finger-nail and said it again. "Hear me? I don't want to have another baby."

He reached over with a heavy hand and patted my thigh. "Go t'sleep."

"The thing is? The boys wear . . . me . . . out. I need to go back to work before I put my head in the oven."

"Okay. So don't have another baby. Go t'sleep."

"I'm having another baby."

"You're not having another baby."

"See? That's the thing. I am having another baby." Bruce sat up straight as a tent pole.

"You're having a baby right now?"

"*No.* That's what I'm trying to tell you. I'm *not* going to have this baby."

"You can't do that." He was suddenly wide awake. "You know you can't do that."

"Shhh! You'll wake up the babies." I kicked off the covers and sat up beside him, reaching in the dark for the stubble of his chin. "Listen. I'm not cut out for all this baby stuff. I don't want to do it again."

Down the hall, the real world started to intrude. Nine-month-old Baby Eric was tuning up. Bruce groaned and eased out of bed to fetch him. Damp with sleep, the baby noodged his way toward my breast until he found the sweetness. His plump face was line-free except for the in-and-out of his mouth.

Bruce climbed back in bed and stroked the baby's velvety cheek. He sighed, and I could hear the slight smile on his face. With his natural instinct for spontaneity and intimacy, I have often thought my husband would have made the better mother of the two of us.

He pulled away from the baby and me and sat up in bed. Even in the darkness I could feel his eyes on me as he spoke. "We are going to have another baby and I'll tell you why. Because this time I'm going to pitch in. Whatever it takes. Yeah, this time things are going to be really different. I will promise you that."

In early August, our third boy arrived.

PERFECT TIMING

David walks into our bedroom at dawn, man-size and swinging his make-believe baseball bat. He is wearing a CamelBak water bottle and his brother's old football helmet. I reach for my glasses for a good look at all this.

"I'm ready for the Metro, Mom," he says.

"Lose the helmet," I say, "and you're good to go."

Because today is the day. The one I've promised him would always come. Bruce and I both take a deep breath. *All right, then. Yes, okay.* At breakfast we agree that I will ride with David to Metro Center, and from there . . . he'll ride solo for the very first time.

For the moment, David's knee is bouncing righteously under the kitchen table, sloshing the coffee in my cup. "It's about time," he says, cramming the clear-cut directions I've typed for him into his pants pocket. The words crinkle up into a chaotic bit of origami.

He's got a point; it is about time. But there will never be just the right time or the right train for him to hop aboard, because in David's world, there is only *right now*. Time doesn't move backward or loom ahead in the distance for this young man. So, in fifteen minutes, we are standing at the entrance to the Metro.

"Cell phone, Dave? Farecard? Directions?"

David pats his pocketful of origami and stares past me into the station's great maw. "Okay, then," I say. "So long!" And off he goes swinging his bat.

Then I pull out my farecard and slip into the crowd after him. From there I shadow him without his knowing it, darting behind a commuter's newspaper like in a bad spy movie. I glue myself to the opposite side of a Metro directory pole, biting my lip as David studies the wrong color line. At that moment I mentally will him to choose the Orange Line. A train comes and goes, and there stands my boy, quietly staring down the tracks as he waits for the right train.

The rumbling grows louder along the tunnel walls, and David's eyes seem focused on the blinking lights that signal the Orange Line train's approach. Suddenly, it is here: the moment I have to let go.

If I hop on that train behind him, he will see me for certain and know I don't believe in him. I make a quick mental note of what he was wearing *when last seen*: the loose khaki shorts, the navy blue Pentagon Police T-shirt, the white baseball cap with the logo . . . *but which team was it?* Unexpectedly, David looks over his shoulder and I think he sees me. But it isn't me he's looking at. It is a lovely Asian woman who has stepped through the doors of his arriving train and dropped a handful of papers onto the platform. David walks up to her, says something I can't hear, then bends down to help pick up the papers. She smiles, nods her thanks, and steps out of the way, just in time for him to slip onto the train in front of me, only an arm's length away. There is still an instant for me to leap into the breach when the big voice comes over the PA system: "Step back. Doors closing."

Through the windows I catch a last glimpse of David, standing there a head taller than most of the other commuters. I can make out his white baseball cap but, *oh, Lord— which team does he like?*

Too late. The doors shut. He is less than ten feet from me now, but on the far side of the glass, heading directly into the dark tunnel. He stands off to himself in the back of the train. I can't see his face from this angle, but I catch the movement of his silhouette as he sets his feet shoulder width apart, stacks his fists together high over his right shoulder, and swings hard.

When I pick him up three hours later, what I deduce from the glint in his eyes is this: nothing bad happened. This is all I will ever know about that first ride alone. The fact is, unless I witness it firsthand, I am not privy to what goes on in David's life. He offers nothing. A closed book. The last time I believe I knew him well was the day he was born.

He arrived on schedule in a quiet delivery the doctor deemed "uneventful," a word choice that brings me a wobbly smile today. Holding his brand-new little body in my arms, I counted his toes, took note of his soon-to-be-circumcised penis, and figured I understood everything about him. Even the name we chose was familiar.

I will always love the sound of the name. It's comforting to me, both strong and gentle. I'd been eager to name our third son after Pop, but our family's cultural traditions clashed. Bubbie came to me shaking her head from side to side. No.

"Eh-eh," she said, "bad luck. You're asking for trouble naming a child after a living person. I'm telling you, don't do this. You'll use the first letter. Call him Daniel, Darren. Anything but David. No, no, no, no, no."

The baby's name would stay. The thing was, I had grown to love my cantankerous old father-in-law for his resilience.

"Teh," said Bubbie, wagging a painted pinkie in the air. "You're making trouble."

IN TRANSIT

It's no trouble at all," I tell twenty-one-year-old David. "I'm on my way."

It's eleven o'clock on a frigid Saturday night. I grab my keys and head out to pick him up from his latest Metro adventure.

Skip the dolphin therapy. Hold the herbal supplements. We have found the cure. After all the expensive evaluations, therapies, and independent living programs for a boy we were told would never grow out of childhood, the best investment we ever made turns out to be a Metro farecard. For $1.35, David has bought himself a ticket to freedom—his own set of wheels.

After a day of riding the rails in the fast-paced underworld of mass transit, he is quick to remind me, "I'm the boss of me now." On the Metro, he chooses where his next stop will be, then steps out into the city a free man. Free to run the length

of the National Mall, free to duck out of the rain to wander
around the National Air and Space Museum, free to trot alongside the Rolling Thunder motorcycle parade down Consti-
tution Avenue. Running longer and longer distances now, he
treks for hours along the river's footpaths, cutting like a ribbon through bikers and walkers. Everywhere he goes, roam-
ing farther and farther into the world, he goes solo.

His first taste of autonomy is a reprieve from the nonstop
commands that fill his days. Directions from me and the others in his life—most of us women—all the teachers, counselors, and therapists who tell him where to go, where to sit,
what pill to take. How numbingly tiresome it must be, year
after year after year, living with the decisions someone else
has made for him.

For hours at a time now, David pores over the Metro system maps he's pinned to his bedroom walls, strategizing the
bus and train logistics for routes that will take him all over
metropolitan Washington. As a backup plan, I have typed cue
cards and planted them in both of our wallets—

Take the 23C bus to Orange Line Metro. Get off train at
Metro Center. Pay Attention HERE! Switch to Red Line.
Go one stop to Chinatown. Exit.

—just in case he gets lost. It still happens, sure, but what
began as my cupping his hand to shove coins into the farecard machine has escalated into my racing to keep up with
him before the train doors shut. These days, the only time I
ride along is for an occasional road test to challenge him with

a destination point: "Eastern Market, please" or "How about the Navy Memorial?" Standing before the large Metro maps, I watch his lips move as he snakes his finger from *You Are Here* to where we're headed. His finger slides confidently down to the fare schedule to find the cost to get there. When the train doors close behind us, I grab a seat. He always takes the trip standing, his back to me like a stranger.

More and more I just drop him off outside the nearest station and say, "Call me."

So here I am at eleven o'clock on a chilly Saturday night, waiting for this young man at the bus stop near our house. He'd left for a run mid-afternoon and has just called to say he's caught the 23A from the Metro station and should be at our bus stop within ten minutes. Could I come get him because his legs are all worn out? Bruce and I take turns on these pickups and tonight's my night, but we both agree: this is progress and it's no trouble at all. I turn up the heat in the car and wait.

Here comes the 23A lumbering down the road. It stops right in front of me and I can hardly wait to see him. In the seat behind the driver is a huddled lump of two passengers asleep with their heads together. From the back of the bus a lone figure stirs. When the doors open, the fellow rises, staggers, and falls back into his seat as drunk as an owl. The doors close and the 23A moves on west with the night. Two more buses come and go and still no David. Because David is sitting at the back of the 23C, headed east to the opposite end of the line.

My cell phone rings.

"Mom, the bus isn't stopping."

"Which bus are you on? Read the sign near the driver."

"The 23C."

"Right bus, wrong way. Ask the driver where you are."

"He doesn't want to talk to me."

"Oh, yes, he does! Tell him you want to get off at the next stop but you need to know the street names."

By the time I figure out where he's ended up, it is just after midnight. I head east. Twenty-three miles later, there is David, standing under a streetlight outside a pulsing pool hall, a perfect bull's-eye for the unscrupulous who prey on the vulnerable. His head is down and his arms are crossed over his chest. One leg is twisted around the other so tight, he reminds me of a barbershop pole.

When I pull up to the curb, a woman in painted-on jeans sporting an epic boob job pushes past David and leans her elbows into my open window frame.

"You know when the next bus is due?"

Eyes down, David fumbles past her to climb into the car. "Twelve twenty-seven," he announces without missing a beat. Holding her fingernails snootily in the air, she notices him for the first time. She screws up her face, pulls away from the car.

As the pool hall fades into the shadows, I ask about his night. "Well, you sure took the long way home."

No comment.

"You okay?"

Nothing.

"David. I said, are you okay?"

An apology for this surprise midnight outing will not be

forthcoming. Awareness of the nuances of causing someone an inconvenience is not part of David's makeup. It's not rudeness, it's just a chapter that's missing from his Rules for Basic Living handbook. And right now I'm too tired to point it out. But it's okay, because tonight goes down as a double victory in the Letting Go Diary I keep in my head. First and always first, nothing bad happened. Second, even though I no more know where he goes than the bus knows where it's taking him, David is learning to keep safe alone in the world.

This is progress. So shut up, I tell myself.

"I'm the boss of me now," he says out of the blue, as if that answers all my questions. But the words sting—hurling me back twenty years to the first time I heard them from a child.

1988

I stood waiting in the morning sunshine for the school bus that would take five-year-old Max to his first day of school. He wore a camouflage backpack and his favorite pair of high-top Keds, one red, one blue. I wore Baby David strapped across my chest and clutched at three-year-old Eric, who circled me on his trike like a mad, wee clown. The bus pulled up and the pneumatic doors gasped open. Max hopped aboard and turned at the top of the steps. "Wave to me, Mom. Wave! Mom?"

But my hands were full of other children now and I could only nod in his direction. With his chin down and an angry look stamped so long forever, Max called out, "Okay, then. I'm the boss of me now."

I stood rooted to the spot as the bus pulled away, pierced by a deep melancholy for the time I'd had alone with my beautiful boy. For the three years before Eric burst on the scene, it had been just the two of us, Max and me—squeezing fresh orange juice for breakfast, reading *The Wonder Book of Myths and Legends* into the long afternoons—gobs of time for folding him into the valley between my lap and arms that belonged to him alone. This was a kind of mothering I could handle, the sun shining across a child's universe, and I expected that closeness to last, not realizing it's a spot of time only for the firstborn. Our sweet alliance was jostled by Eric's arrival, then snapped like a broken rib when David followed eighteen months later.

Max must have figured it out before I did—the fracture brought on by the constant demands of David's baffling needs. And now, as my features were becoming more evident in Max's face, my firstborn was leaving me behind, reduced to a remote star in his wide new universe.

Standing there at the bus stop with two little ones, I didn't have the luxury of time to mourn our old rituals. The next morning, my gloom was a bit less intense. By week's end, with a new specialist to visit with David and more insurance forms to squander time on, the sadness receded even further I was too busy to notice what had begun to go missing.

It's funny. It seems to me that as mothers, we are forced to create the family narrative by scrapbooking together pretty lies. We are expected to carefully record every milestone of the firstborn—the hospital nursery shot, the homecoming, the first holiday. But I was never very good at that sort of

thing. Perhaps it follows that I was less chronically documen-
tative of my second child. Well, then, it should not be a surprise that by the time the third baby whistled down the pike,
I was well past the scrapbook business for good. Not only did
I not take many pictures of Baby David, over the years I got
those mixed up with earlier ones of his brothers, all of them
tossed together in a shoe box, thinning forward from baby-
hood to the present. In my weak defense, all three of my boys
were born with coal-gray eyes and wisps of dark hair. And
each of them came with that same squashed-pumpkin baby
face, so cute. I kept all of Max's baby clothes, cycling each
child through them. What I mean to say is . . . that *may or
may not be* David in his baby pictures. It looks an awful lot
like Max to me.

But I've never been unmindful of the past.

Sitting on my writing desk is a small wooden box. A lifetime ago, my father held it in his hand to paint a castle by a
lake on its top. This is the only keepsake of his I own. Now
inside the small box rest fourteen of Max's baby teeth, each
one yanked gently from its pink gum. There is also a minus-
cule wristband marked *6-17-83@6AM* and an oblong cloi-
sonné earring from a pair I often wore. The earring had gone
missing until it reemerged the next day in Max's diaper. After
sending it through the dishwasher a time or two, I couldn't
bear to ever wear it again or to throw it away. It sits there now
with all those baby teeth, a reminder of the adored child who
passed through me.

THE ROAD BACK

1990

I walked into our quiet house—too quiet. Sophie, our ninety-eight-pound German shepherd, was not at the door to slobber over me. Instead, a white-haired old man sat at my kitchen table drinking a cold Heineken from my fridge. An empty sack of burgers lay crumpled on the floor with Sophie, Baby David's companion dog, asleep at his feet. My father-in-law had broken in again.

Pop never gave me a heads-up on his plans. Just showed up, used his credit card to spring the door lock, then made himself at home. The upside was I didn't have to worry about playing hostess for him—and this night, there was something new. He insisted Bruce and I go out for dinner while he stayed home with the boys. We took him up on his offer, but only after Pop promised the boys he'd put aside plenty of time for bedtime stories. The old man's stories—Goldie Goes to the Racetrack, How Sol the Juicer Made the Vig—usually followed their poker game.

"And you'll be extra careful with David, won't you, Pop? Keep an eye on him?"

"You got nothing to worry about except what to order. Go. Enjoy."

I hugged him, enjoying the softness of his sweater, and passed him nine-month-old David, freshly diapered and meticulously swaddled. Pop stuck him in the crook of his arm like a baguette.

It was nice to see Pop playing the Good Grandpa role, and the boys really did love the old man's stories. But there was legitimate concern about leaving the three of them alone with him tonight. This was the first time I'd left Baby David's side since his latest ambulance ride.

Many low-toned, developmentally delayed babies lack the strength to cough hard enough to clear their lungs. As a result, pneumonia caused by aspirated food is fairly common in floppy babies. Food in, food out—reflux delivers every spoonful right back at you, all within twenty seconds. For their first two to three years, even the loving act of feeding your baby is fraught with harm.

A few weeks earlier I had been spoon-feeding David when rice pudding began to stream from his nostrils. Seconds later a *yuck-yuck-glack* sound sent Max and Eric diving for cover. David vomited so hard his head crashed into the back of his high chair. He turned pale blue and keeled over into the bowl. By the time we'd yanked him out of the seat, called 911, and started him breathing again, the ambulance crew had pulled into the driveway.

This was the second time David needed a week in a breathing tent to heal his fragile lungs. Now he'd come home to us painfully thin, a four-pound loss in a twenty-pound body. I could count the pulse beat in his temple as it kept pace with each pump of his heart.

The image of that tiny chest lingered like a specter over our first night out, and Bruce and I cut it short. We arrived home to a dark house, a single light coming from Max and Eric's bedroom. Bruce closed his eyes and lifted his shoulders. "See? You worry too much."

"Shhh," I whispered, finding relief in the light's path. "Must be story time."

We crept down the hall and found the baby, asleep in the middle of Max's bed with a hot card game well under way over and around him. Wearing Pop's sunglasses, Eric watched as Max stacked a column of poker chips on David's diapered butt. At the foot of the bed, Sophie the shepherd snorted out some some serious *zzz*s. I scooped up Baby David and breathed in the telltale scent of his clean hair. No upchuck tonight. A sweet spot in time.

In the spring, we turned the tables and went to visit Pop and Bubbie in Savannah for Passover. We piled the boys and Sophie into the car for the twelve-hour jaunt down Interstate 95. Hell on wheels, according to Bruce. Forty miles down the road, Eric made the first of many similar announcements to come. "I gotta pee. So does Sophie." At the sound of her name, the big shepherd raised her head and shoulders and suddenly the backseat looked very crowded.

When we finally arrived in Savannah, Max and Eric sprang from the backseat streaming dirty pillows, Transformers, and sticky hands. Pop stood at the front door of his new town house. My in-laws had reunited and moved on up a bit by now, living in a planned community with a pool and tennis court they would never use, surrounded by dazzling hummingbirds and gorgeous azaleas they would never notice. With their sons all grown and out of the house, the two of them had decided to make a go of it again. But after so many years of life on the road, settling down—in a community he dubbed The Reservation, with its designated parking spots and constantly rumbling clothes dryers—seemed to chafe the old rascal. But there he was to greet us.

Pop's knees bent under the strain of lifting two grandsons at once, and he crossed the foyer with a boy on each hip. "Good to see you come," he grumbled, and, because he knew they were waiting for it, "Good to see you go."

On duty, Sophie waited by the car for me to gather up Baby David. My spine was torqued over the car seat, when suddenly at my side, there was Dorothy in living color. Cobalt blue eye shadow that gave her eyes a permanently startled look and orange-tinged hair that was not the color of hair. In the furnace blast of Georgia heat, she had selected white knee socks to complement her high-heel gold sandals. Brass bangles and chunky rings slid up and down her wrists and fingers. I pulled back and gave in to what I loved about her: the whimsy, the chaos, and the hardship of her past. All of her complicated goodness.

Screwing up her face, she loomed in large over David, a two-year-old silent child who hadn't started to walk. "Heh . . . yeah, yeah," she said as she poked his belly with her nervous hands.

David stared back into all that rouge and messy lipstick without making a peep. The baby's tranquillity seemed to agitate his grandmother.

"Why doesn't he cry?"

We shared a stinging memory of the time I picked her up at the airport and her sudden entry into the car rocketed Baby Eric, trapped in his car seat, into ape-shit hysterics. That she could understand. But this?

"Two years old and he doesn't walk? Take him to the doctors in Boston. They'll know."

"He's just taking his time. All babies are different."

"Such a sweet face," she said, pulling away from him, not interested in a second touch. "Reminds me of Jerry. This one's gonna be just like Jerry."

"Who's Jerry?"

"Pop's nephew Jerry. Jerry the Blue Baby."

I had no idea who she was talking about. Always a mystery, this lady. I scooped up my kid and followed her into the town house.

Already the place felt familiar, the old furniture in a new space. It took us a while to settle our bags and run through the oohs and ahs over the novelty of it all. And it was good for Bruce to be in his mother's first real home. I was all set for a cook's tour, but my husband's bloodshot eyes revealed the toll twelve hours of kids' audiotapes take on the adult male psyche.

"Max," I suggested to my most responsible child. "Go baby-sit your brothers in the living room for a bit, will you, kiddo? And careful with David?"

"*Dah-voo*—" said Max, picking up his baby brother and running with him airplane-style into the other room. "*Dah-voooooo.*" A mix of his baby brother's name plus airplane engine noises. This is the place where nicknames come from.

The adults gravitated toward the kitchen. Stuffed cabbage rolls and a noodle kugel cooled on the starchy white table-cloth with a centerpiece of unpaid bills. Dorothy's bracelets clanked together as she opened the oven door to peek at a savory roasted chicken.

The aroma wafted its way into the living room where, at the moment, Max had Eric in a rolling headlock to which Eric applied a series of scissor kicks and other flashy maneuvers. When the body slamming began to rattle the kitchen walls, I went in there to gauge the danger level. Great big Sophie cir-cled the boys like a wrestling referee, barking in happy con-fusion with her head near the floor. Max had stuck David under a table topped with a large glass clown sculpture in order to give his full attention to stuffing Eric's head between the sofa cushions.

"Pull him out of there *right now*," I said.

Max yanked Eric out from under the sofa cushions and dropped him on his bottom with a thud. "We're starving. Aren't we, Eric?"

"Yeah, Max," said Eric, looking to his big brother for their next great escapade.

To pacify them, I reached into my bag and waved red licorice sticks from our most recent highway pit stop. Max could never be fooled by sweet talk and took a pass on the bribe. Eric grabbed two red sticks and stuffed them under his lips for bloody fangs. David opened and closed his little hand, reaching toward the candy in silence.

The next morning I woke up to giggling coming from Bubbie's bedroom down the hall. I pulled away from the warmth of Bruce's body, picked up David from our makeshift crib, and went to investigate. On a hallway table we passed Bubbie's collection of ceramic clowns: a lovesick Pierrot, a drunk court jester, a weeping Punch. Clown art was scattered all over this place.

I put David's tiny feet on my bigger feet and walked him backward along a corridor of painted faces that led us to his grandmother's voice. As we turned the corner to her room, laughter slid along the walls.

Suddenly Bubbie's rubbery face popped out at us like a jack-in-the-box. She stood before a full-length mirror with a finger pressed to her lips, shaking her head as if she had a decision to make. Max and Eric preened at her side, giggling over the silly outfits she had dressed them in: purple hats and flowery silk robes scrounged from her overflowing closet. Because today was the day. The big event.

Eric, the child who liked it best when everybody got along,

tugged at his grandmother's elbow. "Can Dah-voo come with?" The question hung in the air as the boys looked back and forth between their grandmother and me.

"Sure," I said, "if Bubbie thinks she can handle the three of you."

David turned his distant eyes toward Bubbie, offering his sweet face. Blurred and unfinished-looking without lipstick and eye shadow this morning, Bubbie stared down at him like the deer who troubles the edge of my garden.

"Not this time." She shrugged her shoulders and reached out for Max and Eric's hands. "Let's go." She trotted them down the stairs, out the front door, and into the bright sunlight where the air smelled of sharp pine needles.

Top down on her rusty gold convertible, they drove off to the Piggly Wiggly to buy gefilte fish. Because *this* was the big event. After weeks of hounding the grocery store to stock the specialty item for her holiday table, the manager finally caved and, with a swipe of intolerance, placed the glass jars on a shelf beside the scrapple, a southern concoction of boiled pig scraps.

"Pop," I asked as Bubbie pulled out of the driveway with the two boys, "how come the big parade to Piggly Wiggly?"

"That's just Dorothy," said Pop, flicking his hand. "She likes to make trouble."

"I can smell the rain," Bruce said, early the next morning. A mountainous purple cloud had eclipsed the dawn sun. It was time to head home, the car already full with the five of us and a large dog yet to squeeze in. Bruce planted his hands on his hips and looked up into the sky. "We're gonna get clobbered."

An hour into the trip a hard rain took hold. The steady rhythm of the windshield wipers had lulled the boys into a sweaty, fitful sleep. David was packed into his car seat tight as a mummy with Sophie curled on the floorboard. Max and Eric's heads had fallen toward each other, their breathing matched snort for snort. Now was the moment to pump Bruce for everything he could tell me about Jerry the Blue Baby.

Bruce and Jerry were first cousins, that much he knew, but Jerry's mother died young. After that the families lost touch. Bruce was ready to bail out right there, but I pushed.

"Go on, go on."

"O-kaay," he sighed. "Jerry was short and squat, with purple lips. He had narrow eyes, a flat nose, and"—Bruce pinched his nostrils—"talked like this." He shrugged, shot me a "That's it" look, and squinted into the rain.

"And?"

"*Hoo-boy*, this is no fun. Let's see. . . . He had a long head that ended in a real prominent jaw, an underbite." Bruce extended his lower teeth and stroked his chin, studying the windshield wipers. I looked over my shoulder and studied the sleeping David, the shape of his eyes, the length of his jawbone. "And you'd look into his eyes and realize he wasn't connecting. He couldn't lock eyes with you."

Except for David's tendency to avoid eye contact, from what I could determine he was very different from Jerry. Still, I was searching for a connection here, a clue to some genetic predisposition to risk factors, a way to put a name on something I could not explain. Because if I could pinpoint what was different about my son, get to the root of the problem, then perhaps I could stumble into understanding it. Fix it.

"Okay," I pushed on. "So, where does the Blue Baby part come in?"

"Look. Nobody wrote it down. Nobody remembers. My mother just always called it that. So that's what it became. Okay? Now, how about you let it go."

It was raining harder now, turning into hail. Cars had slowed to a creep, some pulling over to the shoulder, flashing their lights. Bruce picked up speed, sending a fan of spray over their hoods. I followed the arc of white BBs pinging off the windshield.

"Why are you so cranky? I'm just after some simple facts here, Bruce. Maybe a family Bible, old letters in the attic, that kind of stuff . . ."

"Damn it!" He banged his fist on the steering wheel and Sophie stuck her nose over the front seat to remind us she was there if we needed her. "You don't know what the hell you're talking about! We weren't like your family, okay? There *was* no attic. Shit, I don't even know how old my mother was because she was always changing the date. She had a bunch of different driver's licenses with birthdays five, eight, even ten years apart. Even Pop didn't know her real age. But who cares? I mean, it wasn't like anybody was ever after us to join the DAR or anything . . ."

Bruce turned up the wipers as high as they'd go. They sounded furious.

"Listen," he said in a tight whisper. "You're just looking for someone to blame. Fact is, *I* am comfortable with uncertainty because I grew up with it—but there's just no explaining it—so you, princess, need to back off. Now. Got that?"

Point taken. It was true: I had been combing through my husband's family history like an accusatory prosecutor, trying to pin David's developmental delays on them. But even if David had inherited some of his family's quirks or disconnects, what then? How could that change things?

Back off, my husband had told me, even though he knew how hard it was for me to do. It was no secret between us that I had unyielding tunnel vision and a host of perseverating tendencies: I'm a counter who swims not for the aerobic high but for the gratification of the silent finger tap at the end of the lane after exactly twelve strokes; I stand on top of my desk and rip the battery from the wall clock because each *tick-tock* is so damnably compelling; I make up my bed while I'm still in it.

What?

I looked at the rain streaking across the window and counted the seconds it took a drop to slide all the way down. One. Two. Three. Then again. I leaned my head against the window and caught a rigid reflection staring back at me from the side-view mirror.

Hmmm . . .

Maybe I'd been looking into the wrong side of the family all along.

THE LEAST OF HIS BROTHERS

When I pick up the phone, the bubbly delight in his voice spills out onto my end of things. "There's a fire at Metro Center," David informs me. "They're putting us on shuttle buses."

"Where are they taking you?"

"Dunno!" he says, even more excited. Here's a new wrinkle: What happens when the Metro system falls apart at the seams? Surely, the bus will take the passengers to the next station down. Then they'll all hold hands and walk in a straight line back onto the correct train. And David will find the way home. Right? Isn't that the way these things are supposed to work?

"Do not get on any bus, David. You understand? Wait for me on the sidewalk. I'm coming to get you."

As I drive through downtown D.C. listening to the radio,

the *William Tell* overture with its "Lone Ranger" theme comes on. Trapped at a red light, I gun the engine. An image springs to my mind that I cannot shake: me giving twenty-one-year-old David a piggyback ride.

This learning-to-let-go business is killing me. Killing me. But it's a good thing: it's killing the old me who rescues David, and making way for the new me who must let him take over. David, whose school evaluations always began with "Does not transition well." All these years my job has been to tighten the slack. To bring order to the chaos he invites. But I will not be here forever, and everyone's life is full of mayhem. Monsters under the bed. Random accidents. The fire at the Metro is a two-alarm wake-up call that the days for giving piggyback rides are gone forever.

1991

It was a sticky August afternoon when the three boys were young. With no advance notice, a friend dropped off four tickets she couldn't use for an outdoor opera at Wolf Trap, a theater for the performing arts located on a sprawling one-hundred-acre farm on the outskirts of Washington.

"Only four tickets, huh?" Bruce quickly calculated a free night ahead for himself. Merciless with a "Gotcha last!" grin, he said, "You can *all* go!"

That meant a blanket among the crickets for me and the guys while the sun dropped behind the trees. As the amphitheater began to fill with binocular-toting operaphiles, I settled three-year-old David in the middle of the blanket and slapped away mosquitoes while Max and Eric munched on fried chicken. When the stage lights flickered on, the first notes of Rossini's *Barber of Seville* filled the night air, and I sensed that familiar uneasiness I always felt when it was three against one.

In all their years as a fighting unit, my boys had never been simultaneously interested in any one thing. Always and somehow, a brawl would break out, bringing with it a bloody nose and a ripe word and silent David, just getting steady on his feet, flapping his tiny scapula wings in the center of it all. But this night felt different. As soon as the music burst across the lawn, the primed fists of my pee-wee warriors froze in mid-blow. Punches were not delivered. Instead, delight beamed from their dirty faces. They unclenched their sticky haymakers, collapsed into a heap like well-fed puppies, and listened to Rossini!

Opera buffs near them on the lawn nodded to each other, radiating their silent approval of me, a fellow highbrow, for breeding the next generation of opera-loving rogues. My heart swelled with optimism.

However. I had not yet realized that *The Barber of Seville* doubled as the soundtrack for the most madcap Bugs Bunny cartoon ever made. Without the visuals, and only the music to guide them, Max and Eric must have had to think really *hard* here, to rein in their imaginations to bring the prized moment to life: Elmer Fudd strapped to a barber's chair with

Bugs Bunny cracking wise and ice-skating across the little hunter's bald head.

The exhausting effort carried the boys nearly five minutes into the first act. Even David seemed to focus as the boys pushed him rhythmically, dreamily, back and forth between them like a floating beach ball. The depth of their concentration was astonishing. Until it went *phffft!* and Bugs's wacky magic kicked in, eliciting hoots, jabs, and sidewinders from my prepubescent cartoon zealots.

Sitting there on the blanket caught in his brothers' cross fire, a sudden high-pitched laughter rolled out of David. I was stumped: he gets Bugs? Whatever the starting place, David was near swooning with the cascading laughter of a child, the universal sound that delights the human heart. It was the first time I had ever heard him laugh out loud.

As Rossini's libretto sparkled along, David's whoops fanned the wildness in his brothers. The dustup from their tennis shoes kicking out at each other hung high in the air, glittering like fairy sand in the stage light. Next came the drumstick-throwing incident between Max and Eric, followed by a tight-lipped usher who helped us pack up our picnic blanket. With the precision of a maestro's baton, he shined his flashlight toward the exit sign for us.

"Hop on, Doodlebug."

I scooped up David for a piggyback ride to the car and felt his tiny heart beating against my back. The sound of his laughter still in my ear. His beautiful laughter. For the first time, I had glimpsed what I had longed to see ever since David was born: the simple joy of my son being silly—a garden variety little boy with his giggle box turned over, the long silence broken.

As I chased down Max and Eric playing tag between rows of parked cars, my heart thumped with fresh anticipation. But my two hands were not big enough to contain this much hope. *Hold on tight, little boy, for the ride of your life.*

David staggered into walking at three and a half. He turned four, then five, tugging silently at my leg for more juice. He tugged without looking at me, as if he was ringing a butler's bellpull.

"Use your words," I would tell him, looking into his blank eyes. It was the refrain in my daily song—just as it is for thousands of other families with autistic children whose voices they long to hear. "Use your words," we say, as much prayer as plea.

After a neurologist diagnosed the combination of autism and a brain pause in five-year-old David, at least we had a name for whatever this was. I told myself he would grow out of it, it was just a phase.

But by the time David turned seven, learning disabilities presented as part of the package along with the ADHD, OCD, and Tourette's syndrome his doctors diagnosed. He was learning to read in his special ed classroom, but against such odds: the force of the tics would jerk his eyes off the page, causing him to lose his train of thought. Though he had very little to say at school or at home, he was speaking in full, brief sentences now. He was using his words. Then, as he grew into boyhood, thin and twitchy, David surprised us again.

During a pre–Thanksgiving dinner football game in a yard full of young cousins and old men, my brother Mac, that long-ago soldier who was now a grandfather, tapped Bruce on the shoulder and said, "Watch this." He threw the ball across the yard to one of the other boys and David followed its path, keeping pace just under it with no pretense of catching it. When the ball was thrown back, here came David again, swiftly and just underneath it, knees picked up sharply with his head and shoulders held high—and again, no intention of making contact with it. Running along the path created by the spiral, David seemed to float, near weightless in his economy of movement.

"That boy runs like a deer," said my brother. And it was true.

Being outside in the fresh air was good for his health, and running brought him a fleeting peace from the tics, whereas the cornucopia of drugs we experimented with either exacerbated them or turned David into a walking zombie. So, starting in second grade, we signed him up for a soccer team. With his bony frame stretched skin-thin across his birdcage chest, he zigzagged up and down the field, oblivious of the ball, picking up his sharp little deer knees to remain three steps behind the general direction of play.

Bruce and I would flip a coin for which of us got to sit through those games. We were really there just in case: if David ever *did* make contact with one of the other players, one of us would be there to sweep up the dust fragments. For me, the mind-numbing boredom was easily handled by a book. For Bruce, it was a sore reminder of how many poles apart David was from his hard-charging, well-coordinated big brothers.

At the end-of-season parties this oddball kid of ours was routinely given the team bench-sitter's trophy for Best Attitude. The pretense went on for three seasons until nine-year-old David finally brought the masquerade to a halt. In a muddy basement packed with players, parents, and cheap brass trophies, in the course of wolfing down pizzas and Kool-Aid, the soccer coach rose to begin his solemn tribute to the loose-legged kid everyone knew glided to a different beat.

David stood up when his name was called, stared at the floor, and finally used his words. Tic-ing like a metronome gone haywire, he announced matter-of-factly, "I don't have the best attitude."

The room fell silent, leaving even the chatty coach at an awkward loss for words. Then David sat back down, nibbled on his slice, and the three of us went home early that Saturday. Sometimes, the inability to read social cues can be a real time-saver.

His differences weren't so noticeable when David was a toddler and could be dragged along wherever we went. But as Max and Eric grew into adolescence, they began to see that the balancing act with the mother-child relationships in our family had gone a little lopsided—and not in their favor.

In elementary school, Max and Eric witnessed for the first

time how their younger brother looked to their peers. In a county ranked among the nation's best for education, a trailer had been set up in the parking lot outside the main building for the special ed classroom—a physical distancing, a barrier wall that fenced off and isolated the learning-disabled kids from the rest of the students. No matter what innovative, first-rate intentions U.S. Department of Education policy makers claimed, for every kid among the rank and file in any public school across the country, the "LD" label and the "special ed" trailers were code for a single word: "retards." Because you can't fool kids. While the confounding terms like "hyperactivity disorder" and "apraxia" that Bruce and I batted around our kitchen table held no real meaning for my boys, seeing their little brother lumped in with the kids in the trailers made it clear for the first time: David was one of them. Special.

Rail thin, David was otherwise normal in appearance for a second grader, but his brothers already sensed the little pills he swallowed marked him as one of those kids at the table set up in a corner of the lunchroom for the lowest social order that no other kid, not even Max or Eric, would pull a chair up to.

While David would have gotten lost in the mainstream classroom shuffle with its larger child-to-teacher ratios, the regular students weren't the only ones to use insensitive language. One late spring morning, I squeezed into a child-size chair for a parent-teacher meeting in the trailer. David's teacher pointed to him at the end of the table, where he was copying the word "dog," and stated matter-of-factly, "Most of the time he just sits there like a vegetable." My stomach lurched. I must have misheard her. I asked her to say that again. She did. And this is me looking you in the eye saying it really happened.

It took every string we could pull to do it, but by the end of second grade he was out of there. We enrolled him in a private school for the learning disabled three miles away, across the river in Washington. A giant statue of Pegasus greeted visitors and a huge mosaic hung from the ceiling. David's new school was big on experimenting with learning styles, building relevance into the curriculum via a sort of living textbook. When they studied the Neolithic period, the students pretended to be cave dwellers. When they studied the Renaissance era, they held jousting matches. No grades, just long letters home at the end of the semester, but there was music to dance to, a stage to tumble across, and a team of kids who ran along the river path. David was intent on becoming one of the river runners. Although his eyes still skipped over the page as his tics wrestled for his body's attention, he made some progress with the daily therapy he received. Of course, the downside was the school's wildly expensive tuition—comparable to the cost of a good graduate school. Parental guilt egged us on to trust that a price tag like that carried certain promise. Somehow we would find a way to do this.

Dinner conversations were now frequently about David's doctors, his school, his medication, his therapy. The doctors all asked the same questions about our family gene pool, and many of them performed identical tests. Time after time we regurgitated the same background information for a new specialist, but left empty-handed. No one was willing to go out on a limb with a prognosis for David's future.

One neurologist decided David reminded him of a patient with a traumatic brain injury. So nine-year-old David was sent for an MRI to determine if there was some sort of a hole in his brain. There, they stretched him out on a table under a coil that looked like a flying saucer. A disembodied male voice remained in contact with David via an intercom system built into the machine's magnet. The lab technician told David he would hear a knocking sound over his head and shoulders. The examination would take about an hour, and any movement could cause blurred images, so he needed to be very still. . . .

After the first ten minutes the exasperated tech showed up in the examining room with his hands on his hips. He looked at me and said, "Can't he hold still?"

Well, again, I'm no doctor, but let's try to figure this one out. First, take a child with overly sensitive hearing, tactile defensiveness, and spatial awareness issues, and place him in a small chamber that knocks around his ears. Now ask this kid with Tourette's syndrome to hold still for about an hour. What do you suppose might be the results of those blurry images? A colossal waste of time and money.

On the way to the next appointment with still another specialist, David asked, "What does this one look like?"

I said, "The doctor? I don't know; I guess he'll be a man in a white coat like the others."

"Oh, a professional stranger," he said, staring off into space.

I was beginning to wonder which one of us should have our heads examined. But we both knew forty-five minutes with another professional stranger had never been long enough to fix this child.

We had waited six months to get in the pediatric specialist's door, and from the moment the Great One walked into the room, it was clear something was off. David began to stare into the doctor's face with the rapt attention he reserved for squalling fire trucks. The fellow vaguely reminded me of someone, but I couldn't place him. The doctor proceeded to ask a series of familiar warm-up questions: Who's the president? What year is it? What do you call your mother's mother? David responded with the emergence of a new string of tics that had not been there half an hour earlier. Time after time he would drop his head over the side of the table and giggle, inching closer and closer to the doctor's feet. You'd think you get used to these surprises, but still you are thinking: *Best behavior here, sweetheart. Show him you're not crazy, and by "you," I mean me.* The head dropping continued until the doctor grew impatient and asked David to wait outside so he could talk with me alone.

It was crystal clear to me that there was no magic pill to fix this boy.

On the silent ride home, the strange new tics disappeared as mysteriously as they'd arrived. We were back to the regular eye blinks and knee jerks we'd walked in with. Always a puzzle, this child.

Then, as we pulled into our driveway, David said, "Mom, why was Inspector Gadget there?"

Bingo! The Great Doctor was indeed the spitting image of actor Matthew Broderick, Inspector Gadget in the film Bruce had taken David to see the night before.

Six weeks later, the specialist's costly evaluation arrived in the mail.

I read the report cover to cover but did not recognize my child in it anywhere. The doctor had diagnosed schizophrenia, OCD, and symbiotic psychosis. That last one I had to look up. My dictionary defined it as "loss of contact with reality, with delusions and hallucinations and often with incoherent speech, disorganized and agitated behavior, or illusions." A Rorschach inkblot test suggested a personality disorder with possible suicidal tendencies. For a moment there, he had me scared. But in my gut I knew this distinguished physician, a rock star in the science of human behavior—or, as David would say, this professional stranger—had completely missed the root cause of his patient's reaction: David just desperately wanted to see the fireworks explode out of Inspector Gadget's left shoe.

By this time, Bruce had sold his syndicated news service. Now he was trying his hand in a new start-up venture with the city to turn old buildings into affordable housing for low-income renters. My plans to return to work full-time had all but dried up, dwindling to various freelance writing projects I tackled at home. Now most of my time was consumed with David's needs, following the latest research in behavior modification, and tracking the effects of the grab bag of drug treatments that left his mind and body either wired on Ritalin or sleepwalking through the day on clonidine. I pressed to the corners of my mind the creeping sense of guilt I felt in abandoning Max and Eric. The two of them had gone baseball crazy by then, and Bruce happily stepped in to support them. After all, this was the sort of game he understood.

Max played the third-base hot corner and pitched the ball in on the hitters' hands, buzzing it up around their heads to, you know, make 'em step in the bucket. That's the way he'd begun to speak, tough-guy lingo mumbled through a clenched jaw blooming with its first down. Spouting stats, he walked through the house swinging his aluminum game bat. David tracked Max from room to room, swinging a make-believe bat that sometimes sent his bony frame careening into the woodwork. But while his brothers whacked the ball at the local park, baseball was out of the question for David. Spatial awareness problems created a tendency to move his face *into* the oncoming pitch. Bruce never forgave himself for smacking David with his first bloody lip under the front-yard cherry tree we called home plate.

As his body began to stretch out of the little-boy stage, David steered clear of his brothers' roughhousing, shunning the physical contact. After school he plopped in front of the TV or wandered into the front yard to hang with his best friend, our dog. Sophie sat like the Sphinx while David listened to her belly noises through a stethoscope. Belly noises were as funny as Bugs Bunny any day. David sank into a stranglehold of laughter at the slightest memory of it. Drowning in laughter was the one thing that trumped the violent tics that came at him like a wild pitch. But it came with a downside. Sometimes David got stuck there and it could be hours before we could set him right again.

It didn't take much.

On an early spring night, just before we sat down to dinner, there was a knock on the door. Our next-door neighbor stood on the front stoop with his two teenage sons.

"Still need help moving that sofa bed?"

It was an offer we couldn't refuse. For the last two days, a heavy old sofa bed had been stuck in the middle of our foyer like a broken-down truck. To get from the kitchen to the front door, we had to climb over it. We needed a few more strong shoulders to lift the thing and take it around outside the house to store in the basement. And now the cavalry had arrived.

I held open the front door and David stood behind me, flitting around the screen like a moth. "Let's do it, then. On the count of three . . ." said Bruce. A dozen knees bent and the impossible sofa bed was hoisted into the air. Bruce and our boys, the neighbor and his—everybody held his own, and the great migration around the side of the house began. Step by step in the dark.

Then somebody let their dog out. A yappy, growly little terrier with that tendency to jump up, and up, and take quick bites out of the air. The troops had made some progress with the sofa bed—had worked their way down the front steps and over to the dark side of the yard—when Buster (that was the name all right) spotted them. The sight of all those hands grabbing that sofa—or perhaps, from his point of view, being grabbed by it—sent Buster into a frenzy. He made a beeline toward the hoisted sofa and the jumping up and biting at the air began in earnest. The troops were operating on the sloping side of the yard now in total darkness, so that although they could hear Buster's barks, no one knew exactly where he might strike next.

"Go 'way, Buster!" somebody yelled. "Crazy-ass dog—"

If one man dropped his edge, the whole operation was in jeopardy. So they trudged on, Buster biting the sofa behind everyone's fingers, everyone kicking out at Buster as if they were blindfolded. All the way down the hill until somebody finally made solid contact with Buster, lofting him into the air with a high-pitched howl. That's when David began to laugh. A gonzo *har-har-har* with his stick drive jammed in gear.

We thanked the neighbors and said good night, everybody still sort of smiling over Buster's spineless howl. Back inside, the house felt wide open as we walked through the foyer without having to climb over the old sofa. David's giggles bounced around the empty hallway, a liberating release that would ultimately deliver his twitchy body some peace, but not before it had exhausted us all.

We sat down to dinner, passed the salad, and ate in silence while David continued to laugh. We tried to talk over him, but David's laughter got in the way. While his brothers piled on second helpings, David kept on laughing. When the eye blinking and head jerking grew too frenzied and the table began to shake, it became unfunny. A full glass of milk sloshed over into the platter of chicken. A menacing growl came from one of his brothers—but which one?—and then all hell broke loose.

"CUT IT OUT, RETARD! IT'S NOT FUNNY!" An elbow spiked into David's rib cage sent him flying to the kitchen floor. Time has gently erased which boy said it and who threw the elbow, but suddenly we were all yelling at one another, pointing fingers, reaching across the table, pushing back from the ruined meal—every one of our dinner rules broken at once. Then all of us miserable as Bruce bum-rushed the boys out of the kitchen—everyone ashamed, confused, and hurting.

After the lights were out and tempers had cooled a bit, Bruce took a long shower in the dark. David's unhinged giggling had come to an abrupt halt in the kitchen, and now, alone in the quiet of his room, he would sleep like the dead. I splashed cold water on my face, climbed into bed, and pulled the covers up to my chin. Having grown up in a house full of careful women, I harbored a vague feeling that I would never be able to understand my boys' cathartic explosions, never master their minimalist language, or quit tripping over their thrashed-about shoes. I had just about given up on trying to figure out boys at all when, skin glistening, Bruce walked into the room rubbing a towel over his wet hair.

"Rough night, huh, kiddo?"

"Oof." It was all I had left.

He dropped the damp towel on the floor and climbed in next to me.

"Hey," he said, punching up his pillow. "David might as

well learn to be tough at home. Besides, you can't keep boys from doing what they've always done. Face it—they're stinkers."

Bruce went quiet for a long moment. I thought he'd fallen asleep. Then he reached his arm around my shoulders and pulled me in close. And there we were again, in the dark, hanging on together.

STINKERS

David is staring hard at his own reflection to see if he's still bleeding. It's hard to tell in the train's dark glass window. He dabs at his jaw with a fresh Kleenex that comes away bright red, and the woman hanging on to the strap next to him peels away to the rear of the car. David presses the tissue back against the cut and holds it there hard, just the way Bruce has showed him over and over.

Doing is learning.

The greatest educators claim that people learn best by doing tasks over and over. I thought about this earlier today, watching Bruce hold his breath while he supervised David's morning shave. The neck so thin and white as the razor slid over the bulge of David's Adam's apple. So easy to slice. Of course, repetition is the key to getting it right, but there are bloody consequences to a hasty shave. I suppose that's why failure makes for such a valuable lesson.

1997

How do you do? And how do you do, and how do you do again?

When I was a child, the singsong repetition of my grand-mother's question signaled she was about to teach me some-thing. Now I tried it on ten-year-old David as we sat at the kitchen table, desperate to stay focused on his math home-work. He'd become a viable reader, but the abstract concept of numbers opened up for him like a vast black hole—the enigma solved in an afternoon counting pennies unraveled into space by the next day.

But homework was still homework. And math assignments mostly came down to repetition. Tedious, mind-numbing rep-etition of a single task. The afternoon's task was to pinpoint the differences between nickels, dimes, and quarters, then sepa-rate them, maybe even add them up. *Repetition*—his teachers swore by it; but all silver coins looked the same to this boy. He will never learn to multiply or divide, but to add and subtract? Maybe so. Yet there was a deeper reason for this focused prac-tice that had nothing to do with homework: the price of a hamburger.

I was sick of walking into the local hamburger joint and demanding the young cashier fork over the right change after cheating David out of the difference between all those silver coins. But it wasn't the lost change that made me crazy.

It was the lost time.

The teenager behind the cash register couldn't possibly

understand the amount of time that went into planning ten-year-old David's solo mission to buy a hamburger. He couldn't imagine how long we'd sat there in the car, role-playing cashier and buyer, before my son had the confidence to step through the swinging door alone. How many times David had practiced saying into the mirrored sun visor "I want a burger, fries, and strawberry shake" before he could actually walk into the joint, lock eyes with a perfect stranger, and *use his words*. And the kid behind the register couldn't fathom what was irking this foaming she-wolf who comes walking in after their transaction, snarling, "What's the matter with you—you cheated my kid?" He couldn't know how devastating it was to lose time in a life where there was no extra time to lose.

So, on this particular Tuesday afternoon, while Sophie slept in her spot under the kitchen table and David's faraway expression drifted in and out of the room, we worked on what David could learn through repetition. We began by separating the nickels, dimes, and quarters. Again.

One floor down, four of Max's high school pals were over: a knuckleheaded mix of sweet jocks and budding nihilists who regularly disappeared into our basement, surfacing only for food. For years I had let the basement be Boy Land, rarely venturing down if I could help it. When the screams and crashes reached a particular crescendo, I opened the door to holler—"Is there blood?"—descending only if the answer was affirmative.

And now the noise from Boy Land had leveled off. I

supposed the boys had popped in a video of car crashes, or maybe they'd found the porn channel again. And, oh, wasn't that a cigar I smelled? Either way, too quiet. With a sigh, I got up from the kitchen table, David and Sophie following close behind.

Faces alert, Max's friends had formed a circle around six-foot-five-inch Phil, who had someone cornered in a boxing match. Sophisticated Patrick held a lit Black & Tan cigar high above the fray. I noticed the animal bloodlust in all of their young faces, a George Bellows painting of a prizefight come to life. The two fighters wore the red Everlast gloves Pop had given the boys for Chanukah. I recognized the contorted face of the recipient of a commanding blow. It was Eric—the classic second brother. Eric, known among Max's friends as the tough little guy who took all the punches and popped back up for seconds. They circled each other for a bit before Phil extended a gangly arm and glommed his hand onto Eric's head like a toilet plunger. While his brother flailed away with the arm speed of Mighty Mouse, David began to giggle. Just as Eric reared back to land a killer blow, Phil sidestepped the punch and, with exquisite timing, released his grip. Eric's head banged into the corner where the two walls met. He crashed facedown onto the floor and rolled onto his back, arms open wide, tweeting birds circling his head.

"DOWN goes FRA-ZHUH!" The ringside announcer was doing his best Howard Cosell into the face of a lit flashlight. Sophie ran in for cleanup duty, barking into the air and licking Eric's face. Max on bended knee, solemnly and for the final count, intoned, "DOWN goes FRA-ZHUH."

I peered through spread fingers. *Is there blood?*

Phil crossed the room toward me in one giant step, like a Great Dane. He didn't appear real concerned about anything in particular.

"Hey, Max's mom," he said, looking down at me with his charming smile. "Got anything to drink?" He bounded past me upstairs to help himself to the fridge. David followed close behind like a happy puppy, contorted by the laughter that would take him through the entire afternoon. Behind him, Sophie's loyal wagging tail.

After dinner, passing Eric in the hallway, David gave Eric's shoulder a little tap and broke into a new round of giggles.

"What?" said Eric, coming out of the shower with a towel tucked around his hips.

Giggling so hard he was near swooning, David said, "Hey Eric, remember when Phil grabbed your head and you kept swinging your arms? Remember he never hit you and still knocked you out?" David cut himself off laughing, not a little tee-hee laugh but one of those body-bending *har-har-har*s that he couldn't turn off. "Remember how you, how you—"

"Cool it, Dah-voo," Eric groused, calling up the old nickname. Eric turned away and started down the hall, his fists pumping blood into a sculpted chest that had evolved overnight from boy into big boy. David trailed behind like Quasimoto, crippled by his laughter.

"Hey . . . hey, Eric. Do you remember when Phil grabbed

your head and you just kept swinging? Remember how your eyes, how . . . *Ooo-wee*." David was gone, drowning in it.

"Shut UP, David." Eric just wanted to forget everything about it.

David's knees had gone wobbly with laughter. He reached over to lean on Eric's shoulder for support. "'Cause Phil's so tall and you're so short—"

Eric swept David's hand off his shoulder and exploded. "SHUT UP, idiot! Just SHUT UP!"

POW! David popped his brother with a jack to the jaw so hard, Eric's head snapped back.

"DA-vid!" shouted Eric, the athlete in him vibrating, primed to uncoil as he held . . . held . . . held the throw-back punch. Still quivering, he squeaked out a whisper of disbelief: "Why the hell did you do that?"

The laughter all gone from his eyes, David stared at the blood coursing down his brother's chin. "I don't know, Eric." But he did know. He knew plenty about what he'd learned through the repetition of ugly words thrown his way.

A single punch from Eric would have sent his skinny brother into tomorrow. Eric dabbed at the blood springing from his lip. He looked deep into David's face, his mind reeling between *What the fuck?* and *Great hit.* But on this night, conflicted by a mixture of frustration, duty, and love for an oddball little guy who'd just thrown the best punch of his life, Eric, the toughest of my boys—Eric, the gentle warrior—let it slide.

LOVE ME TENDER

It's easy now to look back and see where we made our mistakes. The intense demands of parenting a special needs child had left Bruce and me so fragmented that we didn't realize we were creating a second vulnerable crew: David's brothers.

In the shoe box of photographs that sits on my desk, I look long at the only shot I have left of Max as a teen. His chin is resolutely down and his blue eyes, the exact color of mine, stare back with rigid mistrust. Fifteen-year-old Max. It was the year he quit playing football after being sidelined by a couple of broken ribs during a late-fall game. I hadn't been there for him that overcast afternoon: I was in a conference with David's therapist and had no thought to my oldest son's playing schedule. Max huddled outside the locker room in the cold until a friend's mother could be recruited to pack him off to the emergency room. I was unreachable.

When I finally caught up with him, he was pushing himself around in a wheelchair, warily viewing his X-rays with the attending physician. The pain had collapsed his shoulders over his strong frame, making him look like an old man. When I walked into the room, he put up a hand to call off my hug. Leaching guilt, I prodded the doctor for details. Max stared back at me with cold eyes, as if to say, *Forget it. You're too late. Why don't you go wait in the lobby until I'm done?*

Once I got him home, he retreated to his bedroom in a nasty funk with a handful of painkillers. Of course, the only thing to do for broken ribs is to be quite still and let them knit themselves back together—no kissing the boo-boo required. I left him alone. Every child needs to be celebrated, and what I hadn't managed to do was to be present in his life at a moment when he needed me to celebrate his pain, his valiant pain. That's where I went wrong. And he wanted to make sure I understood that.

Although he never took it out on David, Max was right about one thing: the gravitational pull of concern for David's needs now outshone everyone else's light at our house.

During the tedious weeks it took for his ribs to knit, Max pulled even further away, walling himself off behind the cut-rate books he'd begun to gather from flea markets and second-hand bookstores. He read everything: history, philosophy, sports, military battles, Greek plays, the Beat poets. His collection spilled from his bookshelves and climbed from his bedroom floor in stacks of winding columns. Watching his passion for reading take him in so many different directions, I realized he had developed his own support system within the world of books. Who fought the Russians in the Crimean War? Max could tell you. What was Steinbeck's second novel about? Ask Max. I admired that in him, and it dawned on me that perhaps every thought I had did not have to concern David's disabilities. Where does it say that, to be qualified as good mothers, we have to keep giving ourselves away? Maybe it was a good idea to salt something away for myself. So, in a quiet corner of the house, I pushed my freelance work aside, closed the door, and began writing stories that no one would ever read. All of them with vulnerable outsiders that kept showing up and twisting the lives of ordinary characters into messy tight spots. There, behind that closed door, I chose to believe that the book swallower in my sensitive firstborn understood how much the quiet space meant to me, how it buoyed my spir—

"NO ONE CARES!" Max yelled from the hallway. This spot-on review arrived simultaneously with a flying baseball that blasted open the door.

That got my attention.

"Plus, the fridge is empty," he hollered. "That's your job you know, Mom." But this was about much more than an empty refrigerator.

"Okay," I said, squinting over my keyboard to relay a thought to my fingers before it evaporated. "Let me finish this line and I'll go start dinner."

"You're not even listening: we've eaten!" He strangled the doorknob with one hand and wrapped the other around his rib cage. For a heartbeat, I worried how those tender ribs of his might be holding up.

"One sec, hon . . . one sec—"

The door slammed and he was gone. He had cut me off and there was no road back in.

In the weeks to come, late at night like a cat burglar, he began removing photographs of himself from the family collages. Not all of his photos at once, but three or four little ones. Bit by bit I became aware of the emptiness where a child's cherished face had been. The discovery forced me to recall what was once there, and what was beginning to fade away.

I never claimed to be a good mother, just barely good enough. Eric must have sensed that this splintered kind of mothering was too big a job for me early on. Instead of wondering *Where is she?* he looked around and found himself someone else.

Born with a physical intelligence and an unerring sense of rhythm, Eric was a fierce child who drummed on the kitchen table and tap-danced with his shadow outside under the streetlamp. His fingers began to skip across the piano keys when he was just three, coming awfully close to making music. At age six, he begged for piano lessons, so we scouted around for someone much livelier than the arthritic piano teacher forced upon me as a child. Eric needed someone young, someone as fierce as himself. I found Patricia. He found a second mother.

This intense, raven-haired classical musician made Eric believe that music making was an exhilarating, noble, and muscular romp that lay waiting under his fingertips, *if* he would commit to the same hard-core discipline of an athlete that it would take to succeed. Soon he began to mimic Patricia's powerful position at the bench: the delicate curve of her fingers, the strong wrists, the bend of her elbows making a corner with the white keys. There was a certain charm in seeing a boy with a football player's sturdy physique approach the piano with the same intensity he had devoted to the playing field. Eric's nightly practice began after dinner with the repetition of scales and warm-up drills. The rule was to stop playing by eleven p.m., but there was no getting away from it anywhere in the house or even up the street, according to neighbors. A few years into it, Max yelled "Enough!" and moved into the basement to read.

After practicing, Eric would often close himself in his room, pick up his trumpet, and work up something soft and sweet for a little while. Across the hall, lying in bed, David never complained. The repetition seemed to calm him, soothing him toward sleep.

Practicing at Patricia's studio several afternoons a week, Eric learned her explosive technique with crashing chords that she spun out into quiet interludes, milking the music for all it was worth. Patricia and her husband, a cellist, delighted in Eric's enthusiasm and began to take him to concerts around town, introducing him backstage to rising young stars on the classical scene. The piano teacher and her student often shared the recital spotlight in duets that came off like heated dialogues, leaving the audience panting for more. Yet their time together wasn't only about music.

Whenever the noisy drama of high school got a stranglehold on Eric, Patricia was there to remind him where his music could one day take him. And I was grateful. I hadn't been there for Max; I would try to be for my second son, but if I hoped to get anything done for David, from time to time I had to be able to hand off Eric to someone else. Amid the erratic bursts of attention from me during those years, Patricia's steady cadence wrapped Eric in a dependable safety net that regulated the beat of his natural rhythm.

And I was grateful.

WHAT GOD LEFT OUT

What does a wink mean? How can a frown telegraph rage? Why does laughter sometimes cause pain?

Some things are so obvious, they don't need explaining. Most people catch what waggling eyebrows suggest or the tipping of a hat conveys. Most people, but not all. The missing part of David's puzzle is an inability to read facial expressions and body language, a sort of emotional blindness that is the polar opposite of empathy. It would be easy to dislike someone like this, the sort of young man who lets the door slam in your face when your arms are full of groceries, the teen who shoves you out of his way to reach for something to eat, or the child who turns his back when you ask for a hug. But when that someone is *your* someone and no one else's, your heart works overtime.

2000

I thought mine would break the afternoon sweet Sophie died. The gentle shepherd left behind an indelible shine on the hardwood under the kitchen table that has never gone away. For the eleven years that good dog shared our lives, she worked double duty as David's companion in a confusing world and my girl, moving alongside me from room to room. Oh, how we loved her: the claylike smell of her fur, the fluff she left on the sofa, her sandpaper tongue on our toes. Sophie dug up creek rocks with David while I sat on the grassy bank and read. A champion swimmer, she would glide through the water at the seashore, pulling David behind her as he held on to her tail. In the fall she nipped anxiously at Gypsy's hooves while David bounced his way through equine therapy. She sent up a howl if Max and Eric got too rough with him on the living room floor. And she let David listen to her belly noises. She had made a noble career out of being David's best friend.

Toward the end, it reached the point where we had to lift her decrepit hind legs to bring her in and out of the house. At bedtime, her milky eyes and the thump of her tail at the bottom of the stairs tormented me. Every time I brushed her now, especially careful around her aching hips, I hoarded clumps of her fur. I stuffed a pillowcase full of gobs of the golden, black, and gray hairs that free-floated in the air like dandelion puffs. The tufts would become a pillow for David's bed and, as is nature's way, extra padding for a sparrow's nest tucked into a lamppost outside his bedroom window.

I hope we handled Sophie's leaving the best we could. We pulled David out of school that Thursday to go with us to the vet to put her down. Dr. Fox sat cross-legged on the floor with us, Sophie's head cradled in my lap, as he administered the final shot. David and Bruce each held a paw until she was quite still. There was a final slow exhale and I kissed her eyes shut.

Bruce couldn't staunch his own tears as we left through the lobby, and I would be a wreck for the long days ahead. But David walked out to the car in silence and climbed into the backseat, not offering a clue as to how he felt.

For weeks afterward I thought I'd heard the clang of Sophie's collar coming from David's room at dawn and, on autopilot, I'd get up to feed her, expecting her nose under my hand.

"Come back to bed," Bruce would gentle me. "There's no Soph."

One morning I walked all the way down the hall and crawled into David's bed to hold him for a moment, perhaps more for me than him. "I miss our good girl, Dah-voo." He stirred a bit and said nothing. It was like holding a broom, and I didn't stay long. If anything could reach David's concern for another being, it had to have been the loss of this lovely dog who had served him in so many ways, asking so little in return.

"He's got to feel *something*," Bruce said. And I saw how much this hurt him.

Fathers of children with hidden disabilities often struggle with deep denial over their child's label, distancing themselves perhaps more so if it's a son they've attached their own hopes to. Looking back, I realize how I inadvertently added to this distancing. My maternal overprotectiveness created an inherent fissure in our family. Hovering over my frail infant every moment, I had boxed Bruce out of the relationship right from the start.

Of course, it was much more natural for Bruce to throw the ball in the front yard with Max and Eric than to find the way into a closed-off child he couldn't reach. Unlike love, a father-son game of catch has simple rules. You throw out the ball and your son tosses it right back to you. Back and forth. Give and take. The problem is, David has no give.

At a year old, when David's head still lolled about like a full hydrangea, a kind male nurse told Bruce, "You can't put in what God left out." As David grew older, those words took on a deeper level of meaning.

Whether two hours or two months had passed since he'd seen someone last, my string-bean son would walk in and out of a room without offering a hello or good-bye. There was no aforethought or intentional rudeness to it; it was simply his way.

"David," Bruce would say, tapping the cushion beside him, "come sit down and tell me what you did today." David would walk around the edge of the room without answering him, then slink away like a cat. Bruce usually shrugged it off. But year after year, a person has to work hard not to let that sort of thing get him down.

A few weeks after Sophie died, Bruce took David to see the film *My Dog Skip*, a ten-tissue weeper where an only child loses his beloved dog to the ravages of old age. The setup was the boy had been sort of a loner and really counted on his dog for companionship for most of his life. When the houselights came up, many moviegoers stayed in their seats, blowing their noses and taking the time to set their faces straight. David stared ahead as the credits rolled with no trace of emotion, no outward sign of a connection to the movie-boy's loss.

Outside the theater, rain pelted the sidewalk. Bruce pointed David toward the parking lot and they raced through the street, water gushing along the curb and over the tops of their shoes. Chilled and wet, Bruce sat behind the wheel of the car, soaking in the expression on his son's face—walled off, unreachable. Neither of them able to bridge the abyss between them.

The thought triggered a little shudder in Bruce's shoulders and, aching for what he realized would never be there in his son's psyche, he broke down. He crumpled over the steering wheel and couldn't stop crying, not sure which of them he was grieving more for. Because it wasn't only a good dog that would be missing from David's life, but the need to hold a hand, to desperately want a lover's kiss, and to someday comfort his own child in his arms. All the things in the sphere of love and affection that mark us as human in our daily lives. Pressing his forehead hard against the wheel, Bruce wept in great heaving sobs that wracked his whole body and left his hands full of rain and snot and tears.

David stared across the empty parking lot, waiting out the storm.

SOMETHING ELSE

The figure in the mist wore a tattered gray coat that kept on disappearing into the fog between us. He folded his scrawny neck between his shoulders and continued to pace along the shoreline. David and I took a step closer. Swiveling his long neck, the great blue heron peered back at us with a reptilian eye and let loose a *koo-koo,* a moan. He spread his six-foot wingspan and, with two powerful flaps, disappeared into the dark cloud cover. To the casual observer like myself, it was a lucky brush with nature. To David much more.

"That is *something else,*" he said, stumbling along behind me with his binoculars glued to his eyes. He said it slow and clipped, but this phrase always meant top praise from David. In Davidspeak, "something else" translated to "I am absolutely thrilled with this."

It was the Friday after Thanksgiving and just the two of us were out here in the fog, because Bruce had taken Max and

Eric on a road trip to a college football game. So here were David and I, weekend guests at Grey Gull Cottage, a weather-beaten 1940s saltbox on Chincoteague Island, the remote tip of Virginia's eastern shore. The little cottage seemed stuck in time with its undersized furniture and nautical whatnots, every room dotted with wooden bird carvings. A friend and her husband had rented it for the long holiday weekend to witness the annual migration of snow geese. Dedicated birders, they brought along emergency candles, gourmet food, and their eleven-year-old son. I brought along thirteen-year-old David and a good bottle of Scotch.

The Scotch was a well-aged Highland single malt, a pale straw color that lingered on the tongue with the right hint of oak. It went well with the fine cigar my friend's husband smoked outside in the chilly night air. He was feeling good about himself, having whipped up a seafood chowder for us, the potatoes expertly sliced and the oyster liqueur giving off just the right trace of the sea. Before he stepped out to fire up his cigar, he challenged David to spot an oystercatcher when we headed out the next morning. Oystercatchers, he explained, are smart birds that grab oysters in their bright orange beaks, fly up one hundred feet in the air, and drop them on hard surfaces like rocks or asphalt to crack them open. Then they swoop down to eat the meat, fighting with their comrades over the pulpy mollusks.

"That's really something else," said David, and I knew he'd be on the lookout for them in the morning.

My friends' son was tall and thin like David, but he looked you in the eye. This boy was well-versed in the *Peterson Field*

Guide to Birds of Eastern and Central North America. He knew the nesting habits of the local species, he knew to keep his eye on a bird when adjusting his binoculars, and he knew how to use the clock system to direct another birder to what he'd spotted: "Hey! A nuthatch on the loblolly pine. There on the dead limb at two o'clock."

David knew birds by their songs.

On this night, the two boys sat wordlessly on either side of a faded checkerboard. David had one checker left to the other boy's full lineup, most of them double crowned. The father had gone to bed early, a bit bored. I poured a second round of Scotch for my friend and me. There was little to say.

The five of us rose at dawn and draped our binoculars over our hearts to be able to peer at the migrating fowl that come there by the spectacular thousands. Every November they descend on Snow Goose Pond on their stopover between Canada and the Gulf of Mexico. The wildlife refuge is also home to sparrows and warblers and pileated woodpeckers. As we traipsed across the sanctuary, an eagle perched high atop a wooden post that seemed to be sunk there strictly for him. Charming little sika deer with their white powder puff behinds jumped through the marshland like dolphins at play. I focused my binoculars on David, who was looking at the natural world through his. But the morning brought us no luck in our search for the smart oystercatcher.

We returned to the cottage for a lunch of turkey salad on homemade bread. My friend's family life seemed well-ordered, so much more disciplined than my own. While she and I cleared the table, her husband became playful and suggested a little fresh air might be good for the boys. He hadn't been around David before. He scooped up a football and took the boys into the middle of the empty lane to toss it around. David still led with his face to catch a ball, which can spook a person, so soon enough it became a game of toss between father and son.

As David stood off to the side, lost in his own idea of the world, there was a loud *craaack!* beside him on the asphalt street. Then something nearly hit him on the head as a posse of at least a dozen oystercatchers swooped down to fight over the open oyster shells at his feet. With their bright orange beaks and legs and their black-and-white tuxedo breasts, the birds' beauty was stunning. This really *was* something else. David giggled in delight over the birds' ravenous skirmishes, then raced back to the cottage to tell me the wonderful story of the oysters that fell from the sky.

He told me the story from the beginning, delighted by the experience and quite stuck on it. Tic-ing away in happy animation, he banged his ear on his shoulder and flapped his hands in the air. *Ooo-wee!* Why, he could've been a bird himself. He told me again and then still again, when the father and son appeared at the door.

We'd been enjoying a pretty good laugh, David and I. I realized this was something my friends had never witnessed. For most of the weekend David had been silent. Now, as he told the story for the fourth and fifth time, the polite smiles on their faces slowly turned as wooden as the bird carvings that dotted every nook of the little cottage.

When he was finally able to catch his breath, David shook

his head right to left and said to me, "Now, that was really something else."

Yes, my love, wasn't it?

Time to go home. A nasty thunderstorm was percolating between Chincoteague and our drive home to Washington. Counting on making it there before the storm hit, David and I packed up early. As we all walked out to the car to say our good-byes, David asked to hold the car keys, as he often did. He liked the jangling sound they made. I handed them over.

"Okay, kiddo. Pop the trunk."

He pressed the little open-trunk icon on the key ring, then played with all the other buttons, popping the door locks up and down, up and down. I dropped in our single suitcase along with some wooden bird tchotchkes we'd picked up at the village Water Fowl Festival. As I slammed the trunk, in the blink of an eye David palmed my car keys and threw them inside. *Blam!* Trunk closed. All four car doors locked tight, the keys in the trunk with our suitcase and the wooden birds.

I felt the nerve endings I always kept on a slow boil start to heat up and curl in on themselves. Breathless. Livid. "What the hell, Dave? Why did you—why did you do that? WHY?!!"

He seemed as surprised as me. "Dunno, dunno, dunno!" Taken aback by the witchy hiss in my voice, there was something like fear in his face. Tic-ing like mad, his right heel delivered a series of swift kicks to his opposite calf. "Quit staring at me, Mom!"

I could not explain this one.

Neither could he.

My baffled friends looked back and forth between David and me for an explanation, their expressions begging, *What just happened . . . and why?* I could not respond to their confusion and deal with the car keys locked in the trunk at the same time. Oh, but even if I could've bitten through the metal lock and pried open the trunk with my bare hands, how to put into plain words why he'd locked it shut in the first place? How to tell them some things in my life would never make sense and this was simply one of them? One of those impulsive, unknowable, and frankly sad things about my boy that I could not control. Nor could he. It was just another tic.

Most mothers and fathers are under the illusion that we are in control, but parenting David had taught me we are not. Only, my friends could not see that there was no malicious intent in my son's action. They could not fathom that the impulse to toss away the keys was as fleeting as the breeze, and the why of his actions was already lost in this strong wind blowing up. Neither could they grasp that there was no sense of responsibility on his part, no splash of guilt or concern about the stress he had created. This was the defenseless and hidden undercurrent of David's psychological scaffolding. It had often left me adrift like this, exposed and vulnerable, the wind out of my sails. In those dark hours, I saw that the joke was on me: my boy really didn't care.

Ah, if only I were a screamer. Howling into the tides might've done me some good right then. But David's mind was what it was and I could cope with it or not. So. I shook off the devil and started looking for a locksmith. With the clouds rumbling in low overhead, I swallowed my fury and grabbed the cottage's battered copy of the Yellow Pages.

We had spoiled our hosts' afternoon. To pass the time, my friend decided to bake something complicated. The father and son opted for a long walk, even though the wind had picked up and it had begun spitting rain. By the time they returned from their walk, perhaps we would be gone and things would be back under control.

A quiet and remarkably awkward three hours later, a local truck crept into the yard of Grey Gull Cottage. The locksmith wanted me to know I was quite lucky to have found him. Most late-November weekends, he was off shooting the ducks we had traveled so far to admire. In less than three minutes the locksmith popped open the car's trunk, spit a jet of something black into the sandy earth, and up-charged me his hourly holiday rate. "Golden time," he explained.

By the time David and I pulled away from the cottage, the early evening rain had turned serious. He stared out the window in silence. Standing at the edge of the yard, my friend held an umbrella into the wind and confusion sat heavy on her face. Certain there was no way to explain it, I rolled down the window to apologize for staying too long. "So sorry about . . . all this," I called out to her with a flimsy smile.

As the car's headlights swept across her face, the tears in her eyes caught me by surprise.

The weeks passed quickly as the yuletide season lurched into full swing, but this time of year was fraught at our house. The annual confusion of marking both Christmas and Chanukah had rendered the task of decorating way beyond my personal ambitions long ago. As a solution to my seasonal blundering, I leave snappy white lights on the ficus tree in the corner year-round. In December, I plug them in and call it a holiday.

What I couldn't control was the dreaded Christmas letters choking our mailbox, starting the day after Thanksgiving—that ignoble tradition of notifying one's personal Listserv of how exceptional one's offspring are based on the milestones that camouflage the dysfunction in every family's life: trophies ladled out, passing grades scored, community service hours clocked, all the things that create the general *cluck-cluck-cluck* of ordinary lives. Every year, I make it through fewer and fewer of these letters. It's not the self-congratulating spin that rankles, it's the missing truth. After dinner, I asked Bruce about this as I stuffed the latest letter into the kitchen trash.

"I mean, if it's great stuff, you're bragging. If it's bad stuff, you're complaining. Why not just put it on a sticker and drive around with it on the back of your car?"

"People do that," he said, ignoring me by gathering up the dirty dishes with a flourish.

"See, here's the thing, babe. I know all these people; I just don't believe them. 'Cause here's what I really want to know: How about their daughter's DWI that rang in last New Year's?

And let's hear all about the porn site Dad's addicted to. Oh, and what's up with Mom's Prozac prescription? Now, *there's* an interesting holiday letter."

"Would you stop it," Bruce said, retrieving the unread letter I'd just crammed into the trash. "Nobody's life is perfect."

"Oh, hey, I got it. We should send one out—you know: 'Dear Everybody We Know, What a year it's been! Family therapy's going better than ever, and once the meds kick in, looks like our youngest will learn to count nickels and dimes after all!' "

"You really need to get ahold of yourself." Bruce shook his head at me and brushed some coffee grinds off the balled-up letter. "You've got your own life. Just go live it. Don't worry about anybody else's." He smoothed out the crumpled letter and, squinting into the soggy mess, began to read it out loud—" 'We started the year on camelback at the foot of the Sphinx . . .'; JEE-sus"—and tossed it back in the trash like it had bit him.

Of course, Bruce was right. I really did need to get ahold of my bah humbug self. Was I simply envious because I couldn't send out letters like these? Or was it because I ached to write one of my own that said, "This, yes, THIS was the year that David called out, 'Watch me, Dad!' " or the first time he kissed his mother good night. Yes, envy is a sinister form of self-pity, but sometimes the whole world just seems entirely too proud of itself. To fend off my sourness, I needed the strength of an unjaundiced soul.

"David!" My shout came off just a tad unhinged. "David, get down here right now."

A few moments later my boy ambled into the kitchen,

barefoot in jeans and a T-shirt. I reached into the fridge and grabbed two large eggs.

"Outside," I said, jerking my head toward the deck. We stepped into the season's best icy cold.

It was no wonder we never talked about this: throwing eggs was something you just had to do. I could almost hear my mother's voice coming to me from the backyard of my childhood. *Put your trouble inside the egg and let it go.* That woman—a single parent with breast cancer that left her looking like she had her head on backward—had had real trouble, but she had never been a crybaby. I handed one egg to David. Shivering, he stuck his free hand into his jeans pocket and stared over my head into the ether.

I tapped the side of the egg to lasso his attention. He had witnessed this ritual a time or two over the years, but I'd never passed it on to him. It was time.

"Watch."

Squeezing the egg with both hands now, I brought it under my chin and zeroed in on the brick wall beneath my bedroom window. I took a deep breath and held it right there. This part was crucial.

"Pay attention, David." Still tapping the egg. "You gotta take a moment to think about whatever makes you angry. I mean, really take the time to think about that." I pointed to the target and froze. "Then . . . right about *there*, you throw the egg as hard as you can. You watching?"

I took a second breath and held it before I released a double pumper that hit the bricks and blew the egg apart like a firecracker. Ah, so good, so good.

"Now you, Dave. Hard as you can." I backed out of the way.

David didn't question the why of this moment, because this boy had always lived in the fluid present tense, the almighty *right now*. But he approached it in a way that made me proud. There was a hint of a smile, like he was getting away with something wicked. He lifted the egg, sized up the target, and took a deep breath. He paused a second, his lips moving while he mulled things over. Then, arms spinning like a windmill in a storm, he hurled it toward the wall with a force that startled us both.

"You nailed it, buddy. Oh. Yeah."

Pieces of sticky eggshells glittered back at us, making the season bright. As the goo slid down the wall, we shivered together in the frigid air, sporting identical wild-eyed smiles.

"Feels good, doesn't it, Dave?"

"Oh, yeah," he whispered, still wearing my smile.

THE TWO-FOOT RULE

Humans are a curious species. And Metro's unwritten code of silence lends itself to one of our most natural inclinations: people-watching. At twenty-one, David seems to have perfected the art of the fleeting look. Clinging to the low-hanging strap in the center of the aisle, he lets the train's motion twirl him in any direction, keeping a vaguely lost expression on his face. When he picks his target, he looks away a microsecond before contact is made, then slyly out of the corner of his eye to resume his watch. But there's a trick to it. One must never get caught, because staring at people is rude. David gets that. Being stared at has been one of his life's trailing beasts.

When you live with a kid who tics, you begin to pick up the patterns of good stress versus bad stress. You learn to follow what we called his Two-Foot Rule, as in "Stay two feet away or I will tic a whole lot more." You never goose, tickle, or poke the tactilely defensive child, not even in playful fun. And, most important, you do not stare.

During his teens, David's tics came and went like poltergeists, one day tossing him around the kitchen, the next day producing that throaty sound we called his *unhk*s. His classmates would stare and ask what was going on, to the point where he'd make up little lies to appease them. He'd claim "Allergies" when he *unhk*ed. "My nose itches" when he hit himself in the mouth. "My shoe is untied" when his knee shot up to his chest. The cover stories came easy to him, but masking his tics with lies isolated him further from the kids, who stared at him anyway.

The energy he put into trying to stop took its toll. "Mom, I hate my knee," he once told me after an exhausting day of knee jerks. "It's like an itch I can't scratch because my hands are tied." After hours of tensing his neck to hold it still, he claimed it felt like two people were pushing on either side of his head. "My head hurts all the time."

With the Two-Foot Rule in place, comforting David became its own hurdle. His body language created an invisible wall that held off even the tenderest touch. He repelled a hug with raised elbows. An extended hand was left unheld. A back rub? Out of the question.

We experimented with different medicines, but they made the headaches worse and toyed with his internal clock. At night, David would sleep like a cat, conking out for two to three hours until his body jerked him awake. He'd get up and prowl around the dark house, eventually coming to rest at my bedside, his hulking silhouette jolting me awake. He'd flop down at the foot of the bed to pet the sleeping cat. I'd find them there the next morning, snoring in soft tandem.

The drug diary I kept for David from ages five to fifteen reads like an encapsulated nightmare:

- *1992—Ritalin for Static Encephalopathy, PDD-NOS, ADHD. (Headaches.)*
- *1993–94—Dexedrine 10 mg. Up to 20 mg. (Legs shake, hands fisted.)*
- *1995—Prolixin, Ritalin again. (Nervous, miserable, "hurts behind my eyes." Tics escalate.)*
- *1997—Clonidine and Tenex. (Zombie-like, wet pants 1X at school.) Reglan and Tagamet begun.*
- *1998–2001 Desipramine. 40 mg. (Headaches, vomiting, sleeplessness.) Also tried Adderall, Wellbutrin, Catapres, and guanfacine over next two years. (Tics continue, headaches reappear, eye rolling, jaw clenching, throat noises, knee jerks.)*
- *2002—Concerta, 36 mg. (Wired again.)*

But Tourette's is also a slippery syndrome. As the tics spiked and plateaued, sometimes they almost seemed to liberate him. Driving to his school every morning, we would cross into the city over the Potomac River. The traffic often slowed to a halt in the middle of the bridge, over a wild and rocky stretch of white water. We passed the time looking for hawks. David often spotted a red-shouldered beauty in the fork of a tree or at the water's edge, hopping after its prey. When his hawk wasn't there to keep his mind off the long school day ahead, the tics would start up, reinless as a wild-cat. Those mornings, taking a cue from his body's hijinks, I'd crank up the classical station as loud as we could stand it and shout, "Okay, big guy—it's Time to Tic!"

We jumped in our seats, blinked and bit at the air, *unhk*ing and flapping our arms—maestros gone Looney Tunes. While we tic-ed to Beethoven and Vivaldi, commuters stuck in traffic all around us read the newspaper with their morning coffee, chatted into their cell phones, or applied their makeup. Bouncing along with unfiltered joy, David never looked at me and I kept my eyes on the road—a perfect case of hiding in plain sight.

The opposite side of the good stress/bad stress coin was the strain of quiet places. Places like church. Although I struggled to believe, all three of my boys had been baptized. But at our house, where Sunday morning came down to getting up early for church with Mom or toasting bagels with Dad, only David was ever pliable enough for me to drag across the bridge to the Anglican church.

This Sunday, we sidestepped the treacherous patches of grungy snow on the sidewalk outside the church. A homeless man with a dirty foot cast slowed to catch his breath. As I climbed the steps shaking my umbrella, David lagged behind. Limping along beside him came the fellow with the cast, carrying a large plastic sack that jangled with glass bottles.

"Good morning!" the usher greeted the three of us. I smiled, but David and the man with the cast did not respond. Crumpling the *Welcome All* parish bulletin in his fist, the man with the cast dragged off his ski cap. A reddish buzz cut emerged above a heavily lined face. His eyes were distant, but I could see we were about the same age. The nation's capital is full of people like him, shouldering their belongings through throngs of busy folks with warm homes where loved ones are waiting.

The man stuffed a cigarette pack inside his cap, stuffed both of them into his coat sleeve, and took a seat in the last pew. When he set down his plastic sack, glass bottles clanked hard against the wooden floor.

On the far side of the church, the rector nodded *Go* to the organist. I gravitated toward the same pew every time, in the middle space. David sat alone in the back, dropping into the next-to-last row, paying the man with the cast no notice. Every few moments David's head jerked hard to the right, his jaw dropped open, then snapped shut. The muscles in his throat clamped together, forcing out an *unhk*. If he held back too long, his shoulders pitched toward his knees, so whenever he felt it coming on, he slammed his fist against his mouth twice—lashing out against what made people stare. From time to time the organ and choir sounded out, giving David a break from trying to stifle the noise. Then the rector climbed into the pulpit and everybody sat up a little straighter. He got right to the point.

"I'm not going to ask for anyone's wallet." People laughed but avoided each other's eyes. "No, I want you to consider how you use the gifts God has given you." The rector peered into the upturned faces for a long quiet moment. Sporadic bouts of coughing ricocheted around the sanctuary, and David let fly a double-barreled *Unhk-unhk*.

In his purple cape with the gold threads, the rector leaned forward on his knuckles and drew in a slow breath. "When you see people sleeping in the cold night air, do you turn from them?"

He went on like this a while. And David was about to bust. Finally, the rector took off his glasses, swiped them with the edge of his cape, and delivered the kayo punch. "I ask you to remember the words 'Whatever you do to the least of my brothers, you do it also to me.'" He signed off, drawing a cross in the air. The organist thumped away and a whopper set of *unhk*s jumped out of the back of the church.

The man with the cast reshuffled his bottles. In the next pew up, a green bottle rolled by under David's seat, coming to rest against his right shoe. David leaned down, picked it up, examined it. The man with the cast stirred in his seat, muttering. Those distant eyes of his troubled me.

The usher approached the stranger and tapped his shoulder. Surprised by the touch, the man pulled back, his arms in front of his face, and hissed, "You don't want me here, I'll leave."

"I don't want you to go," the usher whispered. "I want you to be quiet."

The man settled back in the pew and the usher returned to his post. People began to look around, nervous. An elderly couple slipped into the aisle and left. I wanted the man with the cast to leave too. I tried to catch David's eye, to motion him to come sit with me, to move away from the man, but David did not acknowledge me.

Up at the altar, the rector was blessing the wine. The man with the cast hoisted himself onto his feet. Hoping he was set to leave, I turned my back on those burned-out eyes of his. But David suddenly stood and walked over to him, handing him the green bottle that had rolled his way. The man took it and held it up to the light from a stained-glass window.

"Aw-*ight*," he said, "that's it," and a half smile faded away into the creases of his eyes. He dropped the bottle into his sack and walked out of the church the same way he'd come in, limping and banging into things. David sat alone in the back of the church, knocking his fist against his mouth, waiting for the service to end.

Crossing the bridge on the drive home that Sunday, I glanced over at David. He had his head turned away from me like a stranger. The parish bulletin was fisted in his lap. It seemed the farther we got from the church, the more his body relaxed. He stared over the railing into the river, preoccupied by a lone red-shouldered hawk circling above the naked tree line. The hawk lowered a wing to glide along the river's edge, in search of something only the two of them could see.

THE BRIDGE

A spectacular September morning. As David and I crossed the Potomac on the way to his school, the sky was blue and full of sunlight. The red-shouldered hawk was there to greet us, perched atop a street lamp. From the top of the bridge we followed a flock of red-winged blackbirds as they swooped in and faded off into the marshland below. A most peaceful way to begin a Tuesday morning.

By eight forty-five I was skirting past the dog food display in my neighborhood grocery store, avoiding memories of old Sophie, when I noticed several half-full carts abandoned in the aisles. A woman raced by with her hand over her mouth. The deli clerk turned on a radio behind the counter and said there were reports of a fire four miles down the road at the Pentagon. "No!" someone else cried, "it's a bomb! There are casualties!"

The cash registers shut down and a sense of fear filled the

air. No one was sure of anything, but in this town, where government jobs are the main industry, there was sudden chaos outside in the parking lot and an extraordinary sharing of cell phones that inexplicably did not work. Driving home, cars weaved across the centerline as everyone had an ear bent to the radio, wide-eyed with the same "It *can't be*" look on our faces.

I got home and turned on the TV minutes before the first tower fell in Lower Manhattan. The crawler on the bottom of the screen announced area schools were closing. *Where are my kids?* Quick phone calls—thank God for landlines. Max and Eric would take the school bus home. David I would have to go get.

Rumors flew that a plane was headed for the White House; no, the State Department; maybe the U.S. Capitol. All of the major routes into the city were closed and government workers had taken to the streets on foot, flooding the roadways across the metropolitan area. All bridges linking D.C. to Virginia became one-way streets out of hell. *I've got to get my boy home. Where is Bruce?* He had flown out of Dulles on a business trip at eight a.m. That would put him somewhere over South Carolina about now. *Inside an airplane. Do not think about that.*

Max walked in first, along with several of his high school friends who lived across the bridge and couldn't get home. The seventeen-year-olds piled up on the sofa and floor, staring silent and fearful at the TV, their everyday Bart Simpson cool evaporated. One boy's mother was an army general stationed at the Pentagon who hadn't answered her phone.

Another's sister was two weeks into a new job across the street from the World Trade Center. Eric called on the house line to let me know he had stopped off at a friend's house. Stay put, I told him.

"What about Dah-voo?" was the first thing he asked.

I had to get David home, but . . . the bridges, the bridges. I called David's school to say I was coming, not knowing how. Hurry, they said.

The phone jangled. Bruce was five hundred miles away in some unexpected airport, safe on the ground, thank God. He would rent a car, get home as fast as he could. No one understood what was happening yet, but we were all accounted for . . . except David, not far from our house, but stuck in the city, on the wrong side of the bridge. My bicycle felt heavy as I lifted it from the ceiling hook and dropped it into the back of our little Jeep. The plan was to drive as close to the bridge as possible, then bike in from there.

At the hill above the bridge on my side of the river, I saw them. A human roadblock: people of all colors, ages, and outfits, surging across Chain Bridge into Virginia. Bureaucrats in rumpled suits weighed down by laptops. Two men holding a ladder with dangling paint buckets that dripped soft yellow paint. Shoeless women tripping along in ripped stockings, cradling pocketbooks and overstuffed gym bags. A one-way pedestrian mob streaming away from the smoldering Pentagon and a turmoil no one could explain. Everyone desperate to reach home.

The only way to David was through the center of the mob. A man in a blue striped suit and a golden tie crouched on the sidewalk and bellowed into a dead cell phone, "Celia? Celia!"

"Helluva day for a bike ride," a woman spit at me as I nosed my bike against the tide of walkers. She pivoted to the right and melted into the throngs.

I reached the Washington side of the bridge and passed a taxi with six people inside and three more squeezed into its open trunk. An elderly woman with sturdy shoes and a walking stick leaned against the bridge railing to patrol the sky through her binoculars. Dropping down onto the towpath that runs along the canal parallel to David's school, I shouted, "Let him be there, God!" I was never much of one to pray, but this came from somewhere ancient inside me as I pumped the pedals, imagining David's confusion. My untested quadriceps caught fire on the steady rise to the school. And soon the building's fanciful murals and magical sculptures appeared, ludicrous in contrast to the terrified teachers dragging kids by their elbows, stuffing as many as possible into arriving cars, shouting in frightened gruff voices, "Go on! Go! Get going!"

And then there he was. Standing alone, right where I'd let him off three hours ago, an empty book bag strapped over one shoulder, a flat look on his face at the chaos surrounding him. I hugged my boy hard, breathing in the sweaty tang of his hair. His arms remained straight by his side.

"David, do you understand what's going on?" I asked him, as if anyone possibly could.

"A plane hit the Pentagon," he said. "Aaron's dad works there."

"Yes," I said. Exactly.

He gazed over my head at the panicky crowd coursing down the middle of MacArthur Boulevard. That was when I realized David had sprouted. Out of the blue, fourteen-year-old David had grown taller than me. My ridiculous plan was to pedal the bike back over the bridge while he sat on the seat and held on to my shoulders. This could only work if one of us was eight years old. At least he was skinny.

So we were off.

The tires flattened under our combined weight as we rolled downhill toward the towpath. With David perched behind me, his constant tics staggered us like a toddler taking his first step. We went as far as we could before I hopped off to lug the bike up the zigzag stairwell to the bridge. I squeezed David's fist around the back of my shirt and begged, "Don't let go, baby."

Once on the bridge, we plunged into the mass exodus of dazed walkers crossing the river, white water wild and rocky. Only, this time I was in step with the rest of the herd, moving in the right direction. With David perched on the bike seat, his light grip on my shoulder reminded me where we were headed. A man with a loosened tie patted David on the shoulder and offered me a grim nod.

"Going home," the man whispered.

Yes. All of us on the bridge were after one thing. Going home.

Five months later, on a bitter cold afternoon, the street where I stood pounding a lug bolt was nearly dark. My left rear tire had picked up a nail and my car sat there as stubborn as a pouty child. I'd already given up on AAA when a white police cruiser pulled up beside me and a cop stuck his buffalo-size head out the window.

"Having trouble?" His voice was deep and I could see his breath in the air.

"You could say that."

The cop pulled in behind my car, aiming his headlights at the flat. As he got out of the car he seemed to just keep on coming, a big man. He introduced himself in a deep baritone voice—a musical-sounding name—then he jacked up my car, struggling a bit before the first lug nut came loose. He said he was off duty, just on his way home from his job at the Pentagon as a K-9 officer. Turned out we were neighbors—his home just around the corner, two of our kids at the same high school. "I'm Isaac," he said, handing me his business card.

He had an easygoing way about him, as if standing there in the frigid cold was not going to bother him one bit. But the cold had gotten to me. The sun was down and my teeth were chattering.

"You afraid of big dogs?" he asked.

"Nope. We used to have a shepherd." I said Sophie had been a companion dog for my youngest, a kid with special needs.

"Then why don't you go sit in the cruiser with the dog while I finish up."

I climbed into the warmth of the front seat. "Hey, good boy," I said to the big white teeth behind the cage separating the front seat from the back.

Grrr-rrr-rrr.

Yikes. But it was that cold. "Sweeeeet boy."

The dog took a good long sniff and settled down. Relieved, I looked around at all the gizmos inside the cruiser. Oh, man, would David love to be sitting here, with the radar, the lights, the computer . . . And there on the console was something for me: a stack of magazines, all of them with 9/11 cover stories. One was open to the iconic photo of rescue workers hanging an enormous American flag from the roof of the still-burning Pentagon. The storyline followed one of the first responders, a police officer with a deep, accented voice and an unusual name. The officer had run toward the smoke, ducking under live electrical wires and sloshing through jet fuel. Using his deep baritone voice, he'd stepped into the burning rubble and shouted, "This way! Come toward my voice!" Eighteen survivors followed the sound of that voice as he led them out of the darkened building. In newspaper stories around the world, the thirty-eight-year-old officer was hailed as a guardian angel and inundated with newspaper and TV requests. Over and over he told reporters, "I heard people crying. I couldn't not help. I was just doing my job."

I remembered the story well from the *Washington Post*'s coverage of the officer. And the man's unusual name? Something long and unpronounceable, with a bunch of vowels and apostrophes to stumble over. Like the name on this guy's card.

The cruiser's headlights held the officer in stark relief as he lifted my spare tire into place. At 250 pounds and six feet tall, Isaac was a brown-skinned man descended from a long line of broad-shouldered Hawaiians with a few seafaring Chinese and Portuguese added to the mix. A poster boy for the look that gets the full pat-down from airport security these days.

I opened the cruiser door and staggered out into the cold air, dragging the magazine along with me.

"You're the Voice, aren't you? The 9/11 Voice."

Isaac stood up slowly, brushing his hands on his pants. He turned toward me, squinting into the headlights, and nodded.

"So . . . so . . . what are you doing standing there, changing my tire?"

"Hey, I'm just helping a lady out." He chuckled and squatted back down to tighten the lug nut.

"But you're—oh, my God, please stop. I mean, can I shake your hand?'

He stood back up and splayed his palms. They were covered in axle grease. "Don't think you'd want to."

I didn't wait to figure it all out. Instead I threw my arms around his neck. When he leaned back and laughed, the tilt of his big shoulders lifted me four inches off the ground.

The letter I addressed to his boss the next day was full of post-9/11 sentiment about what real heroes do when they're off duty, the sort of jingoism that hadn't yet begun to feel corny again. I had nothing in mind except a formal thank-you, but it turned out to be the beginning of a beautiful friendship.

It was two months later, the first Tuesday in March. David and I were sitting at the kitchen table counting those confounding nickels, dimes, and quarters when we heard a loud *whoop-whoop-whoop* from the street. A stern, amplified voice commanded, "DAVID FINLAND. COME OUTSIDE."

David raced to the front door and there in our driveway, next to his white police cruiser, stood a uniformed Isaac and his partner, Marko, the big black shepherd. Isaac held a speakerphone to his lips and his voice boomed out over the yard again, just as loud but this time real friendly: "HEY, BUDDY. I HEAR YOU LIKE BIG DOGS."

I expected David to be shy, to run back inside the house, maybe, but he was drawn to the cop with the big dog. As he walked toward them, his right knee jerked up toward his chest, but somehow his body rhythm factored it into his gait with an acquired grace of its own.

David shook the enormous hand Isaac offered, then knelt down on the grass to get closer to the big dog. Isaac must have read the concern on my face.

"Marko lives with us," he assured me. "My daughters play with him all the time." Isaac took a knee and the big dog flopped down and rolled over, his paws scratching the air, an overgrown puppy with his tongue hanging out, just begging for a belly rub. David sunk all ten fingers into Marko's fur and began to play him like a piano, probably listening for belly noises.

"Does he sit up front with you in the car?" David's head jerked hard to the right.

"This guy? Nah, he's got his own crib."

When Isaac opened the cruiser's back door to show him the cage, David's face lit up. His usual vacant expression had switched to fierce curiosity.

"Want to see inside?"

"Yeah, I do!"

Peering into the front seat, David's eyes blinked nonstop at the gadget wonderland: the tinted glass, the high-tech radar, the map lamps. Isaac opened the glove compartment and handed David a Pentagon K-9 Squad cap and a bumper sticker with the words *9-11-01. Remember*. Then he hit the siren blast a time or two and flashed a light on the console, bathing David's smile in blue.

David stood bent at the waist, looking deep into cop-car heaven, lost in the wonder of it all. Here was an opportunity to ask the officer what was on my mind.

"How come, Isaac? How come so nice to this kid?"

"Hey, you wrote that letter to the chief. . . ."

"Yeah, yeah. No, really . . ."

His expression switched from easygoing to rigid. "The truth?" There was a long pause as his cop's eyes scanned David, whose body was halfway inside the cruiser now and twitching in fascination. "I guess you could say I know what it's like to be different."

The truth was that at the same time the media were swarming over him for being a 9/11 Pentagon hero, Isaac had been privately coping with a different kind of attention. When he was off duty and dressed in civilian clothes, local police often got suspicious of the big dark-skinned man behind the wheel of a Jeep and pulled him over for driving around in the community we both call home. Public perception of him as either hero or terrorist all depended on the clothes he had on. This kept up until he finally figured out a way around it. He ordered himself a set of First Responder license plates so he could make it to the grocery store and back without being profiled.

A squawk came over the cruiser's radio now and Isaac had to head out. But first he made David a promise: he would come to his school and do a bomb-sniffing demonstration with his canine partner in the spring. They shook on it— Isaac and David, David and Marko.

When that day arrived, Isaac asked David to hide a tiny black training bag somewhere among the crowd of students filing into the school's auditorium. Then he slipped out to his cruiser and came back with Marko to let him search for it. The big shepherd—ears up, black hair bristling along the ridge of his spine—nosed his way through the seats. Giddy over an unexpected break from the classroom routine, the kids called out to the big dog, daring him to come closer, squealing in mock terror when he did. With their attention riveted on Marko, David stood beside Isaac at the podium, his eyes blinking like a caution signal. He was doing his best to keep his tics at bay, but it was a losing battle. Uncomfortable in the spotlight, David's whole body suddenly caught fire. His ear slammed into his shoulder. His right knee jerked up to his chest.

"He found it!" somebody yelled from the back of the auditorium. Marko had his nose up in the air now, as he sat at attention beside the training bag. Isaac approached the dog and, in a quick switcheroo, gave him his favorite dog toy as a reward. Cheers and whistles as the dog began his floating trot to the podium alongside Isaac.

Just when it looked like David would make it through the day without his tics being center stage, here came Marko with the toy in his mouth, leading all eyes to the front of the room. Suddenly David croaked out a loud *unkh*. His knee jerked up and his right arm shot out to the side.

In that instant, some kind of hand signal must have passed from Isaac to the big dog, because, as if on cue, Marko trotted past the officer and dropped the toy into David's extended hand. As a stunned smile spread across David's face and the tension in his body evaporated, the kids roared. All part of the show.

While the students returned to their classrooms, I walked with Isaac out to the parking lot. He unlocked the back of the cruiser and Marko jumped in.

"You know, you just about turned David into a rock star back there."

He grinned, but the smile that softened his features was interrupted by the squawk of the police radio. "Well," he said pointing to the dashboard, "I gotta get back to work."

The big cop gave me one of those world-embracing hugs of his and set me back on my feet. Then he slipped behind the wheel of the cruiser and pulled out of the parking lot, flashing a solid thumbs-up.

There you go again, Isaac, I remember thinking. *An everyday hero.*

BE STILL

Not a *thang* wrong with you!"

Sug's voice set off a batch of Monarch butterflies in the early afternoon sun. My mother sat on the broad bench seat of her old blue Buick, drilling fourteen-year-old David on how to bank a turn.

"What about his tics?" I had asked her earlier in the week. "Aren't you worried about him jerking the wheel?"

"*Law,* that foolishness is old hat to me. This boy can learn to drive a car. Let him go."

Sug had retired to a tiny island off the coast of Georgia, a quiet place with mossy oaks and afternoon light like hammered gold that draws painters and writers, drinkers too. The place is so small, if there's trouble, the cops just close the bridge until they solve the problem. Sug believed she'd have no trouble at all teaching her underage grandson to drive. After thirty years as a special ed teacher, my mother had developed a more jaded nervous system than most driver's ed instructor. Throughout the 1960s and 1970s, making sure that her learning disabled students could drive to an after-school job had been her top priority. Sug, your basic outsider, got it.

Now Sug's practice course was a shell-strewn path behind the airstrip that snaked through the island's overgrown Victory Garden. The fifteen-mile-per-hour speed limit was not much different from what most residents managed on the main roads. Behind the wheel, David's focus became unexpectedly fine-tuned. He was careful not to let the car's tires crush the yellow lantana overflowing into the pathway. At the end of every spin, the teacher gave her student a grade. It usually fell in the B range, never an A, because too often David might botch a maneuver: hogging the center of the path or rushing humpbacked Mr. Levy as he crossed the path on his way to the water spigot.

"Pull up here a quick minute," Sug directed David. "Let your momma and me out."

David idled the engine and watched his eighty-eight-year-old grandmother amble over to the birdbath to sprinkle yesterday's bread crumbs. It was a regular part of their lesson, because, like her grandson, Sug loved her birds. Fat little chickadees flitted around her while she stood with her face up to the sun. "*Oooo-eee*—hot to-*day.* . . ."

I walked over to a granite bench curled around a live oak and breathed in the smell of honeysuckle. I usually went along for the ride, hoping to absorb some of Sug's patient technique, but this time she didn't want me along.

"Sit!" she insisted, sticking her bony index finger into my thigh. The bench felt cool against the back of my legs. "You got to give that boy some breathing room! Quit babying him. He can handle this fine." The air was still as soup as Sug climbed into the shotgun seat, cooling herself off with a worn church fan. "Be back in a bit." There was nothing for me to do but "Sit!"

David drove the Buick through the Victory Garden twice, then pulled into the spot where his lesson always began. He sat there a few minutes watching a bumblebee disappear in and out of a zucchini blossom, waiting for Sug to give him his grade, but she had leaned her stiff brush of gray hair against the car's window and, from where I sat, stranded without a cell phone, it looked for all the world like she'd drifted off to sleep.

Nah. Couldn't be.

When she didn't seem to stir, David reversed the car and lurched into gear to circle the garden once more. This time, when he got to the entrance, he brought the Buick to a full stop. He looked over at his grandmother still sitting there as peaceful as a potted geranium. Carefully now, he engaged the blinker, waved bye-bye to me, and turned onto Demere, the island's main road.

"God?" I said to the chickadees. "Please tell me my mother is not sound asleep in the front seat of that old Buick."

Out on Demere, David pointed the big blue sedan toward the village and disappeared from my sight line. In my mind's eye, I imagined him passing through the three green lights and steering the Buick around clumps of jaywalking tourists.

Then easing out of the village he knew so well onto busy
Frederica Road, stopping for three more lights along the way,
then on past the stables and Bennie's Red Barn toward the
island's shady north end. At the northernmost point, where
Spanish moss hangs from three-hundred-year-old live oak
trees filled with snowy egrets, the road loops back on itself.
David would have to cycle back right there, creeping past
Bennie's Red Barn again and the stables, then spilling onto
Demere Road, predictable and steady.

Thirty minutes later, approaching the edge of the Victory
Gardens, here came the old Buick. David flicked on the right
blinker the way Sug had taught him. When the wheels left the
pavement and scrunched back onto the seashell-strewn road,
David guided the car toward the granite bench where I sat
waiting in the shade.

As it drew nearer, butterfly bushes scratched at the doors
and Sug's eyelids flew open with a start. She looked around at
the hummingbirds fanning the hibiscus blossoms, saw me at
the bench, and pointed a long finger at David.

"OK, mister. Pull up over there by your momma and
lemme drive."

David parked the car and hopped out. As he walked
around to the passenger side, I made my way to the backseat
while Sug took her time settling her cranky knees behind the
wheel again. Then she turned and stared hard at her grandson's blank mug.

"B minus," she calculated, already pumping the gas pedal.
"You cut the corner pulling into the parkin' spot."

By the end of the summer, David was driving his grandmother to the post office, the grocery store, the library. Driving that car had flung open a new window in his mind. It was
as if he had set foot on a moving train for the first time in his
life and wasn't about to get off until he got to where he was
going. Sug had figured out that breaking the rules might
someday work for him.

Still. When he returned to school in the fall, it became
clear that no made-for-TV-movie breakthrough was in the off-
ing. His impenetrable silence worried me, and after six years
at the expensive private school, we had no real gauge of progress; David was simply keeping a seat warm. Max grumbled
that the teachers coddled him there. "That place," he said, "is
turning him into a wuss." According to his older brother,
David needed to develop some toughness he could use out in
the real world.

By then I had read everything I could get my hands on
about any connection between Tourette's and autism.
Although the two are considered separate disorders that war-
rant separate treatments, studies show that the vast majority
of people with Tourette's are not autistic. They simply tic or
exhibit signs of attention deficit or obsessive-compulsive disorder. And the majority of young people with ADHD do not
tic at all. The good news is that most young people's tics ebb
between ages eighteen and twenty-one. That would be something to look forward to.

But it was Eric who found the missing piece.

"You know what Dave really wants? He wants to ride the school bus. Get him off the zombie drugs and send him to high school with me, Mom. I'll watch him."

It was true. For years every morning we had driven over Chain Bridge with David eyeing the big yellow school buses that pulsated with the verve of rowdy teenagers.

"When can I ride it, Mom?"

"Someday." I always said, "Someday."

At fifteen, someday was here: time to meet the real world. "Send him to public school with me," Eric had suggested. But could it be that simple? The best advice I ever received from any of David's doctors backed it up.

"Why not?" said the psychiatrist. "Go ahead and pull him out of there now," he said. "Save the money for housing when he's an adult and wants to live on his own—you're going to need it."

But it was the tail end of winter. David would need time to adjust. "When should we do it?" I asked, warming to the idea. "Next fall?"

"Next week," the psychiatrist said without hesitation. "Register him right away. You've got a good public high school in your community with a solid special ed program. Why spend another dollar you don't have to?"

Why, indeed. Of course, every child's needs are different, but here's what was going on with us: Grasping for straws, we had been eager to believe private school was the magic pill we'd been searching for, so whatever it cost, it must be the right thing to do. Instead, it was shortsighted. Nickel-and-diming us for every hour of therapy, evaluations, and extracurricular activities, the out-of-pocket costs for private school were whittling away at our financial nest egg for David's future. After so many years caught up in our expensive search for answers to the mystery of autism, Bruce and I had grown skeptical waiting for clinicians to agree on David's prognosis, jaded by education consultants hell-bent on walling off the learning disabled. We finally decided there is no "best" school; there is only a parent's best instinct as to where his or her child belongs.

Still, the change would not be a cakewalk. In public school with the government's federally mandated Individualized Education Plan (IEP) for special needs students, we'd have to fight for them, but the services would be free. They should be: we all pay for them with our taxes. So now, at the crossroads, we did the math. We took the social, financial, and emotional factors into the equation and made up our minds what would be best for David's future. We calculated how far the tuition fee of a single year of private school would stretch toward a single year of adult David's independent living expenses: his own apartment, food, transportation, an occasional night out. *For the rest of his life.* Then we multiplied that figure by every year of private school David had already attended. Granted, every single child is different, but the numbers proved it was not a wise investment for our kid.

The public school reentry process was a breeze. It was the comprehensive psychological and language evaluations that we found so challenging. David's scattered weaknesses in syntax, his word retrieval difficulties, his inability to read nonverbal cues, his extreme attention deficit—these were the things that defined him here, earning him a seat in a classroom for students with mild mental retardation and the label of "multiple disabilities." Back to being special ed. Nowhere in the evaluation did it mention he was also gentle, handsome, and funny, and knew the sound of birdcalls by heart. But words matter, and the reality is that in public school the "special ed" label translates into services for kids diagnosed with IQ test scores below 70: free speech and occupational therapy, psychological evaluations, and most important, vocational training after graduation. We were also weary taxpayers well past the hubris of saying, "No label shall define my child."

"Call it whatever you want to," Bruce told the school's psychologist. "I don't care as long as it gets him the services he needs."

The transition from the world of private school into public high school would follow spring break. In exactly ten days, fifteen-year-old David would ride the big yellow school bus after all.

In the meantime, we decided David could use a little adventure, a little fresh air. Acting on the conviction that being outside is good for everyone's health, the two of us zigzagged through southwestern Virginia, bumping along a gravelly road toward a 1930s-era wilderness camp nestled deep in the Blue Ridge Mountains. In autumn this mountain cove is a leaf watcher's paradise, but the view that early spring afternoon consisted of stripped hardwoods and sugar maples under dense fog. Only a bare-bones staff was on hand to cook meals and lead hikes because it was mid-March, chilly and damp. David and I had the place nearly all to ourselves. The first night, we sat at opposite ends of a wooden dinner table for twelve. Climbing upstairs to bed, our footsteps echoed throughout the lodge.

Our bunk beds were stacked one atop the other in a room that smelled of chimney smoke. At bedtime I discovered we had left David's Dopp kit at home with his toothbrush and his pills, the little yellow ones designed to scale back the tics. The ones that made him cloudy and listless.

David was supposed to come off these meds gradually to give his body a chance to recalibrate, to avoid headaches, moodiness, even hallucinations. But 250 miles from home, it looked like we'd be experimenting with drug-free fresh air for a few days. I'd grown jaded about the value of the meds, anyway. With each new pill, he had his choice of poison: violent tics or walking zombie. The negative effects seemed to outweigh the good and undermine his natural body rhythms. On the other hand, more and more studies were suggesting that exercise and fresh air reduce the stress hormone that aggravated him in the first place.

So here we were at the wilderness camp, settling in for a weekend of David unplugged. The goal of our trip was the cultivation of independence for David. According to the camp's promise, he would stand on the edge of an outcropping of rocks and steel himself to climb down. But at the moment, the skinny meds-free kid in the bunk above me was tic-ing like a Mad Hatter.

Early the next morning found me dangling from a thin cable looped around a limb forty feet up a poplar tree, trying to stifle a lifetime fear of heights. "Wow, Dave—what a view!"

Don't look down. I hoped to remember which hook to clip and unclip, and in which order. On the alert for porcupines in nearby trees, I tried to sound persuasive. "Come on, Doodle-bug, you really gotta try this. . . ."

David sat with his back to me, not budging from his perch opposite our young guide. Brian, whose forearms looked like maple trunks, informed us he didn't believe in forcing acts of courage on his clients: "You have to want it for yourself."

Brian had brought along his two dogs with us for the morning's hike: a beagle hybrid that nudged its way into David's lap, and a sad-eyed Saint Bernard, a rescue dog named Bear, which I assumed was for me.

An hour after a quick lunch of chickpea soup, I was con-nected to a network of high wires, preparing to step off a wooden platform and zoom out over the Blue Ridge Moun-tains. First came the safety talk on how tucking the legs increases speed and opening the arms and legs slows the body down. Or did I have that backward? David and I were both outfitted in bucket helmets and rope harnesses now, but so far it was only me dangling out there in space. Brian claimed that if David saw his mother on the zip line, he would be more likely to step onto the platform himself. Brian couldn't have been more wrong on that score.

He also said he'd count to three before he let go of the har-ness, but there was a big shove just after "two," and the last thing I saw before I became a flying screech was David doffing his helmet for the day and trotting off into the woods behind the little beagle mix.

"Spelunking" is a curious word to have in your mouth first thing in the morning. On our last day at the camp, two other couples joined us as we donned used coveralls and gloves scented with the smell of red clay. In the back of the van, David's headlamp bumped mine as we jiggled along a dirt road to the cave.

The morning sky was full of dark clouds as we stood under the eaves of an old lady's front porch. The entrance to a beautiful limestone cave was a few steps from her vegetable garden, and protocol was to ask her permission before we began. The old lady liked to know who came and went at her garden. When she opened her door to us, just inside the screen, David got a peek of a big tabby cat nursing three feisty kittens in an open basket.

Heading toward the mouth of the cave, Brian showed us how to flip on our headlamps and asked, "Anybody uncomfortable in tight spaces?" There was a buzz of nervous laughter and I looked around for David. He was not in the garden. But Brian had begun to catch on to David's quirks.

"Hang on," he said, pulling off his headlamp. He made a quick loop around the house and came back with the old lady and David, stroking a gray kitten that bleated like a lamb.

"Where'd you find this one?" I pointed at the fur ball.

"It found me."

Brian set David's headlamp back on straight and tightened the belt on his baggy coveralls a notch.

That's when I became aware that, without the meds, David's tics had begun to taper off. The *unhk*s were still coming, but he'd eaten well and slept less fitfully. He passed on yesterday's rock climbing, ran the other way when it came to the zip line, and sat in the prow of our canoe like a dragon's head on a Viking ship. But there seemed to be a curative value to his time in these woods. For the last two days he'd hiked every trail, pursuing his own little butterflies. He'd spotted an eagle's nest and a Cooper's hawk high in the trees, all the while racing ahead to keep up with the two dogs, tossing sticks to them outside after dinner under the kaleidoscope of stars. Maybe we'd found the good medicine we'd been searching for.

Brian flipped on David's headlamp and said, "Dave, my man, you're going to love the bats."

The underworld of the cave is a cool 54° Fahrenheit and the rocks smell musty and damp. In a place where it never rains, groundwater trickles through the cracks in search of a path to an unseen stream. Calcite dripping from the roof creates whimsical icicle shapes, and diminutive minarets seem to rise from the floor where primitive man once found shelter. As we navigated each boulder and twist, other than the sounds of our feet and breathing, there was silence.

Brian encouraged us to rely on each other for safe travel through the cave's tricky passageways, passing information down the line, directing our flashlight beams to sudden obstructions in the darkness. Our voices lowered to a whisper and the intermittent *unhk*. I brought up the rear of the line with my headlamp centered on David's feet two steps ahead. As we sloshed through an underground stream and squeezed our bodies over and around large boulders, my boy failed to pass back any hint of communication. If the cave's Boogie Man decided to pick me off from the back of this posse, nobody would notice for a good long while.

So I was a bit surprised to come upon a chamber about thirty feet wide and so low-ceilinged one had to stoop to enter. The others were already inside, sitting cross-legged on the cool, dry ground. The light from our headlamps revealed reddish-yellow walls covered by a black cloud that seemed to be breathing.

Brian spoke in a low whisper. "Welcome to the bat cave, but *do not* touch the walls." Because, he explained, Virginia big-eared bats covered every inch of them. Weighing less than half an ounce, with mitten-shaped muzzles and elongated nostrils, they use their sonar radar to snatch flying insects out of the air, and in early spring, according to our guide, females congregate in colonies to give birth. "That's what they're doing here now. But they're fragile—an endangered species—so please, please," he cautioned, "don't touch them. The point is to protect them from *us*."

David let out a fresh set of *unhk*s. In a small act of grace, Brian ignored it and asked for the attention of the others, who were busy staring at David. "Okay, here's the plan. We'll turn off all the lamps and sit here in silence for the next fifteen minutes. Fifteen minutes. It may feel like a long time to some of you."

Oh, Brian, I thought. *You really are something else if you think David can be still for fifteen minutes.* My mind reeled back in time to the technician who kicked David out of his lab for blurring the MRI scan.

First the headlamps and then the flashlights went out and I couldn't see my hand in front of my face. There was a spate of throat clearing and the shuffling of backpacks as we settled in. And then there it was. A blackness—the total absence of the sun's light—like nothing I'd ever experienced. I couldn't be sure if my eyes were open or closed. And with the darkness came immediate apprehension, a void that tricks the mind into an odd floating sensation. It awakened other senses, and what before was simply the musty, damp odor of rock became the sharp taste and smell of iron, or perhaps fresh blood. The emptiness invited sound, and it became plain that our rhythmic breathing was accentuated by something else, faster, steadier.

I honed in on this underlying harmony—a low, organic hum. Several minutes passed in the inky darkness before I was able to process it, until gradually it became clear. It was the beating of ten thousand tiny bat wings coming into their own, struggling to survive. Brian had warned that even the slightest disturbance could cause the endangered bats to abandon the cave and use up the energy reserves they needed to stay alive. And each time a species disappears, he said, we lose not only those benefits we know it provided but other benefits we have yet to realize.

And with that, I grasped the benefit that all bats, birds, dogs, and cats provide for David. It is simply this: their silence. This is not to be confused with some New Age supernatural bond between humans and animals that requires a spiritual leap of faith. Not at all. Animals simply exist without judgment. They are safe for this vulnerable yet impenetrable boy to seek out, and they provide him an unconditional presence that too few humans offer. Yes, the silence of animals is a double pleasure: they do not ask questions and they do not stare.

However, at this moment the cave's dark mystery had blindfolded us all in the subtle game of body language. Here none of us was privy to the unspoken messages telegraphed in fleeting facial or postural expressions. In the mysterious darkness of the cave, we were all mind-blind, oblivious to the workings of each other's sense of self. Perhaps David's worldview was like walking inside a dark cave every day.

I patted around for his hand but he pulled away, leaving only the edge of his boot pressed against my knee. We were close but we could not see each other. And for the first time I was really in his world. Only, David was in this cave for life.

Yet, for a rare moment, I sensed no jerking in David's neck and shoulders, his hands resting quiet. Still. Here, in the shelter of the big-eared bats, the merciless *unhk*s briefly took their leave. David seemed to have found his place in the world.

What was it Brian told us just before the lights went out? "Each time a species disappears, we lose not only those benefits we know it provided but other benefits we have yet to realize."

And so we sat still awhile, deep in the underworld of the cave among the silence of the bats.

TWO A.M.

That was my Eric, the well-built cornerback with the dazzling smile, slouched down in the backseat of the police car. When he climbed out, his hands were cuffed in cold steel behind his back. He didn't look at me. His thick brown hair fell into his puffy eyes and his cheeks were red, just like when I used to pick him up in his crib after a nap. He had smelled of fresh laundry and baby powder then. On this night he reeked of cigarettes and beer. I didn't know this cop. I'd met most of them through all the Saturday nights like this. And here I was at it again. Nearly two a.m. and I was at the top of my driveway in my nightgown, shaking the hand of a man with a gun in his holster. The name tag pinned above his heart read SGT. COURTENAY.

There was something for me to sign about reckless driving, a whiff of beer on his breath, and Eric making no attempt to defend himself. I thanked the cop for bringing him home alive;

things people say this late at night when we really just want to crawl into bed and pull the covers over our heads. But these were the sleepless years. Bruce and I alternated the Saturday-night late watch, and this one he got to sleep through. The trouble would still be there in the morning, fresh and ugly, for us to fight about on the way to the impounding lot.

It's all part of the journey of parenting the neurotypical teenage boy. Trust me, the day will come when your sweet kid looks you square in the eye and lies to you as smoothly as shifting gears. And you will believe him because you want to. *Big* mistake. Where you see your darling, darling boy, a good-enough student with a gentle heart, what you can't see is the bottle of booze he's stuffed inside his backpack.

All of a sudden I noticed my not-so-typical son, fourteen-year-old David, peering over the steering wheel of the officer's car. The car's blue light ricocheting around the ceiling of David's bedroom must have awakened him. To Eric, cops were the problem. But to David, all cops were like his buddy Isaac, heroes who drove fast cars with computerized dashboards and screaming blue lights.

Nearly identical in profile, Eric and David were very different as teenagers go. Where Eric was stocky and muscular and rhythmical, David's bird-delicate shoulder blades seemed to float around his spinal column as if they were out of sync. Tonight he'd attempted to dress himself, although the shoelaces that would never be tied were untied, and the zipper his fingers couldn't quite grasp was all the way down.

Standing next to the police cruiser, David ran a hand through his thick brown hair to settle it down and it popped back up. He watched Sergeant Courtenay choose a key from a ring on his heavy belt to unlock the handcuffs, squeezing Eric's wrists. David leaned into the open back door and noticed the metal screen separating the front seat from the back. There was a flush of excitement on his face.

"You have a dog?" David asked the cop.

Sergeant Courtenay was busy, radioing headquarters with his current whereabouts. "Huh? Yeah, I got a dog."

"Does he ride around with you on the backseat and get sleepy?" David had this big hopeful grin on his face.

"JEE-sus, David—" Eric snarled under his breath. Eric was coming out of his beery fog now, and he always woke up cranky.

The cop lifted his eyes off the paperwork and took a sharp look at David, standing there in the moonlight flapping his hands. Under the officer's gaze, the muscles in David's throat clamped together tight like a fist, and he forced out an *unhk, unhk*. He balled up his fist and slammed it against the involuntary tics that made people stare. The cop stared anyway, then he said, "No, my dog's just a dog. You're talking about K-9 dogs. . . ."

Just what David wanted to hear. He launched: "Our Sophie was a German shepherd, like a police dog, and—"

His brother rolled his eyes and exploded. "Shuddup, David. He doesn't *care*."

Eric shot me the look that meant, *Why can't he be normal?* But David was chirping now, giggling at the memory of the good, sweet dog that used to follow him around the neighborhood and bring him home when he stayed gone too long.

The officer returned Eric's license to me and recommended I keep it until the case came to court. "Don't let him drive till then. The judge likes it when the parents do that."

Yes, I know the drill.

"Why don't you get this boy inside," the officer was saying to me. "Oh, wait a sec." He reached into the backseat of the cruiser and pulled out Eric's leather football jacket with the big varsity letter on it. Then he turned his holstered girth toward Eric. "I plan to call your coach first thing in the morning. I suggest you beat me to it."

Eric mumbled a cross between "Thank you" and "Fuck you," and I dragged him inside the house. Angry and disappointed, I could feel my clenched jaw pressing against my sinuses. I managed to keep it to "Shower and get to bed. And set your alarm to call the coach. You're on your own on this one, buddy."

"He's gonna kick me off the team, Mom."

"Yes. I suppose he will." I flicked the bathroom light on and handed him a fresh towel.

I was too tired to fight. I had never understood why my son limited his worldview to what a coach thought. As the steamy air hit his nervous system, the rushing water in the shower didn't block the sound of Eric retching. Bone-achingly tired, I leaned against the wall outside the bathroom door. Poor guy, he wasn't a bad kid. A couple of mornings a week I still found him asleep in David's bed, his arms wrapped around his little brother.

As I headed downstairs to lock the front door, the silly

bird clock on the kitchen wall warbled out two in the morning. Birds. David loved his birds.

I reached the front door and realized David was still outside in the driveway, talking to the cop. Only now, David was
perched on the edge of the cruiser's front seat, both hands on
the steering wheel of the Crown Victoria. The officer leaned
in to point out features on the control panel. I knew what
David was thinking. He was thinking this was just like the
cop shows he watched on TV, all day if I'd let him. I understood this might be one of the best nights of David's life.

Heading back out to the police car, I overheard David's
cheerful, crazily excited, but somehow businesslike "Yeah,
yeah. I'll be there." He was nodding his head like a pogo stick
and his eyes jumped back and forth from the officer to me,
begging me to jump in to seal the deal.

Turning to me with glittering eyes, David said, "Right,
Mom? It's okay for me to ride in the cruiser tomorrow?" He
was opening and closing his fists now as if he could pull the
cop and me into agreement with them.

Sergeant Courtenay ran a hairy hand over his lopsided grin
and his wedding band caught a glint from the streetlight.

For the first time that night, I saw this cop as somebody
other than the policeman who brought my kid home safe. I
saw a broad-shouldered man who smelled like coffee, with an
out-of-style haircut that was probably regulation length. I saw
a guy in his forties with kind eyes and the beginning of a
paunch who'd probably rather be at home right now with his
own kids than here with mine. I saw a husband who worked

weekend nights and missed the football games on Sunday while everybody else was at home, padding around the kitchen in their socks.

"'Cause I told him about Isaac," said David, his body twisting with possibility, "and how I'm going to be a K-9 officer someday." David's head was jerking hard like he couldn't decide which way to smile. I was cold standing there barefoot in my nightgown. I looked past the cop and lifted my palms to the night sky.

"Ma'am?" said the officer. "Bring him to the station a little before five tomorrow. We'll ride around the parking lot in the squad car."

"Eric too?" David asked. Both of his fists were under his chin and he'd wrapped one leg around the other.

The cop drew a hand over his mouth to pull down the corners. "And his brother."

David seemed so happy, a few more flaps and he'd lift his thin frame up into the night, flying away like a sparrow. A breathy "Sure" leaked out of my mouth, and I looked over at my son shivering and waving as Sergeant Courtenay started to pull away from the curb.

A little after two in the morning. The cruiser's taillights disappeared up the hill into the blue darkness. David set his feet wide apart and the forelock of his thick brown hair fell over his eyes. He turned to me with a brand-new look of cockiness that reminded me of Eric and unfurled his long, nervous body to its surprisingly full height. Looking almost bulletproof, he put his hands on his hips and thrust his chin forward into the night-filled distance between us.

AIMING FOR AVERAGE

Dealing with people has always been hard for David. Still, I don't know if he's a lonely guy or if I just think he should be. Bruce says that's the upside to all this.

"Things that bother us don't bother him. They don't mean the same thing to him, so don't expect him to feel the way you do. He just wants to be left alone." To which he adds, "So leave him alone."

Now, what mother in the history of all mothers, good or bad, could do *that*?

It was another Saturday night at home with the three of us. Max was away in his second year of college, and Eric, in his final year of high school, had headed out with his friends for an evening of mild mayhem. David lay stretched across his bed, listening to his favorite storyteller on the radio, signing off from a little town where "all the women are strong, all the men are good-looking, and all the children are above average."

I looked at the phone that never rings for him.

"Why don't you call Laura and see if she wants to go see a movie with you?" Laura was from his special ed class, someone he'd known since childhood. That caught his attention. I knew because he gave me a second's worth of sliding eye contact. "It's only a movie," I said. "Tell her we'll pick her up and bring her home."

I found the number in the school directory and called it out while David dialed. This wouldn't take long. A phone conversation with David meant awkward pauses that might randomly jump to his passion for police cars. So, when a girlish voice answered, my son shouted into the receiver "It's David!" and bobbled the phone into my lap like a hot potato. "You talk, Mom."

Laura's mother and I chose a movie matinee time. As David and I pulled into her driveway the next afternoon, he refused to get out of the backseat of the car.

"Go on, now," I grumbled into the rearview mirror. "Go knock on the door."

"She's not here. She decided not to go. Let's go home."

"David, you have to go get her. Look, they're watching us from the house. We're not leaving until you go knock on that door."

David did not budge.

And then there she was, standing on her front stoop. Pretty, with a long scarf around her neck and striped socks like Pippi Longstocking. Her mother came to the door, and then her father. "Where's David?" Laura called toward the car.

All of his avoidance tactics be damned, this was actually happening. Miserable and crumpling forward, my boy opened the car door and shuffled out like the next stop was the guillotine.

David rode to the movie in the front seat, Laura straining out the window in back. We planned to meet exactly where I dropped them off and I jotted down Laura's cell in case David made a getaway. "Hold hands," I suggested, "at least until you find your seats." Laura wore a wan little smile as she ran to catch up with David, standing on line with his hands stuffed in his pockets. She reached inside his pocket for his hand and his whole body went stiff.

Two hours and seventeen minutes later, there they were again. Standing right where I'd left them. They piled into the backseat, hugging opposite windows, but it seemed as if they had shared something new. Then I heard the girl whisper to the boy, "I don't want to do it anymore."

He said, "Come on, just one more time."

"*Uh*-uh," she said. Firm.

"Come on."

A harrumph from Laura's side of the car. "Okay, last time."

I heard her move in closer to him and giggle. Wondering what had become of the Two-Foot Rule, I oh-so-casually redirected the rearview mirror to where Laura's hand hovered over David's knee.

Then they each raised a fist and swung it down on the count as Laura chanted, "Rock, paper, scissors . . ."

———

Eric always understood his little brother was wired a bit differently. For the last two years his laid-back watchfulness had kept the inevitable school bullies at a distance, but now that Eric was a senior, he decided to leave some protection for David behind. He nudged his football coach into making David the team water boy—a giant step closer to David being an average guy.

Every afternoon after school, 117-pound David stood in the end zone wearing a TEAM MANAGER jacket, surrounded by a cluster of linemen in skintight pants. After pounding out hundred-yard wind sprints, the athletes drained their water bottles as fast as David could fill them. Then they tossed their empties on the turf while he scrambled to pick them up. I pulled into the parking lot toward the end of the practice, waiting to bring David home.

Out on the field, the coach squinted into the sun, a white-hot blister sitting low on the horizon. He pressed on the accelerator of his golf cart, circling the boys like a cattle wrangler.

"Huddle up there, men!"

The players stood at rumpled attention with their helmets dangling by their chin straps. Somewhere in the herd, dust rose from Eric's head. The coach stepped out of the golf cart with a glide, graceful for a man his age. His dark eyes shone with an intensity that made the boys tighten their sphincter muscles and raise their chins. No matter what he said, the message always had the same effect, working the players into a testosterone-fueled frenzy that sent them bouncing on the balls of their feet, then bursting into the guttural whoops of barking dogs.

A safe distance away, David set down his bin of empty water bottles and perched on his haunches to watch at the edge of the lineup, one knee bouncing hard.

But it turned out somebody had been keeping a close eye on David all along: the school's track coach. A bit of a maverick with a gonzo case of ADD himself, the young coach had noticed the lanky water boy's long, easy sprints on and off the field between plays. At the end of the season he encouraged David to come out for the track team.

By spring of the next year, the coach had instilled in David the thrill of cross-country running, sending him splashing through muddy creeks and long, grassy stretches in the middle of a pack of his teammates. With Eric off at college now, David had gained a foothold in the high school's mainstream. He came home from track practice happier than he'd ever been. The long runs gave him plenty of breathing room and boosted his body's natural supply of mood-enhancing endorphins. The *unhk*ing that had always drawn unwanted attention had peaked. He'd turned what was left of it into an easily faked cough. Mostly head jerks now, the tics flared up when he was stuck behind a desk, but running outside in the fresh air seemed to increase his capacity for self-control. The tics meshed into the beat of his inner metronome.

Now, instead of coming home and stacking nickels and dimes with Bruce or me every afternoon, he kept pace with long-legged athletes, stretching his hamstrings with them and leaning in on the edge of their jock talk. Off the track he was still a loner, but when the team did its six miles of roadwork, there was David looking calm and loose, somewhere in

the middle of the pack. Where he placed in the meets didn't
faze him in the least. It wasn't speed he had but a natural
grace. Circling the track or splashing through the mud, he
finished his races with the same form he'd begun them: head
up, shoulders low, open fists swinging in opposition.

"Running tall," the coach called it.

Still, there were a few glitches. The sound of the starting
gun generated a head tic that delayed David's initial step-off,
but with one foot on the varsity track team and the other in
his special ed classes, he willed himself to shake it off and
move forward. On the other hand, the team's long runs seemed
to nourish rather than deplete him. It was clear the boy liked
to run, and we liked that it was taking him to a place where
the burdensome world of high school might rest more gently
upon him.

At the end of the fall track season, one of David's teachers
asked him to write about how it felt to be part of the team,
how it felt for him to run:

11/21/05

*When I am running I feel that all of my thoughts have
been washed away. All I am thinking about is how many
different trees I can count. It's a time when I can focus
on the important things not when people are asking me
questions right in the middle of it.*

—David

However it worked, it worked for David. A gradual shift from my needing to know where he was every moment had begun. Alone on weekends now, he ran through the rain and over snow-covered sidewalks, offering Bruce and me no details of his treks. Neighbors would stop me at the grocery store and surprise me with David sightings: he might be spotted bounding out of the woods like a deer or running down an empty street at night. Running had become the antidote to our eternal managing of David, giving him his first taste of freedom, the beginning of the private life everyone is entitled to.

Then, sometime during his senior year, unknown to Bruce and me, the track coach handed David a nickname.

"Trust me, Mom," Eric told me years later. "You don't want to hear it."

"Let's have it."

"Sheez . . . oh, God. So. Okay. Coach called him Crazy Dave."

"But, Eric," I asked, the old anger swooping in and banging around my head. "How could his teammates let that go on?"

"You don't get it, Mom. David didn't mind. The coach did him a favor. Crazy Dave meant . . . well, it meant he was cool."

I suppose, wherever you go in life, you have to pick your battles. But there was more to this story. Sometime during Eric's last year of high school, he had been given a nickname too. In a cooking class where special ed students were mainstreamed with regular ed students, Eric sat beside a classmate of David's. They talked about football. This loyal fan never missed any of the school's games, and every Friday night she and several pals created a spirited cheering section dedicated to Eric's time on and off the field.

On cold, wet fall nights under the stadium lights, it was hard to miss them, front and center at the fifty-yard line. When Eric tackled somebody, his special cheering section whooped and clapped. If Eric got tackled, they booed. When Eric sat on the bench, they called out to the coach, demanding number 23 be put back in. Their unabashed enthusiasm did not go unnoticed by Eric's teammates on the field. They dubbed Eric king—King of the Retards.

"Yep. That was my nickname," said Eric. Here we were, all these years later, Eric just now letting me in on the full story. "They used to go crazy cheering for me. Made me feel good."

"But the nickname?" I couldn't see past the ugly of it. "And with David the team's water boy?"

"You gotta understand, Mom. My teammates would've taken a bullet for me. At the same time, their goal was to downgrade me. Jesus, Mom, that's just what guys do." Eric ran his hands through his hair, at a loss to describe what it's like to be a breathing, sweating, average high school boy. "That's the way it is with guys. If you don't grow up with it at home, you just throw that word around. I mean, come on, they're not like *us*."

Fact of life: in the wide chasm between how we'd like things to be and how things really are, there is little room left for the differently abled. As his senior prom night approached and the special ed kids made plans to go as a group, David declined the invitation.

"Not going" is all he said.

The Friday night before the dance I found him rummaging around in Max's old closet. He had pulled on a worn tux jacket that had been re-tailored a time or two, and his bony wrists were sticking out of the sleeves below the cuffs. That's when I realized David had shot up again, taller now than both his dad and his brothers.

"I'm going to the dance," he told me.

"And you should!" I said, thoroughly delighted and terrified for him.

By eight o'clock the next night, he looked about right. The part in his hair seemed as if a bullet had torn right through and, doubling up on his brother's penchant for cologne, he smelled great. Maybe a little *too* great—but we'd lower the car windows on the way there to air him out. The tux pants weren't all that short; the black socks hid the difference. And I thought his choice of a studded black cowboy hat gave him an Alan Jackson look.

But first, pictures. As Bruce posed him beside the tree in the front yard we always use for family photos, I thought about the hand-me-down tux jacket. It had fit Max perfectly but pulled a tad tight across Eric's chest as they posed here in front of the tree on their prom nights. I thought about how, off to the side, David had watched each brother being photographed, quietly absorbing the thrill of anticipation. And I thought how he might have been storing some of it up for himself. Now his day had come.

What handsome boys they were, the three of them! Max with his thick dark hair, Roman nose, and crystal blue eyes. In his photo under the tree, his arm is around a bilingual brunette in a sleek yellow gown, the promise of their youth shimmering in the lush spring grass. When Eric's night came around, he spiked his hair and surrounded himself with friends as a dozen couples squeezed in under the tree for a group shot. Dressed in the colors of painted eggs, the girls squealed as their spiked heels sunk into the lawn, their up-dos already starting to come down. The boys draped their jackets across their dates' bare shoulders and did their best to hide their flasks in the girls' tiny purses. At the top of our driveway, two stretch limos waited to whisk them away.

Tonight, with the last of his high school days on the wane, David stood alone under the tree. The cat settled in under the hosta plants as Bruce moved about with the camera. I stood back to watch. In the spring twilight, my youngest son lengthened his spine as his dad peered through the lens to capture the scene forever.

"Smile," said Bruce.

A moment before the camera flashed, David took off his cowboy hat and held it over his heart. Then he lifted his chin—a fine-looking young man with distant brown eyes, clutching at courage.

Gridlocked by limousines and inching our way toward the hotel's drop-off circle, we had front-row seats for the push and pull of high school romance. Walking along the sidewalk beside our car, a boy pulled his date in close, squeezed her waist, and rode his fingertips up and down her hip bone. When she leaned into him to adjust the ankle strap on her stiletto, he passed his hand over her buttocks and left it there, thrumming his fingers. Trapped in the car with his mother and father, David exploded out of the backseat. No good-bye, just gone. Bruce's voice trailed after him—"Call us when you're ready to come home!"—and I caught David's sharp cringe as he slipped into the swarm of tuxedos and gowns.

Bruce broke clear of the traffic around the hotel and headed toward downtown. "How about the little bistro with the window table in Georgetown? You know the one."

"Perfect," I said, and reached for his hand. Suddenly, Bruce and I had the whole evening in front of us and a good reason to celebrate: shepherding our last child through the precarious hoops of high school. While most of the young prom-goers would soon be heading off to colleges, their résumés filled with the sports and music and languages that would help launch careers, success held a very different meaning for our David. If all went as planned after graduation, David would be heading to Florida for two years—*two years!*—of the independent living skills program, which targeted house-keeping chores, balancing a bank account, and looking someone square in the eye when attempting to ask for a job.

Bruce's cell phone rang as we crossed Key Bridge into Georgetown. Live music roared in the background. "Dad. You can come get me now."

An hour later the tux jacket sat in a heap turned inside out on the floor of David's closet. It was just another Saturday night at home with the three of us—David back in his room, listening to his favorite storyteller sign off again from that distant place "where all the women are strong, all the men are good-looking, and all the children are above average." Even for a long-distance runner like David, it would always be a hard place to find.

SWEEPING UP

Every mother knows the old saying about having children: "The days go by like years, and the years go by like days." But when a child is unable to leave the nest, it challenges the natural order of things. Years and days get mixed up.

After his high school years wrapped up, we packed David off to Florida for the independent living skills program we had put so much hope into. Yet that arrangement fell apart. During that time, David dropped out of photography lab because of the stinky chemical smells, was booted out of the culinary arts class for mishandling sharp knives, and, after the animal shelter job fell through, ended up in the school office, pressing buttons on the copier machine. As for the interpersonal skills, he had failed to make a tight bond with his roommate and never ran a load of laundry, the mountain of crusty T-shirts and towels rising from his closet floor until the counselor's weekly drop-by. On the other hand, he never complained of being homesick. He made a friend he would never see again, an Aspergian student who shared his love of cop cars; and he had learned the hard way that he should never get in a car with a stranger headed into the Everglades. Looking back now, the best thing I can say about David's time away comes across as deeply selfish on my part, but it's the unblinking truth: it gave Bruce and me a chance to reconnect as a couple. It was our first real break in over two decades from the 24/7 supervision of another person's life.

That is no small thing.

So, a month shy of his twenty-first birthday, it was time for David to come home again. Bruce and I made the long drive down to pack him up.

On a steamy July day, in a final sweep through his apartment, I was down on my knees, torqued under his bed, reaching for a forgotten ID. Outside on the balcony, Bruce and David stood together, taking a break from lugging things down the flight of stairs. It was David's last look at the neon greens and blues of the apartment complex that had colored his life the last two years.

"Well, Dave," said Bruce, the sweat trickling down his fingertips. "What you gonna miss most about this place: the weather? Your friends?"

"Yeah."

On the patio below, three teenagers, two boys and a girl kicked back on deck chairs, sunning themselves. Their loud voices floated up.

"Hey, see what's going on?" The question hung in the humid air, clear and distinct. "The retard is moving out."

"Really?"

Pause.

"Good."

Then they giggled.

"My knees buckled," Bruce told me as we dropped off the apartment key in the manager's office. "David had to have heard it too. We both just stood there listening to them laugh." He rubbed his forehead. "It hurts when all you can do is stand by and watch."

David waited for us in the car, slumped over like someone had let the air out of him. He had no good-byes for the woman he'd brought his rent to the first of every month. None of that firm handshake with practiced eye contact stuff he'd been working on for two years. But I wondered how many times he'd been victim to some other casual crime against his spirit, other careless moments we would never hear about. Where does that pain go?

"I'm just hoping—best-case scenario here—maybe David's flip side kicked in on that balcony and he was oblivious to the whole goddamn thing," Bruce said in his glass-half-full way.

We dropped Bruce off at the Fort Lauderdale airport for a quick flight back to Washington so he could get back to work. I pointed the car into the steady stream of I-95 traffic northbound. A half hour later, I looked over at David, conked out with his head against the window. All right, he's sleeping, but God, how it must hurt to be him, forever fighting this mean cycle of try, fail, and try again. Only eighteen more hours and I'd have him home again.

Again.

And then I felt myself start to lose it.

I am no good at this crying thing. I come from a long line of watertight women who mean to persevere against any maudlin thought that pricks our periphery. But a beach ball had somehow inflated in my lungs right then, so while David slept on, I let the steady whoosh of big trucks on the highway mask my stifled blubbering. I was pretty much committed to a messy, full-on implosion when my cell phone rang: one of my sisters calling me out of the blue, asking "How's it going?"

With barely enough time to put up the family's "No whining" shield, I squeezed out, "You've caught me at a bad time."

"What's wrong?"

My siblings and I all have complicated lives now, with extended families of our own to manage—aging in-laws to care for, weddings to throw, and a new generation of babies to delight in—yet our genetic code has produced a clan of fairly private people. We expect upbeat from one another. Fortitude. David's circumstances are Bruce's and mine alone to work through. I am very embarrassed to have been caught in the act of bawling over them. Bawling and embarrassed. *Sheesh*.

Concerned, my sister asked again. "What is it?"

Lord have mercy. Where to begin with the things I would not be telling my sister today? How to explain the raw send-off from the teenagers at David's apartment? Or maybe the squelched promise of David's animal shelter job? How about ciphering the impact on David's psyche after two years at an independent living skills program with so little to show for it? No. I would not be explaining what it's like to watch time be so cavalier with a child.

To do so, I would have to unwrap the dried-up scrapbook of Hope that has toyed with me for years. Early on, Hope had me clinging to reports of edgy therapies and magic pills that promised results for my child. And Hope made me overlook the childhood milestones that weren't reached while we waited, believing he'd get there. Then one day, chin up and a bit impatient, I saw that my beautiful little boy no longer fit onto my lap. The cuddliness of his childhood had vanished and a thinned-out version of all that sweetness had begun to sprout knees and elbows. In its place was a gangly weed with the unsteady vocal cords of an adolescent boy. But this child was different. Although his body had kept pace with its biological clock, his mind remained veiled in a separate time zone. From now on, his social gaffes would go unforgiven and the mother-launched prompts that had worked before—"Got a handshake for the doctor, David?"—would seem domineering and turn me into a nag haunting the background. That thing called Hope had settled into the attic, boxed away.

Nor would I be explaining to my sister that David will make his lifelong journey in this state of being. That my son's present is his future. A solitary life to be lived in the right-here, right-now zone. Because what's not easy today will not be easy tomorrow or thirty years from tomorrow—and, trust me, no one wants to talk about that.

"Listen," I said, tightening my hold on the steering wheel. "Can I call you back some other time?"

"Well, sure. . . ." And that let two watertight women off the hook.

STARTING OVER

Home again. With the Florida sojourn now a yellowing snapshot in time, David is growing restless. He floats through our house like a ghost, a silent presence. He eats at the table alone and exits the room when we enter. And with no job lined up for him, the years of his living at home stretch ahead along an endless road for each one of us.

For now, during the week he is enrolled in a vocational training program, but he will age out of this system in six months when he turns twenty-two. After that, there is the prospect of minimum-wage jobs set aside by the state for disabled adults in the community: jobs such as paper shredders, trash pullers, or mail room workers. Still, a job is a job, and the right to work is a basic civil right. But the terrible rumor is that even these jobs are to be cut from the state's budget this year because of the ailing economy. Every day now, Bruce and I see local news reports about special education advocates protesting at state legislators' offices, demanding these jobs be kept intact. The threat of losing them is no longer on the periphery. It has jumped to the foreground with an outpouring of support from families of special needs young adults like David.

At home, we are bombarded with e-mail solicitations to pressure our congressman to take up the fight to keep the jobs. "Join us," the activists insist, and so we do, calling our representative and promising to stand up as a family at the next public hearing. We slap the group's bumper sticker on our car—*ALLY: A Life Like Yours*—that explains the vital civil right we're demanding. There is new grit in Bruce's voice when he talks about David's future now, and being part of the fight has stirred hope in both of us.

And just like that, we've hopped back on the merry-go-round of possibility that heaves and wheezes into action, finally picking up enough momentum to lift us up and down by the gut.

And what of David's reaction?

David doesn't seem to make the connection that one of these jobs has his name on it. That this is his ticket to work, his chance at a life he can call his own. Instead, Monday through Friday, his mornings are spent straightening shelves in a grocery store, the same mind-numbing task he had in high school. Only now it's called vocational training, he doesn't get paid, and it will soon come to an end. Yeah, Monday through Friday he can pretty much live without.

The real question is: What does he do with the rest of his time?

Like so many young men his age, he lives for the weekends. Saturday mornings he puts on his running shoes and comes alive in the only place where he can be his own boss: riding the rails. He hops on the Metro and stays gone, free to navigate his own course, free from all of us interfering folks who tell him what to do Monday through Friday.

And where does he go? The answer is in the snippets.

Now, all I know of his life I piece together through snippets: the random comments he makes, added to the collection of street flyers and ticket stubs he leaves lying around after a day in the city. These untethered fragments make up the private life this young adult is entitled to—and they are beginning to create a surprising collage:

A drumbeat erupts from the Chinatown alley. "Here comes the dragon!"

The dragon's head snakes its way onto busy H Street, cheered by applause from people swarming to celebrate the Chinese New Year. They stand ten deep on the snowy sidewalks straining to glimpse the orange dragon line coil in and under itself. Sweat glistens on the dancers' faces as they float to the beat. David digs in at the front edge of the spectacle and gawks.

"Conga!" yells a drunk pedestrian in a leather jacket and a Redskins cap, pushing from behind. But now a pair of hands clamps solidly onto David's hips and thrusts him into an impromptu chorus line. A shiny-haired girl turns

her back to him and embeds his hands tight against her
slender hips, gyrating her perfect little bottom against the
addictive drumbeat. Trapped. The music thunders through
David's body. He is surprised how much he enjoys the
girl's firm grip on his hips and the odd little yelps coming
from her throat. The New Year's devotees surge around
them in pursuit of the dragon, leaving the soused conga
line stumbling along behind, David among them, gyrating
like a pack of wild monkeys.

No, I wasn't there, but this is pretty much the story David
offered me in snippets from emptied pockets, give or take a
few adjectives. Perhaps you will forgive a mother's imagined
dread over that "perfect little bottom," but the "pack of wild
monkeys" on that conga line? All his.

"Mom, what's 'born-over'?" Another snippet.

On a busy Saturday afternoon outside the Clarendon Metro
station, David crawls into the front seat of my car. Fresh off a
long run, he smells like sweat and popcorn. He carries a pam-
phlet with a cross and a rainbow on the cover. Popcorn?

The window to hear about his latest adventure opens
briefly. It comes the moment he slides into my car, but slams
shut after the first telling.

"Say that again."

"You know, 'born-over.' "

"Do you mean 'born-again'?"

"Yeah, that's it. I'm that now."

Okay, I think I've got this one. Somewhere between dropping David off at the Metro this morning and picking him up this afternoon, David has had another epiphany at the hands of the experts. I wonder what this one looks like.

"Was she pretty, David?"

"Who?"

"The Jesus jumper."

"Which one?"

Aha, so there were two. He's putty in their hands. Two pretty girls giving out rainbow-colored pamphlets—this time with a helping of free popcorn.

"How much did you give them, David?"

"They said whatever I wanted to give."

"How much this time, Dave?"

"All the quarters and my farecard."

Forget the questions with yes or no answers; this is how we talk to each other. I have to be deliberate and calculated to make it to the next level with this fellow. And I only know I've succeeded when he moves the conversation forward. *Or not*. I'm never really certain about any of this, because not knowing David is what it means to know him.

We toss out the rainbow-colored pamphlets and I manage to talk him down from this one fairly easily, but the next weekend the Metro evangelists strike again. These guys are different. They want more from him than loose change. Two young men have exchanged phone numbers with him and sent him home with a thick book about their beliefs. From time to time they give him a call, just to chat about God knows what. Handwritten prayers crumpled into his pockets have begun to show up in the laundry pile.

But the thick book sits unopened on a shelf in David's room. Although David has become a capable reader, Jack London's *Call of the Wild* better fits the bill. In his teens, I handed him Max's dog-eared copy of *The Catcher in the Rye*, figuring it had just enough dirty words to hook him, but he never opened that one. Instead, his idea of reading for pleasure became maps. Maps of cities, maps of highways. He pores over travel books for maps of subway systems. His favorite book of all time is *Frommer's Portable Washington, D.C.*

"I like the maps" is what he says. "Especially the ones that say *You Are Here*."

There are no maps in the thick book on his bookshelf. So, for the moment, I can put these new "friends" out of my mind. Still, my confidence that David will never open this epic mix of theology and folklore is bittersweet, because everyone's life is about choices. Only, David needs to realize the ones before him now—whether choosing a friend or fighting for the right to work—will create the map to a life he must one day call his own.

ALL CREATURES
GREAT AND SMALL

David takes a giant leap over the rivulet of water that gushes between him and the bottom step of the bus. It's been a blustery, wet week, and the water will find its way beneath the laces of his running shoes. But David likes where he's headed, across town, back with the animals again. Twice a week after his day ends at the vocational training program, he drops by the Washington Humane Society, where a volunteer's slot has opened up. He wears a green STAFF shirt to clean the cages and walk the dogs with another volunteer, a college girl his age. The downside is the ninety-minute commute it takes to get there: a bus, two trains, plus the half-mile sprint from the Metro station.

A month into his shelter stint, posters appear on the bulletin board announcing its annual high-society gala. Fashion for Paws, one of the city's hippest annual events, sends gorgeous models down the runway alongside cute dogs to raise money for the four-footed set. David will be one of the backstage canine handlers. He must wear solid black—shirt, shoes, and pants—in order to blend into the shadows.

On the afternoon of the gala, he dives into the recent history of Max's closet, pushing past a tumble of baseball caps and an empty tie rack in search of a tuxedo vest. To this he adds his own black cowboy hat, lingering before a mirror to angle the brim just so. Still not sure, he walks through the house peeking at his reflection in every shiny surface. Finally, he is set.

The big event comes on the first night of spring at the swank Italian embassy. Out front, fashion photographers snap pictures of silken legs as they sprawl out of stretch limos. Backstage, David's job is to steady the dogs before and after the models sashay them down the runway. All but invisible in this fantasy, David watches from the shadows. These girls aren't like the girls he knows from school, the ones who idly twirl their hair or giggle into their cell phones. These girls come from some other planet altogether.

With tiny dresses wrapped around their flagpole frames, they push off on stiletto hooves and lead with liquid hips. On the return, they collapse their legs like folding chairs and nose-kiss the pooches. Terminally poker-faced, they look straight through David as he steps up to reclaim the dog.

It is well past midnight by the time he's done loading the dogs into their travel crates. The guests and models take their champagne flutes and retreat to the white tents with the smooth jazz. The dog handlers call it a night.

"Mom," he says, calling home. "Come pick me up, but park around the corner from the tents."

A long-anticipated hormonal moment has arrived: mother embarrassment has set in at age twenty-one, a perfectly healthy sign that David is growing up.

"Okay, but did you have fun tonight? Were your dogs well behaved? Did you get a chance to talk to any of the models?"

"Models don't talk to me, Mom."

Twenty minutes later, David is scuttling down the empty sidewalk toward the car. I notice his runner's gait is not as fluid as usual and he's holding his cowboy hat in both hands, covering a hard-on. Poor kid. As the mother of two older boys, I realize my youngest will have trouble sleeping tonight.

At home, I knock on the open door of his room to say good night. David is perched on the edge of his bed, fresh from a shower. His wet hair is slicked back and a towel is wrapped around his waist, the length and beauty of him undeniable. He is solemnly petting our serial killer cat Sammie. She who in springtime brings us a cadaverous flow of gifts: a fresh heart, a tiny lung, a set of teeth edged in gray fur. She who begins the night settled on his pillow with a lusty purr and that blissed-out claw-pull thing cats do.

All creatures have their instinctual desires, so why wouldn't David? The child who resisted cuddling and hold-ing has the same hormonal drive bubbling up inside him as every other red-blooded twenty-one-year-old male. The horny days of high school are not far behind him, and gradually he is becoming self-aware. I often notice him preening in front of the mirror, ranking his chiseled features and deep-set eyes. What he sees there is just about all a young man could ask for, only the small talk is missing, the subtle shades of chitchat girls expect in a romance. Girls like the ones David is thinking about tonight.

So he drops to his knees to confer eye to eye with the cat, his silent comforter.

"Hey, Dave," I ask him from the hallway. "You must have had a pretty good time tonight—right? You had a good time?"

Mesmerized by one of the cat's slow-motion arabesques, David strokes the soft fur of our lazy murderess. Then, without looking up from the cat, he says more to himself than to me, "I decided something. I decided I'm never getting married."

The Fifth Street Ladies Gardening Club is one of Bruce's better ideas. This early spring Saturday morning he is rattling around inside the garage like he's got real purpose, lining up a shovel, a rake, and a watering hose to stuff into the trunk of his big Jeep. David is in the front seat waiting for his dad, ready to get his hands a little dirty.

Bruce, forever the entrepreneur, now works in tandem with the city to renovate old apartment buildings into affordable housing for low-income families. The ladies of Fifth Street—that would be Nicole, Yvonne, and LaRonda—are single mothers trying their hardest to make it alone in a tough part of the city.

Just as Bruce climbs into the front seat, I step out into the garage. "Where do you think you're going with my gardening stuff?" This is the guy who digs up dandelions with my serving spoons and scrapes the ice off his windshield with a bent spatula.

"David's going to do some yard work for me on Fifth Street. Dig some holes, plant some shrubs, pick up cigarette butts. Help the ladies fix the place up a little."

Despite months of knocking on shop doors, filling out job applications in his odd little scrawl, and never hearing anything back, David is still without a paying job. So from time to time David makes a few bucks doing cleanup chores around the apartments, shoveling snow off the ladies' sidewalks or spreading mulch, now that it's spring. Bruce says a little real-world experience might do him some good, because you never know what he might learn from it.

An hour later Bruce calls me from the local gardening store where he and the ladies are standing in the middle of the shrubbery section, undecided. On silent autopilot, David treads back and forth, loading thirty-pound bags of mulch into the Jeep.

"Question," Bruce says into the phone. "What kind of plants would do best along the front of the building?"

"Is it sunny there?"

"Partial shade."

"Impatiens," I tell him. "They're pretty, they're hardy. They should do well."

"Wait a sec. Let's see what the ladies think."

He passes the suggestion back to them and I hear a explosion of whoops. Bruce comes back on the line.

"Ah, no. You don't get it. They need something to protect the first-floor windows. Yvonne says she wants something prickly enough to stop her ex from tossing a concrete block through it."

"A what?" It dawns on me that the harsh reality for too many of Bruce's clients is staving off domestic violence.

"Roses," says David, bending down to lift another bag of mulch. "Roses hurt."

The ladies stare at the quiet, skinny kid and then brainstorm a bit among themselves. Yes, they finally decide, big thorny rose-bushes might be just the ticket. Bruce is right. We never can tell what David might learn from this job. He slings the last bag of mulch over his shoulder and follows his son over to the Jeep to make room for a dozen of the prickliest damn rosebushes he can buy.

Even though the cleanup jobs have given David some pocket money and a taste of the real world, they are only a sometimes thing. Despite his volunteer gig at the animal shelter, there is still no paying job waiting for David once his vocational education program ends in June. But the satisfying weight of the loose change in his pockets has brought a new light into his eyes. Late one night when I'm reading in bed, he suddenly appears at my side.

"You think I'll ever get my own place?"

Finally. A way in to reach this overgrown boy of mine. I put down my book and pat the sheets beside me. "Come here."

He moves to the far end of the bed and sits down, pulling his knees up under his chin. Close enough. I remind him about the state budget cuts threatening to cut the pipeline to businesses open to hiring disabled workers, and all the news stories we've been seeing about the angry push-back from special education advocates. I let him know about the public hearing we've promised to attend. I tell him this is a good kind of angry. Something he needs to be a part of.

"I just want a job and an apartment. With a cat."

"If you really want it, Dave, you're going to have to help make it happen."

The buzz to join the campaign to fight for the jobs is strong at David's school. After spending two decades of special education dollars to become productive citizens, cutting the promised jobs would rob these students of years of progress. They get that. Flyers demanding tough action come home in backpacks every day now, encouraging students to stand up for themselves at a public hearing. Petitions to keep the jobs circulate for students to sign. After-school sessions with tips on public speaking crop up. The red tape surrounding the budget is way past David's grasp, but for the first time now, he is certain one of those jobs belongs to him. When the time comes, he says, he will speak out.

This is war.

On the appointed day, outside the public hearing room, thirty young adults with special needs assemble in ordered chaos. They provoke stares with their loud nasal voices, uneven features, jerky movements, and jangling wheelchairs. To dramatize their plight of having no choice without the job program but to "graduate to the couch," they are wearing their pajamas; many have shown up for the three o'clock hearing dressed in bathrobes and fuzzy slippers, looking for all the world like the Mad Hatters' Brigade.

But not David. No silly PJs for him. Over and over, he smoothes the crease in his khaki pants and pulls at the neck of his Washington Humane Society T-shirt. The word "Volunteer" is stamped across the back of it.

At the clerk's invitation to come inside the hearing room, the brigade creates a raucous stampede as they climb over rows of chairs to fill up the seats with people who walk and talk just like them. They are noisy, giddy with the promise of solidarity.

But not David. Quiet and aloof, he melts into a front-row seat, looking like he'd just as soon sit this one out.

The chairman bangs the gavel and the public hearing gets under way, but not before a board member addresses the spectators with the rhetorical flair of a robo-caller. The seats are hard and David's bony legs bounce against them. His *unhks* have been dormant for some time, but right now his eyes are blinking like a caution signal, and if these gasbags don't wrap it up soon, he will lose his focus all together. Moving at a glacier's pace, the spotlight shifts to the business at hand, and a long line of protesters snakes its way up to the podium.

It is the students' turn to speak, and David is the lead-off hitter. His short speech in hand, he approaches the podium tic-ing mightily. Bruce and I look down on him from our seats along the top row of the amphitheater. Our boy is thin and nervous but, with his slicked-back hair, neat khakis, and tucked-in shirt, eminently presentable. I feel the same mix of pride and apprehension I've known sitting in the bleachers, watching his brothers throw a pitch or block a tackle.

Come on, Dave. Just like we practiced last night, buddy. Word for word.

David's fists pump open and shut and he bangs his left ear against his shoulder. Then he starts to read the speech we wrote. My ideas translated into his language.

"I am twenty-one years old." His voice booms out over the microphone deeper and more solemn than I've ever heard it. "I am a student at the vocational training center and a volunteer at the Washington Humane Society. I take care of cats and dogs and a rabbit." Bruce nods, and I mouth along with every word. "Every Tuesday and Thursday after school, I run to the bus stop from my house, take the bus to the Metro, then take the Metro to Georgia Avenue. From there I run a mile to my job at the shelter. I work four hours, then run back to the Metro for the ride home, an hour and a half each way."

Fine enough, staying on script. Only a half page to go. "I'm good at what I do, but . . . I . . . but, uh, I, uh—"

He freezes and the room gets very quiet. Ten seconds pass and someone clears his throat. *If ever there was a time for you to Use Your Words, Dave, this is it. Just read the script.* David bangs his chin onto his chest twice and then, like an old pro-

peller plane, he starts up again. Only now, my son the ad lib-
ber is righteous mad.

"I'm the Scoop-Up Man. I clean poop out of cages. But I'm
not like the other workers. I don't get paid."

He is holding the mic much too close to his mouth and it
amplifies the growl down in his vocal cords. Bruce looks at
me and I shake my head—*Nope, not in the script*—but the
horse has broken out of the barn, gone rogue. In slow motion
David balls up his fist and pounds it into the palm of his
hand. When he raises his head to speak, I hardly recognize
the young man behind the podium making fierce eye contact
with the panel.

"I want to get paid. I want a life with a real job and my own
place. You gotta keep your promise about jobs for people like
me. It's the right thing to do." He uses the back of one hand
to wipe his nose and waves a handful of paper at the board
members. "I . . . I brought my résumé if you want it."

David turns to take his seat and a garbled voice in the
audience breaks the silence: "Tell it, David!"

The front rows suddenly erupt. David's pajama-clad comrades are reaching across their seats to slap his back, woo-
hooing and high-fiving each other. Caught off guard, David
thrusts out his chin and squints. With a lifetime of being
talked at, never listened to, his delight in the unexpected support radiates an arc of electricity too narrow for most in the
room to perceive. A slow grin crawls across his face. It is
David's own kind who have seen through the prism of autism
to the start of self-advocacy here: *Hey, if this guy can do it, then
why not me?*

The board members stare back at the rowdy young adults with a self-conscious mixture of pity and awe. One member's eyes glisten with tears, and when the video camera tilts her way, she dabs a tissue at them.

"JEE-sus," Bruce mutters, "we don't need any of that BS. Just put the damn jobs back where they belong." But he's savoring this latest border crossing. He's on his feet, too, clapping hard for a kid who has just jettisoned himself into a new dimension of independence.

SURPRISED BY GRACE

The first hint of winter sneaks up in late October, and the days seem much shorter. Beyond my window, the bare branches of a maple tree rise and fall in the wind and drizzle. David is out there somewhere, enjoying the privacy of running in the rain. A weak little voice in the back of my mind makes an instant diagnosis: *pneumonia.* I try to reach him.

He answers on the fourth ring and crowd noise rages in the background.

"Where are you, David?"

"Outside the Clarendon Metro. People are everywhere. It's raining hard stuff."

The sky is slate and it is time to start dinner, but the rain against my window has turned into crystallized darts. Pooling water has formed skins of ice on the front walk.

Don't rescue him, don't rescue him.

I grab my coat and keys and jump in the car. "I'll be right

there, Doodlebug." *What are you doing? If you don't let him figure it out for himself, you'll be rescuing him forever. Is that what you want to be doing when you're eighty?*

My car temp registers 33° Fahrenheit.

Here I come, baby!

It's madness at the Metro. The crowd has spilled into the street, and there are bright lights in the center of it all. As I edge my car closer, I see red, white, and blue campaign post-ers. A TV reporter angles for a stand-up at the edge of a politi-cal rally. And there is David, shivering in his light jacket, running pants, and thin gloves. He's standing between two pretty young women in coats and gloves as they hand out hot chocolate and campaign stickers to commuters. Since he's started these afternoon runs, his cheeks have hollowed out and striated muscles define his long legs. I honk the horn and he makes his way through the crowd to me, beating his gloved hands against the cold.

When he climbs in the car, he smells of hard sweat and the heavy soak of his running clothes. The first words out of his mouth are "Can I vote?"

It's a good question. The 2008 presidential election has piqued my curiosity over how David's mind works. We often watch the evening news together in silence while I set the table and make the salad for dinner. He sits through the entire show without leaving the room, watching the familiar faces; but he's not yet mentioned which candidate has earned his vote. I made up my own mind early on, but so far I've bitten my tongue on swaying David's pick, preferring to see him plunk down in front of the nightly news to decide for himself. But on a cold rainy night like this, David could easily be swayed by a cup of hot chocolate. Do I step in and tell him what I want him to think, or stand by and watch him make a decision based on the pretty face at the other end of that hot cup of chocolate?

Either way, David is twenty-one and in the eyes of the law an adult. And with that distinction, little issues have morphed into bigger ones. This is his first chance to vote for a president, and the right to vote is as important for him as it is for any other U.S. citizen. As fundamental as the right to marry, the right to drive a car, and the right to own a gun. But these rights create a great big tar baby for David: he punches one fist in and it gets stuck, and the next punch traps him in an even stickier situation.

All grown-up now. Sometimes when he enters a room I mistake him for one of his brothers. But the resemblance that is so strong in the physical sense ends there. With Max and Eric, Bruce and I gave our love and saw it returned in the usual milestones: a tiny hand reaching up, an eight-year-old's gushing hugs and kisses, the teenage athlete's minimalist wave from the field. Yet those responses have not come naturally to David. His emotional life is a mystery. Neither selfish nor whiny, he is a consistent one-way street. Along with never having said "I love you," he does not sing, whistle, or hug. He's never needed a night-light or been afraid of monsters under the bed, because he is content alone in his room. He keeps three alarm clocks at his bedside set seventy-three minutes apart. I've asked him about this, but he says it's "a plan," and I understand that's the way he needs it to be. And though I do not know that he loves me, I don't take it as a slight. The gift of his love is not mandatory for my allegiance, because it is loving, rather than being loved, that makes us fully human.

And yet . . . when David comes in from a night run and wolfs down a box of cereal before heading off alone to his room, I sometimes feel a deep ache for what could have been.

Bruce continues to believe the flip side of David's emotional blindness is its own saving grace. He's decided that the disquieting things that keep *us* up nights do not register such concern in David's mind, so unencumbered is he by uncertainty over the future. Perhaps the worry-free bubble in which our boy lives acts as a protective shield from stress. A resident in the perpetual state of Right Now, David doesn't lose any sleep over what would happen if his Supplemental Security payments get slashed or if his Medicaid benefits dry up. These are very real qualms, yet somehow manageable because they do not begin to approach the monster coiled under the bed.

The howling dread for us and every parent of a special needs adult—the singular ache that dries the mouth and makes the heart race—is the growing isolation. Who will offer this human being a healthy touch, chaste and loving, when I am no longer there? Now, as he moves toward greater independence as an adult, who will know if he has not made it home by the end of the day? And if there is no one, will there be safe shelter for him somewhere in his aloneness?

For years we have fought side by side, battling for the right school, therapy, job coach, and, lately, housing. As we champion his quest to become his own man, we have no idea what twists this life will take. He's finding his way in to where he wants to go, but he will be alone when he gets there. On the other hand, how many times have I put down the newspaper with a shudder after reading the latest story about a grim act of parental wrath that befalls so many children and young adults with special needs? That's when I find myself studying the power in my son's legs or the fine curve of his jaw. I feel wonder and a bit of awe for what he can do for himself, and am quietly convinced that some kind of grace permeates the everyday world.

Another tar baby here is our own advancing age, because life turns menacing there. The fact is, Bruce and I are thirty-five years older than David, and we have no way of locking in how things will play out for him after our bones have dried. Nonetheless, knowing what we know, we have made some plans.

"Sorrow is most easily expressed by money," says our Special Needs Trust attorney, himself the father of an adult son with special needs. That means when Grandma doesn't know what else to do, chances are she'll write a check. But when Grandma is a retired schoolteacher like Sug, you better have a Plan B. Under our attorney's gentle guidance, we have begun to explore the practical issues we face to secure David's future.

First, we are to create a narrative of who we think David

is. We must bring a young man to life within its pages, then build a bridge to his future. It is nothing short of reimagining another person's entire life. Aside from the basic quality of life support for day-to-day living, we are to consider his personal happiness and comfort levels that will let him lead as normal, dignified, and fulfilling a life as he deserves. We have been encouraged to think outside the box about what he likes to do for fun, like running, and what his goals are, such as getting his driver's license. And why not? He knows how to drive. And there should be money for an evening at the movies, clothing, the car he's desperate to drive. He wants a cat for a companion. Write that down too. All of this goes into the narrative to give others a sense of David's strengths and needs.

But first things first.

A special needs trust isn't something to rush along. It takes months and months to complete the avalanche of paperwork, an overwhelming but practical necessity. The archaic legal language requires translation into real-people-speak. I read and reread the paperwork, dictionary in hand, to translate the Latinate alphabet soup of phrases like "ad litem" and "per stirpes," at one point asking our attorney, "Am I particularly thick, or is this stuff just hard to grasp?"

He was kind enough to smile.

Round one: David has taught us that life without tough choices does not exist. Still, the question of whom to appoint as his trustees in the unlikely event of our mutual deaths is troublesome. Bruce and I have visited the attorney's office on several occasions, sifting through the legal jargon, considering friends or family members who might be willing to assume a part of this enormous burden. This circle of support would provide a natural bridge to caring relationships for David and a sounding board to assist him with advice about future housing, health, and general quality-of-life matters. The stakes are high and the people we are asking to share the weight are reliable, empathetic, and quietly heroic. My brother was the first to step up to the plate. And Bruce's brother has said yes too. Both of David's brothers have answered the call with an unequivocal "I'm in," but we realize it's a heavy yoke for twenty-something siblings who deserve a shot at their own carefree lives before settling down with families of their own.

And still we're not done, but we're getting there. Three or four times Bruce and I have set a date to meet each other at our kitchen table to wade into the manila folder cataloging David's future needs. Three or four times we've let something get in the way—a silly argument, an evening walk, an unfinished novel—because no one looks forward to carving out time to think about a future they will not be around for. But as mind-boggling as the process is, at the end of the day there is relief, not dread, in wising up and finding new ways to think about securing David's future.

Round two: Gird yourself. The process for limited guardianship can tear your heart out. In creating this practical document, Bruce and I have anguished over our decision to assume limited legal control of David's life. The irony here is it's something neither of us would wish on our son in a million years, but we have to protect him and ourselves from predators who would take advantage of his gullible nature. To do it, we must go to court, appear before a judge, and fight—I'm telling you, fight!—to have him declared legally incapacitated. If a judge grants us limited guardianship, David must have our written consent for each of his constitutional rights: to vote, to marry, to choose a religion, to own a gun. Plus, the rights to drive a car and handle his own finances.

It pains us to think limited guardianship could further stigmatize David as disabled. In speaking for him, we are telling the world who he is when, in fact, we cannot know. On the other hand, this is a legal weapon that will help protect him from the nightmare of a predator's grasp. Here's the thing: the *unhk*s have vanished. The dramatic tics that plagued his teenage years have plateaued into blinking and sharp shoulder shrugs. But the most troublesome trait remains: his mind-blindness regarding social cues—sarcasm, body language, facial cues—especially with strangers. Math-blocked and easy to fleece, David's gullibility is a neon OPEN FOR BUSINESS sign to poachers.

That's how he managed to stop by a health club one afternoon and walk out thirty minutes later committed to a $3,800 contract with a personal trainer. David dropped that bomb on us during dinner that night.

Two hours after the contract had been signed, a fuming Bruce strode into the fitness club to demand the contract be voided. David and I waited out in the lobby, watching taut twenty-somethings pass by, hugging gym bags and water bottles. It seems ridiculous to count on the loose ethics of a vulture, but he claimed to have given David the benefit of the doubt because "he looked like a runner." Inside his manager's office, the trainer slowly caved. The manager just wanted the three of us gone, out of his hair. But to dissolve the contract, Bruce had to put in writing to the corporate office who our son was, what his disability entailed, medical documentation, and why the contract should not be considered legal. Messy stuff. Worse was having to break down the whole fiasco for David, who couldn't see what he'd done wrong.

As we drove home that night, all of us staring out a different window, Bruce gripped the steering wheel like a vise. He took great heaving breaths in an effort to control his anger, but there was no release valve for his built-up steam.

"David," he finally asked, "do you have any idea how much 3,800 bucks is?"

"No, I don't," said David. I flashed back to all of those long afternoons in the kitchen counting nickels and dimes and pennies. "Is it . . ." he asked his father, "a lot?"

It is a daunting task to be an honest witness to another person's dreams, but Bruce and I have just about used ourselves up. The battle for limited guardianship has suddenly jumped to the front line.

On an unseasonably warm evening, the court-appointed attorney, a young man in a seersucker suit, knocks on our door. Bruce invites him to sit on our deck to discuss the guardianship issue. As we step outside, the scent of the next-door neighbor's freshly cut lawn fills the air. My mind wanders to the plat of petunias waiting to be stuck into my garden. But the attorney isn't interested in small talk. He is acting strictly on behalf of his client. That, of course, is David, while Bruce and I, the petitioners, must prove our son's incapacity in explicit detail. The attorney has carefully read through our petition and wants to talk to Bruce and me first. Then David alone.

Now, I have always thought of our relationship with David as an open book: we've cut the kid's toenails for the last twenty-one years—who could be more in his corner? I open with the light stuff: how David's grandmother taught him to drive when he was a boy and how he'd had taken to it right from the start. "A real natural," I say, smiling at the memory.

But the too-young attorney is not moved by this vignette. He says, "Why do you believe David should be allowed to get his driver's license yet not own a gun?"

And so it's time to open up about our personal views on gun control. Why we don't own a gun, won't own a gun, in a family with three sons. But that's not the response he's after.

"Why," he wants to know, "isn't a two-thousand-pound automobile moving at fifty-five miles an hour just as lethal as a loaded gun?"

Okay, a different tactic. Bruce explains why driving a car could be a tremendous asset for David someday. How transportation is the key to his getting and keeping a job and building a more independent adulthood for himself. How David lights up at the very mention of it.

The attorney writes all this down and steers the conversation in a more personal direction. "Why do you believe your son is not competent to manage his own financial affairs?" And "Why do you think it would be in his best interests to take away this particular legal right?"

For the next hour we rip the scabs off the years spent counting nickels, dimes, and quarters on the kitchen table, and the salesclerks who've regularly cheated David out of his change. I scrounge up the voided health club contract to show David's vulnerability regarding money, looking for some sign in this stern stranger's face that he understands—understands we can't keep going back and doing cleanup for the rest of our son's long life, fighting to break every unsavory contract David signs, including one for marriage. The attorney writes this down too. Then he comes up with a question that stands to make a mockery of our whole effort here.

"If you believe your son does not have the good judgment necessary to own a gun," he asks, "then why do you believe he should have the right to vote?"

My heart drops like a stone into a well. Where to begin? There is a simple reason here involving intellectual freedom, but I cannot push the words out fast enough. It's like pulling a huge gob of bubble gum out of my mouth and turning it back into a single flat stick. Gasping for air, I look to Bruce for help.

"Because," he says simply, "everyone is entitled to their own opinion." Bruce's unshakable support for a son I know he doesn't understand brings a quick sting of tears to my eyes. We both realize the playing field has changed now.

I look out across my backyard at the weeping cherries that

have blossomed more lovely every spring over the last twenty years. I see the sloping garden where I've planted tomatoes, buried a cat or two, and broken an ankle. But now I feel like a new arrival on unfamiliar ground. We are the outsiders in our own home.

And now the attorney wants to interview David privately. I stand in the kitchen with the window and my antennae up. But David's back is to me. I cannot hear his answers, only the occasional question from the attorney. They hit me like a gut punch.

- *Do you believe your parents are acting in your best interests?*
- *Do you want them to handle your finances?*
- *Do you trust them?*

Imagine having to convince a perfect stranger about everything that is broken, weak, or missing in your child's life—and handing over this kind of power to him in the hopes that it will protect your child after you die. The young attorney gathers his notes, shakes each of our hands, and says we will meet again in court.

A month later, David, Bruce, and I stand before the deciding judge. The attorney's twenty-page report is spread out before her on the bench. The judge leans forward giving us a hard once-over.

"I have read this report quite thoroughly." Her gaze shifts

between Bruce and me before landing on Bruce. "It says you've asked that your son retain his right to vote because you believe everyone has the right to his own opinion?"

"Yes, Your Honor," Bruce says. "I do."

The judge gives him an unreadable nod, then turns to David, peering at him over her glasses.

"Young man," she says. "Do you know how old you have to be to get a driver's license?"

"Yes, I do," says David. "Sixteen."

"Well, according to this report, your grandmother taught you to drive when you were still underage. Let me see—you were only twelve or thirteen at the time. Is that true?"

"Yes. Yes, it is," says David, nodding yes and tic-ing a wild no.

Suppressing the slightest hint of a smile at the open face before her, the judge looks down and reads the ruling. "Then you, David, are a very lucky young man. Drive carefully."

Turning to Bruce and me, she says, "Limited guardianship is granted."

On the first Tuesday in November, I rise early, surprised to find a lump in my throat as I anticipate standing in line to vote. It's such an old-timey, hopeful thing to do. Five miles from the White House, it's cold at our house, but the sun sparkles as the three of us make our way to the neighborhood precinct. At seven thirty the parking lot is already jammed with cars and people calling out a spirited "Good morning!" On the sidewalk, heavily caffeinated campaign workers hand out last-ditch-effort sample ballots and red, white, and blue stickers with their candidate's names on them. David accepts whatever political buckshot is thrust into his hands. Right now, he is studying the names in the boxes with a big red check mark beside them.

"David, have you made up your mind yet?" I ask, noticing the party logo.

"Nuh-uh-uh," says Bruce, wagging a finger. "You promised you wouldn't do that."

"But . . . I'm just asking—"

"Nope." Bruce is enjoying this. "Not a word."

I bite down on my tongue and taste the blood of my ulterior motive.

David waits on line, tic-ing like mad in anticipation over his first look inside a voting booth. I'm nervous too. Even if I don't know who he's going to vote for, I like the idea of his being part of a larger community, because it takes all kinds. This is when I notice one of my neighbors, the mother of two teenagers, staring sideways at David. This lady has watched him grow up, but right now she sucks in her cheeks and lowers her jaw.

"Is *he* voting?" she asks us, tilting her head in his direction.

"Yep," Bruce tells her, fixing her with a scowl. "That's why we're standing here."

She turns her back on us and makes a little *hmphf* noise.

It seems like every new adventure with David offers us a chance to see the best and worst in people, and too many seem to think differently abled folks should accept a lesser life. It's an ongoing stealth battle against subtle slights, but sometimes you have to push back a little on those who think they own the blueprint for what it means to be human. Otherwise I'd be compelled to walk over there and give my neighbor a good choking.

The line moves forward. All around us, elderly volunteers work the precinct with a keener awareness of the human toll it's taken for every one of us to be here this November morning. They chatter about voter turnout and the chance of afternoon rain, bubbling over with the pleasure of their services being needed. A tall white-haired gentleman with a booming voice and eyes the color of blue Popsicles is checking voter registration cards. When he calls out David's name, David lurches forward in anticipation, knocking his ear against his shoulder and blinking. The older man stares hard at the thin fellow across the desk from him. He seems to be searching David's wiggly face for something.

"Ah—got it," he says. "You wouldn't be related to a Max Finland, now, would you?"

David's elbow shoots out to the side and he nods his head three, then four times. "Yes. Yes, I would."

"Tell Max his old history teacher sends his love, will you?"

The tension in David's shoulders drops like a load of books, and I realize kindheartedness can be just as subtle yet every bit as empowering as prejudice. David steps into the booth and draws the curtains closed behind him.

He is in there a very long time.

Bruce and I have finished voting and are waiting just beyond the ropes. We look at each other with the "What now?" look we've honed over the years. Suddenly a burst of campaign paraphernalia explodes from David's booth, and a flutter of elbows pokes through the curtain divide. When my citizen son emerges, he is wearing a huge grin and a red, white, and blue sticker stuck squarely between his eyes. It reads: CHANGE WE CAN BELIEVE IN.

SPECIAL

Kicking back on the sofa after dinner, my feet rest in Bruce's hands. The cat is sleeping in the crook of my arm and that second glass of wine is settling in nicely. As a TV talk show host begins his opening monologue, David stands at the edge of the darkened living room, reeled in by the music and the splash of bright lights.

We're already laughing when the host mentions the fuming member of Congress who shouted "Liar!" at the president during a televised speech on health care. The three of us chuckle when he dubs the congressman a "shit-kicker from South Carolina." Then he purses his lips and looks over his shoulder, going in for the kill, "Oh, yeah, this asshole with Tourette's syndrome—"

The studio audience bursts out laughing while the host makes two fists and jerks his body around for the audience.

"*Man*, Bill, don't *do* that," says Bruce. We swivel to catch

David's reaction, but the hallway holds only his shadow. There are quick footsteps as he retreats to his room.

I throw my hands up and send the cat flying. "Since when is Tourette's funny?" But the talk show host has already bounced on to the next topic, the audience galloping along with him. "People don't see the fallout, do they?"

What lousy timing this comic has. Ever since the county decided to reinstate the jobs program for special needs workers, David has been feeling pretty good about himself. Pretty, pretty good. Upbeat about finding a job and moving on with his life. But it seems even in good times, there is always a reminder of what he is not.

I toss Bruce the remote. "Change it, will you?"

The next afternoon I walk into the kitchen just as Bruce hangs up the phone. He's pulled his tie loose from his shirt collar, and his hands are in front of his face like he's trying to get a grip on something. "My son," he says, "the gift that keeps on giving. . . ."

The psychologist at the vocational training center has called to say there has been an incident. A threatening note to a teacher has surfaced with David's signature on it. We should come in tomorrow to discuss it.

Suddenly everything that we don't know about David comes galloping back toward us like the Headless Horseman. David has always been a loner with an impenetrable interior life, but I have reason to trust that he's as gentle as a mockingbird, more Boo Radley than The Misfit.

I knock on his door. "David?"

There is no response. In this house that means *Why, come on in!*

I enter into his world of the drawn blinds, the mildewed towel that is becoming one with the carpet, the rank socks, and the unmade bed. The making of a child's bed is an easy act of maternal love. Stopping that automatic chore is the harder duty, part of a gritty weaning to which the stronger mother must commit.

He's sitting in the dark playing Grand Theft Auto, wheels screeching. I stand at his shoulder feeling as see-through as the Invisible Woman.

"Look at me a minute, Dave. C'mon, eyes up."

No response, except for the police sirens. "So I hear you've been suspended for three days." He cuts his eyes at me and goes back to the game. The reek of his running socks tossed on the closet floor permeates the air. "What'd you do?"

Tic.

"Tell me what happened, Dave."

Tic, tic. Tic.

He has clashed with this teacher before over losing focus in his monotonous task of shelving items in a grocery store. I know this teacher is a caring professional and she's not the problem. David does not like to accept even constructive criticism from her because he has zero interest in this particular job. Just like at home, when he loses his interest in something, he needs repeated reminders to finish what he's begun.

"The note, David. They say you wrote a threatening note." I stick a pencil in his hand. "Show me the exact words you wrote." He bends over a sheet of paper and holds the pencil so tight, the point breaks. I hand him a pen. His tongue slides in and out over his lips as he struggles to get each word down. And he writes:

Miss P makes me so angry I think I'm going to explode.

—David

"That's it? That's everything?" His herky-jerky body language is going full tilt. "Nope. There's got to be more to it than this."

There is that odd flash of anger in his eyes that he rarely permits. "That's all—"

"No, it isn't, David." Just like his father, David is no good at lying. I think of it as one of their better traits. "What happened when you wrote that?"

"Then my friend took it. He wrote something on it and gave it back to me. That's when the teacher grabbed it."

"What did your friend write on it?"

David takes the paper back. "I have to have a green pen. He used a green pen."

"Forget about green. Just write down every word he wrote."

He bends over the paper and a powerful set of tics cracks his shoulder into his jaw again and again. Here comes his tongue again, sliding over his lips as he writes the boy's words across the top of the note:

I'd like to fucking mess her up.

Every word spelled right. Points there. I have spent a good deal of David's lifetime trying to overlook, excuse, or ignore what makes people stare at him. Not this time. I am suddenly very afraid for this tall, skinny boy who still walks away from the mirror with a plug of shaving cream in his ear. This child who sometimes forgets to wear socks. When he turns his back on me to resume playing Grand Theft Auto, I am enraged.

"Damn it, Dave! You have to talk to me this time. And you have to be clear. What does this friend mean when he says 'mess her up'? What might he do?"

"He told me, but I can't say."

"You sure can, buddy. You have to say it." I take hold of his jaw to force his eyes on me, but he is the master of avoidance. His eyes shift to the wall. "Tell me, David!"

I feel a fury swell up that I rarely permit myself when it comes to my third son. But autism can drive even the best mother crazy. I'm shouting as I twist my fist around his collar, much harder than I mean to, dialing it up just enough to squeeze out the truth.

"You're not getting away with this!" I have his attention now and it hurts to see the fear I've created in his eyes. But tonight the stakes are too high for any maternal guilt. "Tell me!"

"He said—my friend said—he said . . . someday he might put a tack in her chair."

Oh, just kill me now, God.

A flurry of follow-up meetings over the next several days results in a torturous handwritten apology letter from David plus a three-day suspension, a cooling-off period for what I assume will go into his record as tack threat by proxy. This punishment suits David fine: three days in a row to run free.

Day one of the suspension: David gets up before dawn and takes off, dressed in running gear. His bed is unmade, the radio on, the front door left wide open. He will be gone for hours, blowing past what has been holding him down for most of his life. But that's all I can be sure of about this boy with Bruce's smooth skin and a Roman nose from somewhere on my side of the family tree. But his dark eyes can flash with sudden anger as if there's a mysterious switch behind them. And, suddenly I realize, I have been blind to his anger all along.

But how could it be otherwise? He has spent his whole life on a low boil. Since his earliest days in grade school, the developmentally different kids were lumped together by their challenges rather than their psyches. Walled off in a trailer, he sat in silence as a teacher called him a vegetable. A decade later in the high school cafeteria, a prime breeding ground for social humiliation, David felt the sting of other students staring at his tics. Masking them behind a free hand, he sat alone and ate in huge, quick gulps; but as his hand crossed from ear to ear, the façade worked against him. It only drew more stares. The anger must have hunkered down deep inside him as his body's hijinks grew stronger, descending on him at will. After a while, he quit eating at school. He'd come home angry, befuddled, and ravenous, tearing through the fridge or pantry for food. His sudden harsh attitude had stumped me until, quite recently, I noticed the word "retard" falls between "retaliate" and "retch" in *Webster's*. Seeing the words so close together, everything fell into place about his early high school years: deep down inside, where hunger finds emptiness, there is rage.

"Don't call me special," he begged his teachers time and again. He did not want the kind of attention it brought. He longed for average, to be a regular guy like his brothers. Yet no one listened with ears that understood. How many times had I insisted he was mistaken that students wouldn't talk to him after they heard he was "Special Ed"? How often had I told him to just ignore the one who shouted "Hey, it's Ed!" when he saw him?

Too many times.

There is simply no way to measure the powerful psychic injuries endured in a lifetime of overhearing one is inferior. And now a young man has fought back.

Day two of the suspension: I walk into David's bedroom after dinner. Aside from the light filtering in from the hallway, it's dark in here. He is stretched out across his bed, recuperating from the day's long run. *Aackk,* those stinking socks. I sit down at the end of his bed, as far away from them as I can get.

"Dave, look at me." He doesn't. "Here. I'm here. Look at me. I'm going to tell you a joke. Tell me if it's funny to you."

"Okay," he says, staring at the wall.

"Three cannibals are eating a clown." I say. "One says to the others, 'Does this taste funny to you?' "

I love this hoary old joke. I'm already giggling, but he doesn't make a sound. Just stares off somewhere.

I ask him, "Isn't it a good joke?"

"No," he says, dropping back into that quiet place of his.

"Why?"

"Because clowns are not really funny. And people don't mind seeing them get hurt."

Okay. Perhaps David is on to something. It is much too easy to treat carelessly those who don't measure up to our standards. My favorite old joke is not so funny when you look at it from his point of view.

Day three of the suspension: I'm sitting on the kitchen counter, noshing on olives and feta. Bruce grabs a sharp knife out of the blade box and settles an onion on the chopping block—*wham!*—cleaving it into perfect halves. A bold series of two-handed dicing maneuvers follows as he lines up little onion bits for the skillet. The garlic is already sizzling away, eager for company. Bruce sautés and scrapes the mash into the tomato sauce bubbling on the stove.

"Needs another half hour," he says. He picks up my glass of wine, takes a sip, and hands it back to me. "Go sit in front of the fire. Watch your news."

In a few minutes he joins me on the sofa. David is there, too, stinky ripe from a cold twilight run. He sits on the hearth pillow, staring into the flames. The cat is beside him, drunk with sleep. Bruce's eyes drift from the blue shadow of the TV to the twitching motion of David's head in the firelight. He walks over to David and sits down next to him.

"Dave, let me just massage those shoulders for you. Get some of the tension out of your neck. Come on, buddy. I know how tight it gets."

It's as if Bruce is begging him to let him work the kinks out, but David's body tenses at his father's touch. He pulls away. There is an awkward bit where Bruce moves in closer to start up the kneading again. This time David tolerates it, leaning his face miserably against the fire screen. But he can't stand it a moment longer. He leaps up and disappears into his room.

"I wish he'd let me touch him." Bruce sighs and comes back to sit down next to me. Bruce's attempts to connect with David are always more about fulfilling his own needs than his son's, but that doesn't make it any easier on him. "I know what it feels like to be that tight and twitchy. I hate that I passed it on to him."

"How do you know it was all you? I must have had a little something to do with it," I say.

"You kidding? You descended directly from some slow motion, blue-eyed blond ape named Glorp. Five thousand years ago my ancestors looked exactly the same as I do now and ran around twitching and yelling, 'What? What?'"

I snuggle in close and situate his hands on the back of my neck. "Right there." He squeezes the spot for a moment, then lets go with an abrupt little shove. He stares into the firelight.

"What are we *doing*?" he says. "Just waiting around for the county to find a job for David? It's up to us to make something happen." His fingers return to the same spot on my neck, kneading it over and over again, and I can feel him thinking. Before he wears through to the bone, I grab his hands.

"Okay. What, then? What are you cooking up?"

This three-day suspension has highlighted the reality that David will have absolutely nothing to do once he finishes his vocational training in June. Nothing at all unless a county job opens up.

"Hear me out. I've been thinking . . . I've been eating at the same barbecue joint for twenty-five years. I'm going to call the owner and tell him about David. Ask him to find something for him to do. Anything—washing dishes, busing tables, sweeping the floor. They don't have to pay him at first, just give him a chance and then decide if they might be willing to take him on part-time later. Why not?"

"Wow," I say. "You make it sound so simple."

"Hey. The worst they can say is no."

The glimmer of that barbecue joint job weighs heavy on my mind tonight as we head up to bed. I crawl in under the covers next to Bruce and grab a dog-eared magazine. There's an article in it about happiness. Claims it feels good to laugh because laughter distracts us from what bothers us. I flip over onto my belly and the cat lump slides off the bed onto the floor.

"Bruce, listen to this: it says here looking on the 'sunny side of life' puts our minds on a more positive track. You think that's bullshit, or what?"

Bruce doesn't answer me. The Red Sox are looking strong for this early in the season and he's locked into the latest issue of *Sports Illustrated*. The cat bounds back onto the bed and stands in the middle of Bruce's chest. He raises the magazine above her head and keeps reading.

"Well," I say, just in case he's listening, "I'm not feeling so happy." But he's not listening. "I mean, let's be honest for a minute. We got us a challenge with ol' Dave here. Trying to explain the unexplainable to people. *Christ,* if there was just *some* way to say it simple. To make it easier for people to understand how he thinks—"

"You think too much," he says, and turns out the light.

A month later Bruce is peeling back the wrap on a sandwich at his favorite barbecue joint. Across the table from him sits Brad, the restaurant's manager. They are eating and talking in that vague way men do. Right now David, dressed in a white apron and a red hat, is sweeping up peanut shells around the bar. For the last two weeks he's been training at minimum wage to bring plates of barbecue out to customers and bus tables. David can handle the work, Brad says, but . . . well, something's come up:

"David says everybody's staring at him."

"Uh-huh," says Bruce, reaching for the hot sauce.

"Well, what's up with that?"

"You understand how autism works?" says Bruce.

"No, not really," says Brad. Brad is a fair man. A navy vet who is used to giving orders and seeing them carried out.

"Well, David's not paranoid. People do stare at him," says Bruce. "He's just reacting to the world the way the world reacts to him."

Brad doesn't say anything. Just waits for Bruce to say more.

"David can't make the leap that people are staring at him because they're hungry. He thinks they're staring at his tics. He doesn't get that they're just waiting for him to bring them their food."

"But people are staring at him *because* they're waiting for their food. That's the job."

"Yep." Bruce takes the last bite of his sandwich. He looks across the table at Brad. "Now you got it."

I KNOW A DAVID

My editor friend and I were catching up over a quick lunch at the end of September. As soon as the waitress took our order he said, "So fill me in. What've you been up to lately?"

"Oh, not too much," I said, rewinding the hot blur of last August in Washington. "My kid and I spent most of the summer riding the Metro."

"Where to?" He has never met any of my sons, but like any good friend he knew which one I was talking about.

"Well, just riding *around*. You know—here, there."

"Have you ever considered writing about this?"

Teh! I had to laugh. "Who'd be interested in reading about a twenty-year-old guy learning to ride the Metro?"

Who'd care, indeed. But my friend's instincts had already kicked in. He convinced me to give it a shot.

A few months later, on Mother's Day, a feature story about

David learning to ride the Metro appeared in the *Washington Post Magazine*. When I gave David a copy of the magazine that Sunday afternoon, he shrugged, handed it back to me unread, and headed outside for a run. While he was gone, Max showed up on the doorstep. I hadn't seen him for months but, after all, it was Mother's Day.

It's jarring how little it takes for our grown-up kids to make us happy, and not just happy but wildly so: a touch on the shoulder, the rare phone call when they do not ask for money, or the best thing ever, when they simply show up. It's just as curious how often sadness accompanies those moments. Still, it was good of Max to drop by.

We shared a stilted hug and took up our posts at opposite ends of the kitchen table, where we'd laughed and argued for so many years, over what I could no longer recall. Was it the time I threw a girl out of his bedroom? Or the time I picked him up from school and handed him a box of condoms? The smoke has long since cleared from those old battles. But now, every morning as I sit here and drink my coffee, my fingers trace the ridges from fork tines stabbed into the wood throughout the years. Bruce recently suggested getting the old table resurfaced, but I said no. An unvarnished kitchen table holds a family's history that no scrapbook could ever reconstruct.

Now I looked at my firstborn—who I suspected still slept with his baseball glove—but I didn't recognize his clothes, his scruffy beard, or the names of his friends. The only familiar thing about him was the guarded look in his eyes, which had been there a long while. During college he'd been unreachable for weeks at a time. The distance was bridged by occasional phone calls, then morphed into missed holidays. There would always be a fragile love between us based on a shared understanding of the lighter side of things, things that might appear bleak or even dismal to others. We'd always have that. But the cost of all those missed moments because of David have added up. Those many times that teenage Max received second best from me or, in truth, nothing at all.

We sat together at the table until silence crept in. Finally he spoke. "I have something to tell you," he said, looking directly at me. "Are you sitting down?"

Our old joke.

Then came fine news. He'd gotten himself into law school and figured a way to pay his own way through on student loans and his waiter's salary. Thrilled on both scores, I thanked him for the best Mother's Day gift he could've given me. I was intensely happy for him and let him know this family would always need a good lawyer to help take care of David down the road someday.

"Mom," he said. "I think about that all the time. If he needs to be protected, you know Eric and I will protect him."

I didn't know it for certain until that moment, but I do now.

Max rose to leave, but there was something else he was struggling with. He reached into his jacket and plopped a copy of the article I wrote about David down on the table.

"Nice work," he said. It was enough.

Suddenly the front door banged open and we heard David's footsteps cross the foyer. He bumped into the kitchen holding out a bouquet of flowers—a dozen long-stemmed red roses tied round with a curly white ribbon. Max and I stared in disbelief. He knew as well as I did that *this* was a first. The first time in David's life that he had marked a special day—Christmas, Chanukah, a birthday—with a gift for another person. Every special day in each of our lives had always passed without a gesture from him. It's what we expected. And suddenly here were red roses on Mother's Day.

"Mom," said David, dumping the flowers upside down on the stove-top burners. "You owe the lady at Safeway twenty bucks."

Click. In one fragmented moment, Max, still and forever my second heart, witnessed the contradictory nature of his quirky little brother. This was twenty-one years of Happy Mother's Day, Chanukah, and Thanksgiving—maybe even an I love you—all thrown into one upside-down bouquet of red roses. And it must have unlocked something inside Max too. Had he finally understood that my pushing him into the background all those years ago had not been by choice but a duty, and the only thing I could have done was to watch five-year-old Max climb on that school bus and become his own boss?

My firstborn pushed back from the scarred kitchen table and tromped over to David, pulling him in close. Max let loose a low growl and began to rock him side to side in an unrelenting bear hug that zoomed way past the Two-Foot Rule.

"Dah-voo . . ." Max murmured, calling up the near-forgotten pet name for his little brother. "Dah-voo."

At first David fought the embrace, pulling back with eyes

shut tight, his trapped arms jerking at his sides. But Max was not letting go of the skinny kid brother who stood two inches taller than he did now. Hell, forget about the Two-Foot Rule altogether. Max was holding on for his own sake, rocking David back and forth, back and forth, with laughter and forgiveness brimming over the rims of his eyes.

David slung his head away from me with shuttered lids while Max rocked him. Finally his shoulders dropped in total resignation, allowing his mad-twitch body to give it up and submit to Max's stronger arms. To submit to the pigheaded reliability of a big brother's love.

Three nights later, I was still hearing from readers who had read the article in the *Post*. For me, telling David's story was a way to bear witness, an attempt to peek under the veil of separateness hanging over the lives of the differently abled. But I was hearing from people dealing with all kinds of pain—heartrending letters from people coping not only with physical and intellectual disabilities but also schizophrenia, drug and alcohol addiction, Alzheimer's, depression, divorce—all types of human frailty to which our society attaches a stigma that sets us apart. The connecting thread seemed to be a common sense of isolation.

The response was particularly strong from the families of young adults who fell somewhere in the wide-reaching spectrum of autism. Many of them wrote in simply to say "Your story is my story" and "I know a David." The mother of an adult son with Asperger's wrote:

> Every time people are exposed to stories like this, there is
> a chance they will view autistic people as more human,
> less alien.

The father of a six-year-old with pervasive developmental delays wrote:

> I spend so much time wondering if I am doing the right
> thing. As a father, I feel that so many dads are dealing with
> grief and loss, but I know that our son has made me a bet-
> ter man.

I was just shutting down my computer for the night when a new e-mail popped up with the subject line "David and my son's similarities." It came from a woman named Martha whose insight would bring real change into David's life. Martha wrote:

> I could really identify, remembering what it was like the first
> time my son took the Metro by himself. . . . Larry is 29, so
> we've had a little more fun experience in the job world than
> you have had to endure, a few more years under our belts.
> (Much to my delight, ha ha ha.)

And it came with a job offer. Martha, her husband Rick, and son Larry are a baseball family with part-time jobs helping fans find their seats at Nationals Park, home of the Washington Nationals baseball team. My mention of David's habit of swinging an imaginary baseball bat when he was happy gave them an idea. Martha asked and, easy as a pop fly, the Washington Nationals created an opening for David as a paid ballpark usher. It turns out, when Martha gave the article to her boss, he said he wanted to "see the kid swing his bat."

RITES OF SPRING

May 2009

To get the whole experience of what the Nats job will mean for David, I take a dry run on the Metro with him down to the ballpark. Of course, when I say *with* David, that would be somewhere in the vicinity of the same crowded car. Once we board the Metro, it doesn't occur to him to sit beside me. He keeps walking straight on to the end of the car. But he's easy enough to spot through other commuters, with his brand-new Nats jersey. Across the back is the word SCREECH, the team's eagle mascot.

The train rumbles along, shaking everybody's bones to the same beat, until it grinds to a halt. The conductor calls out, "Navy Yard Metro station. Welcome to the home of the Washington Nationals."

As the throngs of fans make their way toward the stadium,

I sprint to catch up to David. As we head toward the escalator, a blind man sporting a tuft of chin hair and a red-and-white cane makes a beeline straight toward me. Not wanting to bump into him, I freeze. But he doesn't need my help. Some sixth sense must have kicked in for him, because he sidesteps me. But only barely, and his cane slips inside the toe strap of my sandal. As he changes his course, his body weight shifts and—*Ow! Ow! Ow!*—he pivots off my bony foot, stabbing the tender skin between my toes with the nub of his cane.

David witnesses the whole thing: the foot stabbing, my grimace, my claws coming out after the guy walks off to listen to a game he cannot see. Now what're you gonna do about that? The whole scene hits David square in the tickle box.

"Mom," he giggles, shaking his head. "He didn't mean it, Mom. You know that—right?" The look on David's face says, *Believe me, I get this one in a way you never will.*

"Well, ye-ess," I say, giving up. The soft flesh between my little tootsies is already purple. "Okay, yeah. I guess so. . . ." David pokes me in the ribs hard enough to make me go *"Ooof!"* and he's off toward the ballpark at a fast clip. Even though my foot will remember this prick, empathy for a stranger is something brand-new for David. Good stuff.

While David finds a seat in the five-dollar section on this perfect sweater-weather night, I'm going ahead with my plan to meet the ballpark ushers' manager, to thank him for offering David a job.

Forty-five-year-old Kynny Sutton is a physically fit, self-described neat freak in a sharp bow tie. He has served twenty-one years in the air force, more than a dozen of them on presidential color guard duty, and he's got the ramrod-straight posture to show for it. In other words, if David's shirttail is hanging out, Kynny is going to notice.

"Then why, Kynny?" I have to ask him. "Why take the chance on a kid like David?"

"All people," he says, pausing before he finishes his thought, "are surprising, complex, and deserving of a break." He actually talks like this.

An African-American who pegs Stuttgart, Germany, as the nearest thing to a hometown, Kynny says he grew up in the military's "purple world" where color barriers had no place. His purple worldview includes a commitment to hiring people of differing abilities. So, here at the baseball stadium, he trains his employees to do the job by the same standards he learned in the military: to the best of their ability.

"But we don't let up, either," he says. "We'll pull our employees aside: 'Be on time! Tuck that shirt in!' We stay on 'em."

That's good to hear. Staying on 'em has been my job for the last twenty-one years with David and, frankly, I could use the extra help. I look past the bright lights of the ballpark into the velvety summer air and take a deep, stabilizing breath. This is shaping up to be one of my best nights ever as David's mother.

From our ground-level seats behind home plate, Kynny is gracious but all business. While he talks to me, his eyes do double duty. They scan the action on the pitcher's mound, zoom in to the $300 seats behind home plate, and gradually make their way up into the nosebleed section where the hoi polloi are enjoying their beer. The stadium's forty-one thousand seats are only a quarter full tonight, but that doesn't tell the whole story about this park. Washington is a city that has ached for its own professional ball club for thirty-three years—ever since the Washington Senators forfeited their final game to the Yankees in 1971 and fans poured out of the stands to steal bases and scoreboard numbers for souvenirs.

But right now there's a weird crack of the bat, and Kynny's already up and sprinting toward home plate. The bat has splintered, spraying wood shards across the first three rows of fans. And Kynny is there. He squats down to eye level to speak with several ticket holders and taps into his cell phone, explaining the situation to the field command post on the opposite side of the ballpark. Then he holds up a green card signaling that everybody seems to be okay in his section.

Kynny returns to our seats, but I can see he's itching to get back to his rounds, where he regularly racks up five miles a night circumnavigating the park. He gives me a friendly smile and a sharp two-fingered salute before he disappears into the stadium tunnel. As he melts into the crowd, I realize I haven't told him what I came to say. I haven't told Kynny what this job means to the kid he's just hired. But I'll have to wait to tell him face-to-face, because it's not the kind of thing you can say in an e-mail. It needs hands flying and happy shouts.

Because I need to tell Kynny that the day Bruce picked David up from the Metro with news about the job, it hit that boy like a bolt of lightning. As if the years and years of waiting for his life to take off had evaporated and now, suddenly, here was the first day of the rest of it. And I need to tell it to Kynny exactly like Bruce told it to me.

How it was the happiest shout Bruce ever heard from David, how our kid screamed, "Oh! Fun!" and shot up out of his seat, banging his head into the roof of the car; and how that started a surprise giggle fit in the both of them; and how the car careened off the road, nearly plowing over somebody's mailbox; and how Bruce was so happy for ol' Dave, he nearly cried himself, saying it was a good thing David was there to grab the wheel. *Oh, man, oh, man*—that's how I need to tell it to Kynny.

WASHINGTON, July 31—Now 103 games and 71 losses into their season, the Washington Nationals know the anatomy of defeat down to the can't-believe-it loss. They know the embarrassing. They know the feel of being bummed in almost every variation.

—Chico Harlan, *Washington Post* (2009)

You go to Boston's Fenway Park, the tension is palpable. People have to watch every play. The only break comes in the middle of the eighth when the pretty drunk girls shake it to "Sweet Caroline" and, leading, tied, or trailing, they're out there, baby, just givin' it away.

Here at Nats Park—not so much.

It's just a fun midsummer's night game in D.C. And a sparse crowd at that on this clear Wednesday evening with two teams that aren't going anywhere this season. That's okay. Bruce and I are here to spy on David tonight.

What is it about strolling around a ballpark that makes us

all equal? You got your blue cotton candy on a stick, your hot dogs/pizza/wings and chili along with your ice cream and cold beer, all of it walking right up to you in your seat. There's that sense of trust in the air as change for a $20 bill passes through a dozen hands before the Bud Lite meets its rightful owner. There's Washington's version of celebrities, politicians, and journalists, stepping out of the Presidents Club, which is famous for its historic photos of baseball greats. There's the charming imprecision of a local color guard carrying the flag out onto the field and everybody rising to mangle the words to the National Anthem.

You gotta love this game. Wins and losses get locked into the history of a city's heart that keeps on beating regardless of the final score, sorta like David and me. As hard-core fans straggle out after every loss at Nationals Stadium—and there are a record number of them—the DJ plays Bob Marley's "Three Little Birds," with the lyric "every little thing gonna be alright."

Baseball makes room for everybody—the Rubber Chicken man, the Bag of Peanuts man, the tiny girl in the wheelchair singing the National Anthem, the Reefer Jersey guy, the lopsided young war vets from Walter Reed Hospital, the *John 3:16* guy in the rainbow wig, and, somewhere among them, David. He is welcomed with all the other strange birds and optimists who flock to a baseball game on a warm summer night to celebrate life itself. And the plus side of having the losingest team in the league is there's always a seat at the park. But hey, the Nationals hired our kid, and that makes me and my Red Sox–loving husband major-league fans.

Bruce has scored two cheap tickets from a scalper with a plan for David to slide us into the good seats he patrols between third base and home plate. David is easy to spot. He stands at the top of his section with his hands on his hips and a blue towel hanging out of his back pocket. We hunker off to the side behind a mustard and relish cart, unnoticed by him. It's a little after seven and he'll be there until midnight, but there are just enough flashing lights, TV screens, and unpredictable looniness in the park to keep his attention focused on his job. It's funny how that works.

The stadium TV crew spotlights a man wearing a donkey head and flashes it on the giant screen beyond the outfield. There's an official-looking sort of giant white chicken character. The donkey-headed man is celebrating slugger Adam Dunn and the white-chicken-thing is Screech himself, the Nats' eagle mascot. *John 3:16* tilts his rainbow wig dangerously close to a young boy's blue cotton candy. They're both mesmerized by the T-shirt Toss. A leggy brunette in short-shorts fires the Ts toward the crowd via a bazooka gun. It's warm tonight and, besides this, there's not much energy in the park until the bottom of the third when the Nats shortstop ropes one out into center field.

The organist hammers out *Da-da-de-dah-de-DAH*—and the ballpark erupts in *CHARRRGE!*

We got a ballgame.

Bruce shows up with a cold bottle of beer from where he's been hovering at the grab-and-go bar. He holds it against the

back of my neck just under my ponytail. He breathes out a
happy, slow breath, "Red Sox, 2 to 1 in the bottom of the
second."

Then I point toward David standing at the top of his half-
filled section. There is a studied nonchalance in the way
David crosses his arms and looks out over his territory. Bruce
says, "Let's go sit down."

Strolling ahead of us into Section 113 comes one of the
team's wacky presidential mascots that are scattered throughout the ballpark. It's ten-foot-tall Honest Abe, top-heavy and
mute. Oozing cool, David casually fist-bumps Mr. President,
then steps aside to let him down the steps to bewilder the
fans. Honest Abe looks a little lackluster tonight. His eyes are
glassy and his enormous foam head lists slightly forward on
its axis. By contrast, clean-shaven David looks sharp in his
uniform even though his loose shirt and boxy Dockers could
hold two or three Davids. His tics seem to mesh well with the
staccato-paced atmosphere of the ballpark, and when his dad
and I approach I see how serious he is about the job.

We are deeply happy for him.

"Hey, Dave," says Bruce, beaming. "You look great out
here, buddy. Mind if we join you?"

"Let me see your tickets," says David. I laugh and hand
over my stub. He glances at it and doesn't miss a beat. "No,
Mom. You don't have tickets for here."

"Dave!" says Bruce. "It's your mother!"

"Come back at the top of the seventh. We'll see."

"*DA-ave!*" I say, slack-jawed, but of course he's not looking
at me.

There's the crack of the bat and someone yells, "Incoming!"

A foul ball screams over the left-field line and lands in David's section. Frantic hands bobble the stinging ball before it plops into the lap of a woman with two young children, one of them asleep in her arms. Just the kind of unexpected turn of events Kynny Sutton has trained the ushers for. David races straight into the melee.

As David reaches the woman, she holds up the ball and grins, ecstatic that it has found her, leaving Baby unscathed. David looks her over, then reaches into his back pocket and pulls out a green card. He holds it high in the air and turns around for all to see, including the grounds crew, park security, and the television cameras. For a nanosecond, his picture flashes across the ballpark's enormous video screen. The lady's safe and sound, no damage done here. Everything is under control in David's section of the park tonight.

FINDING HIS WHEELS

Think about it," I say to Bruce, "his own set of wheels!" Bruce gazes off into the middle distance with a twitchy sort of smile.

Bruce once said if David could just learn to ride the Metro, then he could travel to a job site, and when he locked down that job, he could pay his rent. With a job and an apartment, he would have a real life. And who knows? Maybe even find somebody other than his dad and me to love him well into the future. The three of us still agree on that.

With a summer job at the ballpark nailed down and three lunch shifts a week at the barbecue joint, David is rolling in minimum wages. And he knows exactly what he needs to happen next. He cashes in his first couple of paychecks to buy a little motor scooter to get him back and forth to the Metro. While Bruce and I are all for this positive thinking about his future, we stammer over the what-ifs of David behind the wheel: the snap judgment needed for a quick lane change, the vague facial cues swapped in a four-way stop, the liability of carrying a (*gulp*) passenger. The only thing standing between David and this terrible new freedom is the driver's test at the Department of Motor Vehicles.

You can take the test up to three times. For weeks, the test manual sits open beside the computer in his room. Every evening he takes a trial exam online while the perky yellow scooter waits in the garage like a carousel pony. He's getting better at it every night. But at the DMV, when he stands in front of the computer screen, the tension and stress that have always been his enemy take hold of his hands. They begin to flap across the screen, tapping it in all the wrong places. Twice this week, we've spent the morning in hard chairs at the DMV, waiting for his shot. Twice now, his tics have reached out and hit the wrong buttons for him. This morning is his last chance.

When his number is called, David approaches the computer testing area, banging his left ear in wicked slams against his shoulder. Oh, never a good sign. A guard with slitty-eyes and heavily muscled arms zeroes in on David. It must be part of his job to stare down the nervous types, or maybe he remembers him from the week's previous attempts? As we wait our turn again in the rows of linked metal seats, David's legs are so lively that a kohl-eyed girl with a tattoo of a naked angel turns around in her seat and brays, "QUIT. THE. BOUNCING."

"C-378, C-378."

That's his number. David smoothes out the crumpled

ticket and follows the directions from the loudspeaker to approach the computer screen for the test.

As David passes him, the guard opens his hands and bounces on the balls of his feet. "Good luck," he whispers through a clipped Caribbean smile.

From where I sit, my boy looks like every other young guy standing there with his eyes on the prize. But the stakes are different for David. If he fails a third time, what positive spin can I possibly put on this? *Lots of people fail the driving test,* I tell myself. He's come so far. But how many times and in how many arenas can he keep getting knocked down before he starts to believe he shouldn't bother getting up?

I look at him tic-ing away over the computer screen and I telegraph him every positive beam of energy I can muster. He's got the same look on his face as the first time he rode the Metro alone. That same gritty determination he had when the doors shut behind him and he swung his imaginary bat. I cross the fingers of my right hand and slide them between the covers of the book I'm pretending to read. I'm so nervous I have to drop my chest over my knees just to stay in my chair.

Come on, Dave. Swing that bat—poke it right outta the park!

We step out of the DMV into the punishing heat of the day.

The very first victory call goes out to Sug, the woman who set David behind the wheel of a car at age twelve. Gripping his new driver's permit like he's just won the lottery, David hoots the good news into the cell phone. But when she presses the receiver against her ear, Sug can't quite recall who David is.

At ninety-four, despite the crossword puzzles that have always been her quiet way of getting through life, forgetfulness has taken root. All day now Sug sits, reading with a Kleenex stuffed into the sleeve of her sweater, her cropped-off nylons pulled up above her ankles, and the sides of her shoes cut out for her twisting toes. The smell of old lady is in the air. She stares openmouthed into the turned-off television and says to no one in particular, "Look at all those children in there, singing 'Swing Low, Sweet Chariot.'" My once strapping mother has broken her hip in a fall and she's rusty now. Long legs that once cut a mean scissors kick and climbed Blood Mountain are bent deep at the joints, her basketball player's toes curled like the overgrown vines in the garden she has left behind. Now, when she lifts her knee and the hip replacement clinks into position, it makes a metallic burp as she grunts *"Oww-oww-ow!"* Her days are spent in a sunny corner of her room at Magnolia Manor, melted into a Barcalounger surrounded by her One Hundred Greatest Books series. Today she is reading Aeschylus.

Again.

"I b'lieve I've 'bout read all his stuff," she told me years ago, hugging him to her chest. Up until ninety, she rode her bicycle to the library every day before the fleas of life ganged up on her and took a big, leeching bite, trapping her in that chair. She is closing in on her One Hundred Greatest Books journey now, many of them read twice and forgotten, and once she has finished all one hundred again, my mother can die happy.

But today the young man's voice Sug struggles to identify is strong and triumphant. The exuberance of youth manages to turn the wheels of the old teacher's mind one more time.

"Did ya hear me, Sug?"

"Is that David?"

"I got my driver's license! I aced it on the third try!"

"See there?" And I could imagine her reaching for her crossword puzzle and pen. "Not a *thang* wrong with you."

So the driving lessons have begun anew—this time on the art of the scooter.

We have waited until midnight for the roads to clear. Bruce and I creep through the empty city streets top down in the same beat-up little Jeep that somehow survived the driving escapades of Max and Eric. Close behind, David follows us on his brand-new scooter. The tiny yellow bike is not much bigger than a toy. It sports the latest *Remember 9/11* sticker his cop pal Isaac gave him when he ran over to his house to tell him he'd passed the driving test.

At the Jeep's wheel now, Bruce tracks David's every move in the rearview mirror. I ride shotgun, twisting my neck. All long legs and pointy elbows, David reminds me of the mini-biker in a Shriners Day parade who is overly fond of his horn.

Suddenly a car filled with teenagers zooms into view, flashing its brights ten feet behind David's scooter.

"Uh-oh," says Bruce. "Here we go."

David's tics make it look like he's challenging the tailgating car to bring it on! The teens are quick to suggest what David should do with his little toy.

"*Damn*, son," Bruce says to David's herky-jerky reflection in the mirror. "You gotta knock that shit off. . . ."

I hang my head out the window like a wild-ass dog and bang an arm on the door, desperate to keep David's attention on his driving and not the threatening teens.

"Get in the slow lane, Dave! *Yikes!* Blinker, blinker!" I shout. "Okay! Turn it—*JEE-SUS!*—no, the other way! Oh! Just turn the blinker thing off! *Aiyyyyeee*. . . ."

The carful of teenagers squeezes by in our lane with a long horn blast. One-finger salutes emerge from all four windows and the moonroof.

At the red light David pulls up alongside our little Jeep wearing a million-dollar grin. Being considered a public nuisance is something new for him, bringing him *this* close to cool. This really *is* something else. Straddling his 50cc scooter, he tics his silver helmet at us and coaxes a pesky *meh-meh* from the tiny engine.

"Wait'll I tell Max and Eric!"

Eric is home this weekend, so the house is shaking with music again. Though his knuckles are big from once catching footballs, he's got his grandmother's ten-note stretch and, better yet, Sug's play-it-by-ear gift for letting loose. He has surprised us with a quick turnaround from Boston, where he's in grad school studying music, playing at local blues clubs up and down New England.

And, as usual, his best friend, Ryan, has showed up at the front door with his guitar. He lets himself in like family, calls out hello to me from the foyer, and heads straight for Eric, bent low over the keys. He and Eric have been making music together since they were five years old, Eric at the piano, Ryan on all kinds of strings. Ryan is pale, quiet, and funny. He takes his regular spot near the long windows in what we call the music room, a room full of sofas and chairs facing a shiny piano that sprawls out of the corner like a sedan with its hood up.

Somewhere in that room is a clothbound book of photographs of these two friends over the years, playing at every holiday or birthday or any day their music made better since they were five years old. My favorite snapshot is of twelve-year-old Ryan on the viola, Eric blowing a wicked trumpet in his right hand and playing the piano with his left. In the lower corner David sits on a red pillow, a kazoo pressed to his lips.

The two old friends speak in a private lingo based on sharps and flats, so Ryan has only to say "B flat," to jump-start a whole new thread of sound between them. As I pass by the music room from the hallway, I lean in against the door-jamb and bob my head for a little bit.

About a half hour into their jam, I'm settled into the cush-ions on the purple sofa in the far corner of the room, happily committed without even realizing it.

"Finland," says Ryan, on hold for a moment while Eric

pencils something on the sheet music. "David blew past me on the way over here. What's up with that yellow scooter of his?"

"Huh?"

"The scooter, man," says Ryan, picking up the beat again. "So, when did David get cooler than the rest of us?"

Eric's eyes are closed while he hovers over the keys and experiments with a Herbie Hancock trill, the pencil stuck behind his right ear. Fifteen seconds fall in potent silence before he starts a new line, apparently ignoring Ryan's comment. "Hey, check this out, Ry. See what you can put over it."

Eric starts the groove and Ryan plunks down a bass line. They find the pocket and they're away again. Then Eric smiles.

"Yeah, Dave's scooter," he says, still tapping his foot. Genuinely tickled. "Oh, yeah."

David's new set of wheels has brought with it a smug new attitude, and it dawns on me that my third son is not just embarrassed to be seen with me in public. He has finally developed the "My mom's an idiot" smirk, a textbook milestone that is not too far off the mark from the average teenage bear. And there are other encouraging signs too. For example, when Max and Eric were teenagers, our cable TV bill used to be full of the soft-porn movies that the boys swore they never ordered like clockwork every Saturday night. With David, it's *Mall Cop* and *Shrek*—same thing, only different.

"David . . ." I'm standing in the garage, straddling the

scooter with the key in my hand. "Doodlebug, how do you start this thing?"

David rolls his eyes and *tsk-tsk*s me. What an impossible drag on his life I have become. He's right. I vow never to call him Doodlebug again.

"Didn't you read the manual, Mom?"

As a matter of fact I'm reading it now. In what must have been translated from Chinese to French and then into English, it offers this:

Way of Using—

1) Open seat and wrench off it.
2) Tie the metal key into the hook.
3) Put down the seat, and it auto lock.
4) When bring out the helmet, please operate in contrary way.

Okay, so we kind of led David to a low-end model based on what he could afford from his barbecue job earnings. And while it all seems foreign to me, somehow it makes sense to him. He turns the key, guns the tiny engine, and, with a weird and wonderful little he-man's swagger, disappears around the corner.

He's headed over to Harry's. David spends a lot of his time at Harry's now, dropping by at least once a day for some expert mechanical advice. Harry is the Korean-American guy who owns the gas station in our little village, and a throwback to the days when small-business owners had a real stake in the community where they lived and worked. Harry, who knows about every fender bender, DWI, and car-in-the-ditch my three sons have ever had, is the decent sort of man a woman can look in the eye and say, "Harry? My car went *bonka-bonk-a-bonka* last night when I pulled a U-turn on Wisconsin Ave. Is that very bad?" And without making you feel stupid or scaring you to death, he'll just say, "Let's put it up on the blocks and take a look." Then he'll fix your rusted-out, ready-to-catapult-you-to-your-deathbed brake coil for a fair price, pump up your low right front, and throw in some windshield-washing fluid because he notices you're running low.

And Harry keeps an eye out for David. Lately, Harry's become David's vehicle guru, teaching him to read the dashboard meters and check the tires. As he supervises my son's clumsy handling of the gas pump, Harry seriously mulls over David's fantasies about what kind of car he will buy himself one day. A Honda Civic or a red Ferrari? Then David follows Harry inside to the cash register to pay. David leafs through the car deodorizer trees, chooses a Nutter Butter to go, and pays cash. Harry always hands David back the right change.

LUCKY

G ood morning, beautiful. It's six forty-five."

   I lift my head and a face drifts into focus through my one eye that opens that early.

   "Coffee's ready," says Bruce. He is smiling.

   God, I hate an early riser.

   It's often said that keeping warmth in a marriage calls for one person to be kinder than the other. That would not be me.

   I flip the pillow to the cool side and cover my head with it. I can hear my love whistling a tune as he walks outside to pluck the morning paper from under the bushes. He wears a billowy white T-shirt over striped pajama pants and loose slippers, and his uncombed hair is like wild-goose feathers, so that flapping down the driveway with the newspaper, the man of my dreams, the fire of my loins, looks like a visiting clown.

But the aroma of fresh java lures me down to the kitchen. As I reach for the coffeepot, Bruce leans in close and sniffs my neck. "Wow. You smell good." He says this without expectation, then zeroes in on what's new with the Red Sox.

From the other side of the table, I tighten the focus on the bones of my marriage, sitting there with the box scores, digging into his grapefruit. He squeezes it into a funnel. A pink rivulet escapes his lips and courses down his unshaven jaw. Using the back of his hand now, he wipes it away. I hold my coffee cup in midair, taking all this in. When he lowers his chin, he finds me glaring at him through my specs, all sour-pussed and squinty-eyed.

"Ye-ep. See there? You did it again," he says, his gentle eyes loaded with the comic side of things. "You got prettier overnight. Too much beauty rest." Then he chuckles, picks up the sports section, and begins to whistle again, entirely disarming my snit.

He says this every morning and, Lord, it gets me every time.

Of course, the truth is, I'm not getting any prettier, only increasingly nondescript the way most women tend to age. But this, I have decided, is Bruce's kind way of telling me he's sorry. Sorry we can't just run away together next weekend or next year, sorry we can't even make love in the kitchen. And behind that sorry is the big one that says sorry for any twisted cerebral hardwiring his DNA may have contributed to David's blueprint.

Yet more and more I see myself in David. Although Bruce would never say it, I see how my inflexible traits may have bled over into David's life, tangling him up. How hard it is for him to summon the cool logic needed to guide his reaction to a new experience, and how this rigid nature of his gets in the way of his ability to empathize with others. But every child comes wrapped in his or her own surprise package, and rather than one gene being the culprit, it's more likely that our genetic stew is responsible.

The unspoken secret is that this blame game can fray the edges of a marriage. Here is the pattern: Following a diagnosis of autism, parents of young children often bond together in a "Hey, we will beat this" pose, soldiering forward into every therapeutic frontier available. But once this puzzling child starts high school and the years of battle fatigue have set in, the struggle can tear holes in a marriage because we parents are only human. We want quick fixes. We want someone to haul over the coals for how the course of our lives together has diverged. And when no perpetrator can be found—no quirky ancestor, no sinister vaccine, no environmental threat—the couple's relationship too often takes the hit. By the time the teen reaches adulthood and the long-term financial picture has become a permanent strain on the family pocketbook, the tension may be too much for many relationships to absorb. Divorce becomes a conventional way of stepping aside because just checking out emotionally is socially unacceptable. The fact is it takes an enormous amount of maturity to care for a disabled child's needs. There is little time left over for the kind of happy-go-lucky love that may have started things off.

For couples who choose to stick it out, the never-ending

challenge is balancing the emotional exhaustion somewhere
between backbone and collapse while struggling to make
sense of it all.

So what will become of Bruce and me? Will we stick it out?
Of the two of us, I'd say my husband is the grown-up here,
the pragmatic one who secured the special needs trust and
nailed down a job for his son. The one who is willing to think
outside of the box when it comes to figuring out independent
housing for the adult David. But there is one more thing.

It is the thing that God did not leave out of Bruce: his long
habit of kindness to me. If this is the key to keeping warmth
alive in a marriage, then a future with this good man, with
his frank and open capacity for empathy, speaks to me of
staying power.

So here we are on Open House Night at a local independent
group home for five developmentally disabled adult men.
Bruce and David and I have come to see if group housing
might be a good fit for David.

"It could happen," Bruce tells me, and I want to believe it.

The lively man who answers the group home's door seems
to be bent funny somewhere along his spine. A big grin splits
his face. "Name's Ernie." He grabs Bruce's hand and starts to
pump it. "Come on in, why not, goddamn it. Want to look
around?"

Ernie's still pumping away when the house counselor, a
sturdy Nigerian with an easy smile, introduces himself. "Welcome, I'm Jeremiah. And I see you've already met our Ernie."

Bruce has at last extricated himself from Ernie's grip and now Ernie has turned his sights on David. "Want to look around? Well, come on." And off the two of them go straight through the kitchen door and out into the unlit backyard.

In a brief tour of the home, Jeremiah tells Bruce and me the five residents are between twenty and forty years old, each of them working day jobs in supported employment with mentors or job coaches. These are jobs set aside for the uniformed ghosts we see in public places every day: the custodial workers who empty the trash cans we stuff latte cups in, the faceless folk who clean public bathrooms or shred and dispose of our tossed-off paperwork.

I stick my nose in the kitchen, where the countertop sparkles with a fresh spritzing of some strong lemony cleanser. The eating area is clean and spare. Neatly labeled pantry shelves boast a long list of food items, cleaning supplies, and paper products: cereal, detergent, toilet paper. Instructions for their use are straightforward. Simple. Looking around, I realize everything is labeled and there is a special place for everything here, including David, as long as he's willing to wait for an opening. He's already been on the county's group housing list for over a year, but openings in group homes are rare. These men aren't here because they want to be; they're here because they need to be.

"Look around," says Jeremiah. "Please take your time. I'll be in the living room."

We poke along down a hallway leading to the men's bedrooms. The sign on the open communal bathroom door says BATHROOM. The sign over the hall closet says TOWELS AND SHEETS.

The residents' private quarters are neat and tidy, and I sense a practical woman's touch with throw rugs, framed pictures, and CD players in each room.

As we turn to leave, a door at the end of the hallway opens and out steps a heavyset man, peering at us as if he was expecting a knock. A large dollop of drool rolls out of his mouth, stretches thin, and splats on the floor. He locks eyes with Bruce and points to a sports poster curling at the edges and pinned to his bedroom wall. In the black-and-white photo, a long-haired, rakish football player poses in a jersey with his hands on his hips, looking over his right shoulder.

"You know who that is?" the fellow asks Bruce.

"You kidding me?" says my husband. "Namath was the best."

The heavyset man grins and retreats behind his door, closing it without a sound.

In the living room, the mismatched sofas are comfortably worn. A flat-screen TV is tuned to ESPN while a resident dances with his sister to a loud José Feliciano song playing in the background. A middle-aged woman and a young girl nibble at the pizza slices balanced on their knees. As we enter the room, several others look up from their conversations, and Jeremiah, the counselor, introduces us around. They smile and nod hello, then turn their backs, picking up where they left off. Although this is an open house, we seem to be the only strangers here. It's like a family dinner party and we are first-time guests, unsure of where to light.

Beyond the dancers and into the dining room, a raven-haired woman holds the back of a chair where a young man sits staring into space. The woman looks my age. I introduce myself as David's mother, pointing to him as he follows bent-funny Ernie into the living room. The woman doesn't notice the hand I've extended her way; she just looks me hard in the face as if she's searching for something. I know what it is because I'm after the same thing from her: a quick synopsis of her son and if this is a safe and good enough place for him to carry out a meaningful life.

"I am Mrs. Singh," she says, unsmiling. The name tag on her blouse explains she is Prem's mother. The party has ramped up a bit, the TV suddenly louder than the music, so she must raise her voice. "My son has lived here seven years. We like it."

"Seven years? That's a long time." I bend to catch Prem's eye. His lashes are dark feathers. "Hi, Prem. How do you like being on your own—"

Mrs. Singh interrupts me. "Does your son speak?" she asks, and I see that hers does not.

"Yes," I say, and it feels like bragging. Mrs. Singh raises her gaze and sends it off into the next room, our conversation at a standstill.

How different this gathering is from those parent-son open houses I'd gone to for my other sons in years past. Talk there centered on sports and colleges, not sheltered employment and group housing. Of course, Max and Eric were children then, and now David is a grown man.

The little girl on the living room sofa has left her mother's side to join in the dancing, and the local TV sports announcer is screaming football stats over Feliciano's frenzied guitar playing. It's a pity blind José can't be here to witness this for himself. Mrs. Singh lifts a tray of homemade sweets off the dining room table and begins to pass them around. She calls to the heavyset Joe Namath fan down the hallway to come and join the dancers, slowly enticing him out of his room with the sweets. As he plods down the hall toward her, Mrs. Singh's eyes take on a softness that had not been there for me. She is smiling now, calling everyone by name. These are the people she trusts, her son's circle of support. And there is plenty of room for her peace of mind inside this house. The insiders know it. The outsiders see it.

Tonight, an outsider sees the group house is spotless, it is safe, and the home's counselor is kindhearted. But this outsider can't wait to get out of here. I want to believe that life holds more for my David than this.

I spot Bruce and David by the front door pulling on their jackets, saying good night to Ernie, still bent funny and pumping away on Bruce's hand again. "Leaving?" says Ernie, the perfect host with that wide grin. "Well, goddamn! Come back and see us soon, okay?"

On the drive home, Bruce and I are silent, but David is noticeably upbeat, near giddy with fresh ideas. He announces that he likes Jeremiah's clipped accent, the neat bedrooms, and the bright kitchen and bedrooms with all of their easy-to-read labels. The imagined freedom of it all. Can it be that where I see for him a disappointed life, he sees the open road?

"They have a fenced-in backyard, Dad. Think I could have a dog if I lived there?"

"I don't know about all that," says Bruce. "But first, you

need to think about what living with four other grown men would be like. Think you'd be happy doing that?"

David chirps from the backseat, "Oh, yeah. I'd really like to live there."

How could I misread my son so completely? Why do I think that such careful supervision would come to mean a dead-end street for him?

"Yeah, yeah. I'd like it a lot." He's leaning over the front seat now and his legs are bouncing with anticipation. "I mean, except, you know, for the *people*."

Bruce and I go numb. Whacked in the head again as sure as if we'd stepped on the wrong end of a rake. At the next red light, Bruce reaches over to squeeze my hand a little harder than I'd like. "Think about it," he says. "Do you know how lucky we are? We are so goddamn lucky."

Funny he's saying that, because right about now I'm thanking my lucky stars for all the good things David has going for him that give him more choices than any of the men in that house will ever have: his straight back and two strong legs that can take him wherever he needs to go. A brand-new driver's license with a picture of him that pleases the eye. And, most important of all, a built-in circle of support with Bruce and me and, after we're gone, Max and Eric. But for the time being—the *right here, right now* of it—he's got our clean-enough and cluttered home where no matter how long this young man continues to live with us, nothing and no one will ever need a label.

TURNING
THE WHEEL

Three weeks into the Scooter Age, the phone rings late on a Monday afternoon. "I had a little accident, Mom. I got to go inside an EMT ambulance. It was *really something else.*"

With the artery in my neck pulsing like a jump rope, I yell out the shorthand to Bruce. We hop in my car and race toward the busy intersection the emergency tech has given me. It's a white-knuckled ten minutes away.

The ambulance has pulled into an empty bank parking lot where an emergency technician leans against the vehicle's hood. The lazy way he's hugging his elbows suggests there is no emergency here. Still wearing his silver helmet, David sits on the sidewalk between a second tech and a taxi driver, smiling and wrapped from thigh to calf in a bulky bandage that slips to the ground when he rises and limps toward me. His knee looks like it got caught in a garbage disposal, but the

taxi driver who narrowly avoided squashing him tells me it
was only a pothole. He says he's from Sierra Leone and he's
seen worse.

The little scooter lies on its side near the curb. It's not
much bigger than a bicycle. The yellow paint is scratched and
there's a busted-out taillight, but it starts right up when Bruce
straddles it and turns the key.

"Here," says David, and he hands his dad his silver helmet,
which I notice has gotten pretty banged-up too. David eases
his aching body into the front seat of my car, more interested
in talking about his face time with the emergency tech than
the torn-up condition of his bloody right knee.

Driving home, I pretend to listen to every word, but it's
Bruce's reflection in my rearview mirror that's really got my
attention. His heavier body weight has slowed David's tiny
scooter to a crawl. As we crest a hill, a string of passing cars
overtakes the scooter and the engine's *meh-meh-meh* gradually fades off into the distance. There goes my knight in shining armor, a bit dented by the eternal watch-and-rescue duty
of being David's father, but just steely enough to make it
home on his own.

It takes three weeks for the tough scab on David's knee to
shed itself. I am quite surprised when the phone rings early
in the evening and a polite young male voice asks for David.
Fifteen minutes later there is a honk at the top of the driveway. David bounds down the stairs and lands in the foyer

with a loud thud. He looks handsome in the collared shirt his freshly shaved chin bleeds on.

"Where are you going, David?"

"To a cookout."

"With who?"

"Friends."

I draw a complete blank on that concept. I would love it to be so, but here is just another random snippet of information in the patchwork collage that is becoming David's private life. Soon enough, in our driveway, two clean-cut young men in a short-sleeved shirts and dress pants appear in a car.

"Who are they, David?"

"Friends."

The young men smile and wave our way. Friendly like he says.

As I watch David climb into their car and drive away, I have very mixed feelings. In the past, youth groups haven't appealed much to him because, by nature, he's not a joiner. We'd signed him up for Best Buddies, a local offshoot of the Special Olympics program that matches intellectually disabled young people with college-age mentors, but the contact had been sporadic and rather last-minute. In fairness, this is probably the result of David's missed social cues as much as anything, but I could never quite shake the troublesome feeling that a callous college kid is working off his required community service hours by sharing a ten-minute Coke with David once a month. A short-term friendship, another one-way street for him.

But David is an adult now, and Bruce insists he make up his own mind about these new friends. "Leave him alone," he tells me. "If these guys think they can take him on, more power to them."

"Okay," I say.

And so it begins again.

A real gully washer has softened the parched ground late this afternoon, and the weeds come away easily as I reach into my bed of hostas. The street is still wet and slick when I hear the reassuring *meh-meh-meh* of David's scooter rounding the corner. Here it comes—still new but, oh, dear, the little bike has another broken taillight, a mangled rearview mirror, and now a ripped leather seat. The *Remember 9/11* sticker is unscathed, but it appears more paint is scratched off the front end and David's left pant leg is rolled up to accommodate the sloppy white bandage hanging from his knee. Following close behind the scooter is a little red car driven by a cute brunette. David pulls into the driveway and turns to wave good-bye to her. With a toot of her horn she drives away, ignoring me altogether.

"David?" Blood has soaked through the white bandage and turned it a purplish black. He's already begun walking away from me, pushing his scooter into the garage.

"Whoa there, big guy. Hold up a minute. Lessee that knee." The thin film of scabs healing his knees and elbows has been ripped away. "*Yikes.* What's going on?"

"I went to the church. They wanted to talk to me about

baptism," he says, "but the EMT guy says I don't need stitches." He parks the scooter and disappears into the house. Case closed.

Baptism. Church. Stitches.

As he's taught me time and again, nothing is ever exactly what it seems with David. First impressions are not to be trusted because with him you only get part of any story and rarely do the parts you get fit together quite right. There's his quixotic little habit of saying the opposite of what he means when he's stressed. "Yes" often means "No." Keeping this in mind, from what I could gather about this latest scooter accident, he was on his way to a youth service with a group of young people he'd met on the Metro. Regardless of who these people are, somebody has patched him up, fed him, and kindly followed him home, driving slow behind his little scooter all the way. There is true compassion in this act and I appreciate it. However, there is now a fresh scrap of paper in his pocket with an inked-in prayer on it, and I suspect the return of the Metro Evangelists.

Or not.

There appears to be some genuine concern about this odd little fellow. Several times they have invited him for a hamburger cookout, which a guileless David misinterprets as friendship. The thick book remains unopened in his room, but now they are talking baptism.

Or not.

Regardless, attention must be paid to what is *not* being said here. Although Bruce and I know David better than anyone on earth, we have come to realize that the older he gets, the less we will know him. Here is a young man who never speaks abstractly about any idea. He uses simple, concrete language. Because most human reactions are too cluttered for him to figure out, his stories often feature animals and rarely people other than himself. Empathy does not come to him instinctively. As for his spiritual journey, when I remind him that he was baptized as a baby—and that I dragged him across the bridge to church for years—he looks away blankly, as if I'm trying to force math on him again. It's pretty clear that one more dunking will not affect him either way. I'm not a moral referee here, just a realist who's been at this a long time. Before things get any more complicated, somebody has to tell it like it is.

It is dinnertime at our house on a warm Tuesday night that happens to be our wedding anniversary. A half dozen boxes of Chinese takeout are spread across the table and we're nearly done eating.

"I don't get it, Dave," I say, chasing the last glop of rice with chopsticks. "You've had their big book on your desk for a couple months now and I've never seen you touch it. So explain it to me. Who are these people and why do you care?"

"Friends," he says.

"No, no, no. I mean, what is it that they believe?"

With his complete absence of sarcasm, hurting David has always been like shooting a mockingbird—no sport in it— but I need to know what he thinks. He gazes down at what's left of his Kung Pao chicken. This is a decision he needs to own, but he has nothing to say. Unable to stop myself, I point my chopstick at him and lay it on the line.

"Listen, buddy. You got to know they're not after you to be their friend: they want you to follow their religion. Is that what you want?"

No response.

I realize I'm staring at him too hard. He could use a shave. A shave and a run. Since the accident, a loose network of scabs has formed over his knees and elbows but the road rash hasn't quite healed enough for him to go for a long, soothing run.

"Okay, then answer me this, Dave: Do you really want to do that or do you just want to go to their cookouts? 'Cause Dad can make us great burgers right here."

That sets off a flurry of his head tics. He gets up from the table. It's too easy to be cruel.

At the edge of the kitchen he turns around and says with a trace of relief, "Okay, it's the burgers. The other stuff is too complicated."

He walks away with his head down and I want to bust out crying, but I don't. Bruce's silence from the other end of the table cools what's left of the meal. He doesn't have to say a word. Every move he makes telegraphs what a royal jerk I have been tonight. He knows the silent treatment is killing me because that's my game, not his. Finally, he sort of huffs, nods his head, and winks at me extra hard. Then he says, "Way to go, champ."

He cracks open a fortune cookie, pulls out the sliver of

paper, and stuffs the cookie shards into his mouth. I hate the way he's crunching on them and pretending to read the fortune.

"Oh, cut it out," I say, my eyes shooting daggers. "Somebody had to tell him the way it is. I mean, come on. Our kid a holy roller?"

"I've said it before and I'll say it again: if those guys were willing to take him on, more power to them. They'd sure do a better job than you're do—"

"Whoa, goddamn it!" I slam my fist on the table and a chopstick flips out of my hand and catapults over Bruce's shoulder. Dodging the stick, he continues to read the fortune.

"Hey, looks like I've got *your* fortune here," he says, all calm and cool. I'm thinking I may go for his throat—maybe flip the table—until he gets in the winning shot. " 'You have a natural grace and are careful with the feelings of others.' " When he looks up at me, his indulgent expression reflects the way the years have aged us both. "Happy anniversary, sweetheart."

We stopped giving each other anniversary gifts about ten years ago. No need to put a ribbon on it anymore; we'd just keep holding on. But tonight I need to get away from all the craziness in our house. Anniversary or not, I need a walk.

It's about nine o'clock as fat clouds begin to steal across the moon and the air in this neighborhood smells like rain. Already, porch lights have begun to dim. Up the street, the wind whips open the bathrobe of a shadowy figure standing at the end of his driveway in pointy-toed black shoes. In the streetlight I catch a glint of reflected steel. The man turns toward me, spotting me with his one good eye.

"Evening," says the old colonel, a neighbor who lost a hand and an eye somewhere in the Pacific. In the grass at his feet, his ancient black pug squats ugly. I smile at the familiar faces, and the colonel brandishes his hook in a crisp salute.

I pump my arms to crest a hill that ends in a cul-de-sac where a shiny coupe is parked. Inside, behind the wheel, a young man sits with a determined expression on his face. A tousled head of hair and shoulders thrust up and down in his lap. Giving that one a wide berth, I follow the footpath that leads to the neighborhood pool.

Beyond the lights of the tennis court, the sweet scent of honeysuckle mixes with a faint hint of bleach. I pass the darkened swimming pool area, empty save for a forgotten towel stuck in the chicken-wire fence. From there, it's a long, flat hike to the front gate, at least a quarter of a mile down a pitch-black drive.

No old men out with their feeble dogs now; it's just me and a hot night wind that suddenly comes to life, stirring the pine needles beneath my sandals. But I am not alone. Looming ahead, there in the distance, is Randall, a middle-aged loner who takes the bus to his accounting job every day downtown. Several mornings a week, I drive by him and wave. Randall does not wave back.

Randall lives nearby in somebody's basement. The landlady says Randall does everything in threes: Randall snaps his light switch on/off three times before he enters a room, he toe-taps three times before hopping the 23A to work, and he washes his hands a lot. Tonight, Randall doesn't look up from counting his footsteps in the pine straw until the moment we pass. When he spots me he flinches, and I realize with a fellow counter's pang that I have thrown him off his game.

I wave once, twice, and then once more. "It's okay—it's just me," I say, wishing that meant something more to him. Rattled by the unanticipated interlude, Randall doesn't acknowledge me. He turns on his heel and heads back in the direction he came, subtracting.

The moon tucks itself under a cloud and disappears in the darkness. I pick over the familiar shortcut through the woods toward home. I know each root bump by heart. At the end of the path a streetlight shines through trees. My feet find the sidewalk, returning me to the land of manicured lawns. A garage door rumbles up and a teenage voice shouts from his car, "Just out! I'm going out!" As the car screeches out of the driveway, a matronly figure stares after him into the empty street.

All of a sudden I want to be home. Home with my gentle, quirky Dave and practical, funny Bruce. I finally get why Bruce swears we're some of the luckiest people on the face of the planet.

On the home stretch now, I duck under a deafening boom of thunder. The first drop of rain lands cool in the bend of my elbow, and a thousand shots splat down onto the bare street to soak me clean through to my skin. I pull off my sandals and splash through the streaming water, delighted to be caught off guard by a warm night's storm.

Heading down the last hill toward home, I am blinded by the lights of a car threading through the downpour. The driver bears straight down on me, flashing his high beams for a really good look-see through my wet white T. The wind whips at my face and I stare back with a puckered brow, my sandals crossed over my chest.

Then I recognize him.

The only person in the world who really cares if I make it home tonight is out in the rain looking for me. He slows the car and I bend down to take a long look at the face I know best. I climb into the front seat next to him, as wet as a kiss.

A SHIVER OF
RECOGNITION

June has arrived, and here is David sitting onstage in the
second row of folding chairs. He's among twenty-seven
other special needs young adults poised to graduate from the
county's job training program. Tonight he will walk off the
stage with a diploma in his hand, straight into a lifetime of
bills for rent, transportation, clothing, food, and health insurance, but no job. With his twenty years in special education
coming to a close—ten of them in private school, the other
half in public—here's what educating Our David has taught
us: We should have kept our son in public school and our
money in our wallet as long as possible, because we will need
it for what happens next. Because what happens next is the
rest of his life.

And here is David, up on that stage, dressed in his father's
suit and with an ear full of shaving cream. I might have
cleaned that ear for him, but tonight he invoked the Two-Foot

Rule—*keep your hands off me!*—and the ear full of shaving cream is just the sort of thing I'm working hard to let go of. As we make our way to our seats, I am surprised at the strong turnout for the graduation ceremony. Even so, Bruce and I are the only ones here for David. Max is waiting tables somewhere in the city and Eric is in Boston, playing his regular midweek piano gig at Wally's Café. So tonight it's just us.

"Our next speaker . . ." says the principal, but that is all it takes to bring up David's classmate Wahid. Wahid leaps from his seat with a heartbreaking smile, exuberant Old World manners, and a king-size suit on his slender frame. He races to the podium and shakes the principal's hand with both of his. His dark eyes are shining, and as he turns and bows to the spectators, he beats a fist against his heart. Wahid hasn't spoken the first word and Bruce is already a goner. In a brightly lilted accent that reminds us he has traveled a very long road to get here, Wahid begins to thank every vocational training teacher, every counselor, each school cafeteria worker and building custodian he knows, for getting him to where he is today: a restaurant greeter with a local hotel chain.

"With benefits!" he says, zigzagging over the podium.

And we are charmed, pulling for him in the long journey ahead, wanting to believe Wahid is one of the few who will actually make it. Then, from out of nowhere, still at the podium, Wahid deviates from his prepared text and bursts into a singsong rift of "Yankee Doodle went to town/Riding on a pony . . ." To this, he steps back from the podium and adds a neat little dance step. The audience freezes in a shiver of recognition, sliding its collective eyes right and left.

We parents get used to these charming departures—autism's little non sequiturs—in the privacy of our homes and cars, but, *oh Lord, why here and why at this particular moment?* Mostly, the rest of us are relieved, quietly thinking: *It could've just as easily been my kid up there taking the detour . . .* until, one by one, Wahid's three sisters rise up in their dark hijabs and swirling skirts, and they begin to clap—deliberate and hard—in complete allegiance to their brother's happiness, their chins lifted in a show of support as indelible as blood.

And so we all join in.

At first it is only polite applause, until gradually we see there is more to this than "Yankee Doodle Dandy" and we are rising to our feet in an ovation that swells into a wave of sustained cheers and whistles that come not just for Wahid—whose arms are now raised high over his head with his fists punching the sky—but for all of our kids on that stage, pushing, shoving, wanting, hoping.

And here is David. So different from the others as he walks across the stage with his ear on his shoulder. Yet so like them in his prospects for the future. Bruce and I are corresponding flotsam in this sea of parents tonight, all of us mired in the sheer eternalness of it, working our jaws to keep our emotions intact. But here we are.

We are here to bear witness to these young adults, hoping mightily that this night will *not* be the very *best* night of the rest of their lives.

The following Tuesday evening finds Bruce and me sitting at the bar in our neighborhood Italian restaurant. It's early and there's nobody else here except the four young men we've brought along with us. We have orchestrated a graduation celebration for David and three of his classmates from the vocational training program.

They sit apart from us at a corner table, studying their menus. They are loose-limbed, broad-shouldered guys in baseball caps and T-shirts. Years of Special Olympics soccer have toned their muscles if not their coordination. Earlier, on the drive to the restaurant, Bruce had told them, "Order whatever you want, guys. Tonight is on me."

While it's no Beach Week, it is a night out to honor their achievements. So I am dressed for fun—chunky jewelry and a shimmery blouse—and Bruce looks interesting in jeans and a dark blue shirt with a loose tie and his sleeves rolled up. He signals the bartender, a young hipster with slicked-back hair and a fluid way of moving. Wiping down the bar in lots of circles, the bartender spins his towel back our way.

Bruce says to him, "See those guys?"

The bartender looks over at the quiet foursome and nods.

"They're all over twenty-one. Give 'em whatever they ask for tonight."

The bartender, who on a slow night like this is also the waiter, says, "Sounds good, boss."

He heads over to take their order and tells the guys the drinks are on "the dude" at the bar. One of them nods toward Bruce and waves. When the bartender asks to see their IDs, the four of them dig into their back pockets and open up their wallets, willing to give him whatever he asks for.

I take a sip of my martini and sigh at their compliance, knowing quite well that none of them drink alcohol. Bruce tips his Coke at me and says for the thousandth time in our marriage, "You, on the other hand, have the drinking gene in this family."

"Funny," I say.

The bartender reappears beside us, a bit agitated. His lips are in a fat pout. He taps his waiter's tablet with the tip of his pen.

"So. They ordered two ginger ales, a root beer, and a Shirley Temple—two cherries," he says, and one side of his mouth curls up. "They're jerking me around, right? The four of them?"

"No," Bruce assures him. "They're not jerking anybody around."

The bartender tosses back his shoulders as if he's been personally let down. "So, what are they—like, religious?"

"Nooo . . ." says Bruce.

The bartender wipes the bar in an ongoing circle, trying to work out the last piece of the puzzle. A lightbulb in his head switches on. "Aw-right. I got it, I got it . . . AA."

I shake my head from side to side and look at Bruce who is smiling into the bottom of his Coke glass. He lifts his chin and tilts his head at me as if to say, *Okay, then, so what ARE they exactly?*

I look over at the quiet young men we came in with. They

stare off in four distinct directions. Indeed, who are they exactly? What do they really want? What sorts of secret things do they long for? I'm guessing they'd all like to drive around in a fast car on a summer night, the music up too loud, with a funny, pretty somebody else beside them. And maybe find a job one day that could lead to a place of their own. Not so very different dreams from Max or Eric or most young men in this tough economy. Either way, these four fellows seem perfectly at ease in their own skins tonight.

And all of a sudden it seems really simple. It isn't up to the bartender, or to Bruce, or me, to pigeonhole these young men into worthy or unworthy groups. They will always live their lives on their own terms, in ways uncharted by the rest of us. And, God willing, maybe somehow they will find a way.

"No," I tell the young man behind the bar. "They're not jerking anybody around—that's just the way they roll. And don't forget the two cherries on that Shirley Temple."

Soon it is midsummer. Sticky hot. With the relief of David's graduation behind us and the endless battle for a full-time job looming ahead, Bruce and I have decided to take the afternoon off.

The first stop is Jack's Kayaks in Georgetown, where twenty-five bucks gets us two hours of quality time on the river. We slip into a wobbly boat and push off from the dock. Paddling upstream toward Chain Bridge, we disappear into the lazy glint of sunlight and water so we can float our single getaway rule for two full hours: *No talk about David.*

With the sun on our backs, we dig into the current at a forty-five-degree angle and push past Fletcher's Boat House. We keep our distance from a flotilla of powerboats tied together for a beer-fueled deck hop, and nod hello to four Latino fishermen in a flat-bottomed boat. Their radio plays a few bars of "Livin' la Vida Loca" in time with the slap of our paddles. Bruce smiles what we don't have to say about that.

We skim our way toward the cool shadow of Chain Bridge and pause to watch a flock of red-winged blackbirds swoop in and fade off into the marshland. I think of my usual top-of-the-bridge view and the avalanche of water that roars over the rocks every time it rains.

In rhythmic tandem, Bruce and I come up to and easily overtake a bobbing canoe. The life-jacketed man at the stern is belting out "Elvira" at the top of his lungs. *Oom poppa mow mow.* His look-alike little boys giggle as they bang out the beat on either side of their canoe, rocking it side to side. Bruce smiles, squinting at the trio. Everything on the river is a bit blurry for my nearsighted husband, who has left his glasses in the safety of the car on purpose. Things have a way of disappearing out here on the river.

We push on farther north of the bridge to the base of the rapids. Paddlers often gather there to gawk at top-notch kayakers as they slice through the white water and massive rocks, then navigate smart U-turns for a repeat performance in total control.

With an hour left on the clock, we point our kayak downstream and head back real slow. Again we pass the Latino fishermen in their flat-bottomed boat, all of them smoking cigarettes. Only now, sitting on a cooler in the middle of the boat, a woman with very pale skin holds a blue umbrella against the sun. Bruce notices her, too, and, minus his glasses, strains hard to see her pretty face.

We paddle past the public boathouse again and are surprised to see the singing dad and his two boys have made little progress. But now their clothes are soaking wet, and the father's dark hair is plastered across the side of his glasses. With their canoe bobbing in the direction of the boathouse, the older boy sits in the bow and weeps. The dad is reaching his cane pole over the bow to try to reclaim a drowning baseball cap before it disappears for good. He gives Bruce a sheepish thumbs-up as we slide by in silence.

The heart of Georgetown looms in the distance, but a nude man standing knee-deep in the water just forty feet away has caught my eye. He is taking his bath. He rubs a bar of soap gingerly across a washrag, then begins to scrub his nether regions with unmistakable vigor. I slow the kayak and stare back, completely enthralled by the surprise of him. He wears his white-blond hair short against his head. His chest and belly are thick and his arms are well-muscled. His penis is at half-mast. It is at this point that we lock eyes and I recognize the fine madness there. He gazes over his shoulder at me with very little interest, as though he were sweeping off his front porch and I am a local in a passing car.

Near the shoreline, I see the wreck of his home, a sleeping bag under a blue tarp and dark bottles scattered about. Behind that, the bright colors of a line of cyclists' jerseys wink through the trees along the canal's paved bike path. Runners are also drawn to the shade-dappled trail. We don't speak of it now, but Bruce and I know that somewhere out there, David is running, because this is his turf too.

For the moment, my nearsighted husband can see only the blur of a human form and offers the naked man a token "guy" kind of salute.

The man ignores the gesture and climbs up out of the water onto a large sunning rock. His skin is a burnt pumpkin shade made shiny all over by the splash of soap and water. Meticulously, he smoothes out his washrag on the rock to dry in the sun and, in no apparent hurry, bends over to slip his feet into a pair of heavy combat boots. Then he turns his bare ass to me, takes a few careful steps down from his rock, and fades away like sunlight into the darkness of the trees.

INTO THE
WORKPLACE

August third. It's David's twenty-second birthday. The phone rings. Eric is checking in from his summer job in Boston where he teaches music to inner-city summer campers. He's on a bus filled with tired kids on their way back from an all-day outing, but there's so much noise, I can't hear a thing he's saying.

"I can't hear you, either, Mom," he says. "Hold on a sec."

Eric pulls away from the phone and I hear him bellow at the top of his lungs, "Anthony! Charmaine! Shuddup!"

A squeal that sounds a lot like "Bite me!" leaps out of the background, followed by a shower of giggles.

Eric returns to the line, composed now that order has been restored. "Sorry, Mom. You were saying?"

"Well, um, I was saying, Eric . . . don't forget to call your brother tonight at dinnertime to wish him happy birthday. Seven thirty. Like always."

"Gotcha. Later."

———————

We've just sat down to grilled swordfish when the phone rings. A lively arpeggio leaps out of the receiver before any word can be spoken. Bruce passes the receiver to David. "Guess who."

"Hey, Eric."

When Eric finishes the third octave to his satisfaction, his voice comes on the line. "Dah-voo—Happy B-day, bro."

"Hey, Eric?" says David. "I'm going to run a marathon. What do you think?"

Bruce and I stare at each other, bug-eyed. First *we*'ve heard of it.

"That's cool, man. Yeah. Do it."

"Hey, Eric? Can you tell me what's special about this birthday? I mean, what's gonna happen to me now?"

Eric fires a huge glissando straight up the keyboard and hammers high C. "Now," says David's big brother, playing backup for himself, "you're officially a man."

"Sweet."

This morning, a set of gray waffle-shaped footprints has appeared on my kitchen floor. I track them across the hallway rug, over the black-and-white ceramic mudroom tiles, and out through the garage. I'm looking for David anyway to tell him the good news, and I know the tracks will lead me right to him. I step out into the brisk sunshine. His scooter is on a plastic tarp in the middle of the driveway. Cramming a brush into a can of gray paint and dripping it across his pants leg, David is just putting the finishing touches on the scooter's underbelly when I approach. The cat sits on the edge of the tarp, tracking each stroke as it oozes onto the bike's black leather seat. Above the front wheel the *Remember 9/11* sticker still claims its prominent position, carefully outlined in gray paint.

"Well!" I say. "*We-ell!* How come you're painting your scooter?"

"Dunno."

With all the dents and scratches the little scooter has suffered, I don't suppose a coat of house paint could do it much more harm. I also realize at this moment we are way past negotiating a fair-market resale price for this beat-up critter.

"Tired of yellow?"

"Dunno."

Hmmm . . . house paint? Might it melt on a hot summer day? Could it catch fire when the engine heats up? We'll have to ask Harry, because I don't know about these things—I know about the gray waffle paint marks across my kitchen floor.

What we have here is one of our "Jesus *moments*"—one of those enigmatic David gifts I am learning to transcend; a moment when Bruce smiles, opens his palms like a mystic, and says, "Just lift it up to Jesus. Isn't that what you people do?"

But that can wait. Right now I have some important news. Big news. The county has come through with a shot at a custodial job for David at a federal office building.

"It's the big one, Dave. The one we've been waiting for. You've got an interview first thing Thursday morning."

"Will there be soldiers there?"

"Well, it's a military base. I suppose there will be soldiers. The job is cleaning their offices. You up for that?"

"Oh, yeah. Oh, yeah—that's really something else." He articulates this quite formally, like he's somebody's Great-uncle Wellington-Smythe, but he looks like he's about to bust with pride. Oh, the stubbornness of hope.

As I turn away, David picks up his cell phone and punches in some numbers.

"Hey, Isaac," he says. He's called his friend the Pentagon cop, who picks up on the first ring, and I can almost see Isaac's big dog Marko, ears pricked, leaning over his shoulder in the police cruiser. "Hey, it's me, David. Guess what?"

It is early October now, the night before his big interview. David has gone for an extra-long run this evening, followed by a steamy half hour in the shower. He lays out his clothes and insists on a coat and a tie. When I say he "lays out his clothes," this means they are stretched like Flat Stanley all the way across the floor of his room, starting with the first thing he'll slip on—shirt with tie already knotted under the collar, jacket, pants—down to his socks and shoes, so he won't miss anything in the morning. I imagine him slithering out of bed feet first, sliding his toes and skinny torso through the knotted tie, coursing snake- like beneath the shirttail and on down into the pants legs until his toes slip into socks, then shoes, until, voilà, he's dressed.

Wasn't it Byron who claimed we are all differently organized?

"Oops," I say, noticing a tiny glitch in the layout. "You'll need black socks with your dress shoes, not white anklets. So remember. In the morning, look in Dad's drawer for a pair of black socks. Don't forget, okay?"

Silence.

"Black socks. Now, get some sleep." I flip off the light. "Night."

Silence while I stand there in the dark.

"Hey, Dave. When someone says good night to you, you say good night back at 'em. So—good night, David."

A head shake, maybe a tic.

"Okay," I say. "Black socks. Dream about black socks."

Very early the next morning, he walks into the kitchen looking sharp for the interview. I'm impressed. Then he begins his circling routine. He's missing something, but not really looking for it, just circling me until the repetition of his nearby footsteps permeates the op-ed page of the *Post* and I snap out of it and say, "What? What are you missing?"

"My smart card." The Metro pass that goes missing at least once a week.

"Look, you can't be late today. Just use cash. C'mon on, I'll drop you off at the station."

I'm driving him down the road, fiddling with the radio buttons for the weather report, when I look down on the floorboard and see his bony ankles. It's 39° outside on this mid-autumn morning and he's barefoot, his pearly-white ankles sockless inside his heavy dress shoes.

Emily Post said you can only make a first impression once.

Well, I'm not going to explode. Nope, not going to do that this morning. Because I know when David gets stressed, he begins to tic. He's due at the most important job interview in his life in forty-five minutes, and I'm pretty sure Raging Tourette's is not the first image he should project when he walks through that door. Just thinking things through here, not stirring things up . . . staying calm on my end. Also, I happen to be wearing a pair of black socks.

"David?" I swallow hard. "Listen, you. I'm not gonna ask why you're not wearing any socks this morning. Too late for that. You'll just have to go with me here: I have on black socks. Grab the wheel so I can pull 'em off and you put 'em on. Got it?" My clenched jaw quivers. "Just . . . keep your eyes on the road."

I keep one foot on the gas, and channeling some serious yoga, pull the other foot to my chest and yank off a sock. As David leans in to take the steering wheel, I pick up the fresh scent of shaving cream. His eyes are scanning the road and I give him a good sniff. Oh, there it is. A plug of Barbasol in his left ear.

"Wipe the shaving cream out of your ear—quick."

He lets go of the wheel and swipes his ear with a black sock. That's when I notice his fingernails looks like a female hand model's. Clean, but there's way too much of them.

"Ah, jeez, Dave. You didn't cut your nails. They're longer than mine. You can't go to a—oh, forget it! Bite 'em off! You heard me—bite 'em off right now and spit 'em out."

As David chomps down on his nails, I feel the months of

anticipating this interview twisting in my gut. The job may be cleaning bathrooms and dusting stairwells, but the stakes are high. We gotta get it right the first time. I have reworked his résumé for this interview and droned on and on about how he should shake hands! Look 'em in the eye! Speak up! How he should highlight his unique strengths with a positive spin, such as being physically fit and having no earthly interest in interoffice politics. But now we are both nervous.

I pull into the Kiss-and-Ride at the Metro station and turn on him, schizy as a cheerleader with the game tied and the clock winding down.

"All set? Got your ID? Can't get in without your ID, you know. There might be more than one David! Ha-ha-HAH!"

As he hops out of the car I call out to him one last time, the game in the balance. "Go get 'em, Dave. Handshake! Eye contact!!"

He walks off without a word, his lips pursed weirdly in place. As he turns away, I see that his tie is upside down, flipped inside out.

Twenty minutes later, I'm back home in the kitchen, sipping cold coffee and assuring Bruce ("Hey, it wasn't so bad. Yeah. No, really! It could've been a whole lot worse . . ."), when the phone rings.

It is David.

"Mom. Guess what? I left my ID in the car."

I have lived this moment before.

I put down the cup of cold coffee and hand the phone to Bruce. "Here, Big Guy. It's for you . . ."

I gaze outside into the swirl of October's leaves. The open

kitchen window is full of the cool fall air. I hear them before I see them. Crunching leaves with their patent leather hooves, a family of deer glides across my backyard, sashaying through the sloping garden that has wrecked my knees and ankles time and again over the last twenty years. The four of them have come for their breakfast. "Git!" I whisper from a place buried deep in my southern childhood, but the vigilant mother deer understands this means *You are a delight to observe, eat what you will.* I stand at the window and watch.

"Try the poison ivy," I suggest, eye to eye with her.

The angle of the wind whips the whirligigs into a mad dervish as the trees release ever more of their offshoots, a timeless reminder of nature's easy way of letting go. Inside this house, I was once the mother deer. Leading a pack of look-alike sons who ate what they wanted and moved on when they'd had enough. Only now, it seems, one of them has stayed behind.

I rifle through the fridge for a couple of eggs and step out the kitchen door onto the deck. The wind has picked up and it floats my breath in the brisk air.

Splashed in fine morning light, I slip out of my shoes and plant my sockless feet flat on the boards. I bring the egg up tight against my chest and inhale. Squeezing it with both hands broadens my shoulders. And here I pause.

First, to breathe in. I will never fix any of this. I can only accept it. On the other hand, David's ingenuousness has softened the hearts of his older brothers. His resilience has earned the respect of his father. And, time after time, David has taught me to do what has to be done and to simply do it. It's as uncomplicated as a pair of black socks.

I zero in on the brick wall under my bedroom window and exhale in a slow release. Packing everything I can inside the little egg, I reach back and fire off a real haymaker.

Thwack! I shake it off like a wet dog.

Bruce, on his way out to rescue David yet again, steps onto the deck and blanches at the exploded mess sliding down the wall. "Damn, kiddo," he says. "Who's the crazy one now?"

There is one more egg left to throw. It feels smooth in my hand, solid as a rock. I pook it into the air, throwing like the girl that I am. It sails upward, misses the wall entirely, and settles in a deep pocket of pachysandra with only a thin crack around its base. Damaged and less than perfect, somehow the little egg has managed not to break apart.

For six months there is no news about the job. But over the years, David has taught me to grow accustomed to waiting a long time for people to tell him when he can move on. He's waiting too long right now, here, behind the wheel of the little Jeep. He looks hard at every driver at this four-way stop, waiting for the subtle signal that means it's his turn to move forward. Somebody finally honks *Go!* at him, and he taps two jaunty fingers to his forehead and presses into the intersection. He displays a focus I admire and it dawns on me that he is reading facial cues now. He is changing out of the lost little boy I remember, gradually finding his own way around. Driving, he is in complete control for the first time, making choices for himself and doing what he wants with his life. And I am comfortable in the passenger seat, no longer needing to be the driving force in his life. Truth? I feel much safer with David behind the wheel than I did with his brothers at this age, because there is no hint of road rage inside him. Whenever he gets spooked by another driver, instead of getting agitated or combative, he simply puts on his blinker and slides out of the way. Like he once said, he finds trouble "too complicated," so he steers clear of it.

In early spring, we get the great good news: hired! David will become part of the huge American workforce that cleans office buildings for the military personnel at a local army base. He will quit the barbecue job but keep ushering on weekends at the ballpark. The new job comes with a starchy uniform and a steady salary with health benefits that might someday enable him to live independently. Most important, the job offers David a little dignity.

Now, every morning he sets his clocks for 5:20. He dresses and steps out into the darkness, cranking the little Jeep in the cool dawn air, the radio blasting for his stop-and-go commute. Just like everybody else. He builds in time for coffee along the way, pulling out a $10 bill to pay for a single cup, then walks away. His generosity is not because his custodian job gives him such deep pockets; it is because he still wants to avoid the unworkable math involved in the exchange and, even more, the eye contact that goes along with it. Whose pocket that leftover chunk of change ends up in is totally dependent upon the scruples of the particular cashier. The easy solution? I set David up with a slim wallet full of one-dollar bills, and they can keep any change.

All this and he hasn't yet gotten to work.

Two steps forward, one step back. With his intense focus on military vehicles and repetitive tasks, David seems to have the makings of a model worker at a military installation, but my confidence does not last long. After a rocky start, a few months into the custodial job a human resources officer phones to invite me into her office to discuss why my son is not "a team player."

Here we go again.

David is becoming an unpeggable coworker and, according to one supervisor, "a pain in the neck." He tunes out detailed directions from his boss and takes his lunch break alone. When the task is to vacuum under a desk, he insists that it's faster to go around it. When his job coach shadows him to make sure he does the job right, David brushes her off, making it clear he doesn't like "being stared at." Leaving work one afternoon, David stops by to inform his supervisor, "I'm off the clock now. You can't boss me around anymore."

Hoo-boy. Surely the next thing coming is a little pink slip with David's name on it, but the thoughtful human resources officer has something else in mind. She assures me that federal law protects the rights of disabled workers. It also means that reasonable accommodations should be made for them.

Instead of tossing my kid out, she wants to talk candidly about autism in the workplace.

"Come in," she says. "We should talk."

Here is a golden opportunity to peel back the layers on two decades of life with my quirky son. But it's tricky. Her opening question is a doozy. "What does it mean to be autistic?"

The face-off begins with my mantra: "I'm no expert, but I can tell you this: If you've met one autistic person, then you've met one autistic person. Each with his or her own quirks."

"But what should we do different for him?" This woman gets points in my book for really trying.

So, using what David has taught me, I decide to be blunt.

"Don't talk so much," I tell her. When she nods okay, I go for it. "Don't be subtle. Just say the thing clearly, then watch his face for a clue when he shuts down."

"What about his lack of focus?"

"He needs structure. A consistent work schedule and intensive training."

"You know, he's very rigid. Doesn't like to take directions from his supervisor."

"Yes. So your flexibility is the key. Give him a little more physical space than you think is necessary. And when things go well, it's a handshake that he can see coming, not a backslap."

"I understand the 'Don't touch' part," she says, "but what about his rudeness?"

I stifle either a giggle or a sob, a too-familiar lump in my throat.

"Yeah, well . . . there is that. All I can say is, he's not aware of what others are thinking. The rudeness is actually missed social cues. It can't be fixed; it can only be worked around. So here's the thing: Try to take yourself out of the equation—because it's not about *you*. When David steps through a door ahead of you and lets it slam in your face, don't take it personally. Trust me, it's not easy, good Lord, not easy at all. . . . You can expect to have your feathers ruffled from time to time."

We look at each other and hunch our shoulders. She fiddles with her notes a bit, then says, "And what's all this about being stared at?"

Now she's hit on one of his stronger quirks.

"You know, my kid has tried to stifle Tourette's his whole life, and being watched has made him extra-sensitive to it. So tell your staff"—and I work hard to say this without a trace of sarcasm—"tell 'em to quit staring."

She shakes her head and smiles a little smile that doesn't come packed with any laughter. Our meeting has become an exercise in counterintuitiveness, but two things are clear: First, most people don't have a clue about what it means to be autistic. And second, it is not David who will have to change, but the way others might perceive him.

Wrapping up, the woman has one more question. "How likely is it," she wants to know, "that we will be seeing more of these sorts of employees in the near future?"

Oh, this one I've got. How many times have I read statistics that show that today alone—yes, this very day—roughly 110 American families will be told by their doctor "Your child has autism," and 70 of those children will be boys. So I tell this considerate counselor she can expect a steady stream of résumés like my son's to be crossing her desk. And soon.

"Our kids are growing up."

One step back. Despite my talk with the woman from human resources, David still has trouble interacting fluidly with his supervisors. He has been transferred to a mobile work crew. His hourly pay is the same, but he has a much shorter work-week and has lost his health benefits. This pushes back his dream of moving out on his own for a while longer. On the bright side, he's still got his weekend ushering job during baseball season, and being on the mobile work crew has its good points. So now, every morning, rain or shine, he hops in a van with a gang of four men charged with cleaning public parks. They pull trash bags from sidewalk bins and clean the grounds as they push on, moving at a fast clip through their daily route. Working outside, David can watch the seasons change, feel the wind against his face, and maybe get in a little bird-watching. A good fit for a guy who longs for the freedom to roam at his own pace, away from too many watchful eyes.

GOING THE DISTANCE

Marine Corps Marathon—October 2009.

His finish time is three hours and fifty-two minutes, but that's not the story. Because we already knew the boy could run. We just didn't know how far he would go.

The night before the race, around midnight, he asks me to make a sign with his name on it for his running shirt.

"Good idea." I switch on my bedside lamp and reach for my glasses. "Let's do it."

With him hanging over my shoulder, we create a flashy DAVID F sign to pin to the back of the shirt. In every corner I type in my cell number and name, I tell him, just in case. Jesus Christ, in case of what? He slips the shirt over his head, takes it for a tight spin around the bedroom. Then he reaches behind his back and rips it off.

"It makes too much noise," he says.

"Right . . . hand me my sewing kit."

I sew the red-and-black sign across the back of his shirt with a big looping backstitch. I hold it up for him and he seems pleased.

When David takes off at dawn for the pre-race warm-ups, the sign lies crumpled on the floor of his closet, snippets of thread still clinging to my cell number.

The weather is perfect for the runners' long day ahead: sunlight bursting through the leaves, fall in the air. With the streets blocked off to cars, hordes of pedestrians travel along the monument trails to cheer on the runners. There is a roving excitement that snakes along the Jefferson Memorial, up the hill, and around the U.S. Capitol. Crowds gather beside the Lincoln Memorial and wander across Memorial Bridge with its gilded bronze horses that spur the runners toward Arlington Cemetery and the finish line at the Iwo Jima statue. As we crisscross the city on foot, the cool beauty of this granite city lifts my spirit.

With us is Eric's girlfriend, Kelly, a former college runner who's driven in from her home in Pennsylvania to watch David's race. Neither Eric nor Max could be here today, so Kelly has come to represent their part of David's small entourage. I like having her here because, while David is sure to ignore Bruce and me, he might make a special effort to let the lovely Kelly notice him run by. I'm hoping he'll even look for her at the end of the race.

At mile sixteen on the approach to the Lincoln Memorial, Bruce picks David out of the field of twenty-one thousand runners. David is more than halfway done and he still looks good out there. Running tall. He is easy enough to spot because he runs elegantly, upright, with his elbows tucked neat against his ribs. As he passes I wave and shout his name. To the casual observer it would appear that we had not connected.

But we have. He's aimed a head tic my way—two jerks to the right. All mine.

Behind David is a tall, lanky guy in a flowing black beard and wig topped off by a baseball cap, beat-up shoes, and floppy shorts. A spectator, the young man next to me in the crowd, gets a kick out of the runner's clever wit and yells, "Run, Forrest, run!" It is one of many silly costumes on this late October weekend, but the runner suited up for laughs is now being outpaced by my real-life Forrest Gump.

Coming up well behind David, a man pumps his hand-crank past Lincoln's big chair. He sports a BE ALL YOU CAN BE T-shirt and a red, white, and blue flak helmet. His dark-skinned biceps are the size of the pumpkins I've just set on my front porch for the trick-or-treaters. The vet's left leg ends at the knee in an Ace bandage, and when someone on the sideline calls out "You got this!" his grimace turns into one helluva wicked grin.

It's time for Bruce and Kelly and me to trot our little posse across Memorial Bridge toward Arlington Cemetery. David has been running for nearly three hours now. Approaching the Iwo Jima statue, the three of us press in among the mob of onlookers to watch and wait for him on a legendary hill one hundred yards from the marathon's finish line.

Before they reach the end, all of the runners must endure the racecourse's most cruelly macho quirk: a grueling 45° incline with the end mile marker close in sight. It's the ultimate gut check as calves and Achilles tendons, quads and hamstrings, shocked into fatigue by the previous twenty-six miles, get a welcome home from the Leathernecks.

The first competitor to cross the line is U.S. Navy, breezing in on tiptoe with a smile and an extended fist. Then a U.S. Army runner gallops in, followed by the day's best marine sprinter yelling "Ooh-rah!" A half hour later the first woman jogs up the hill, determined and fresh-looking. Her spunky smile sends the crowd into a frenzied cheer.

Other elite runners follow by the dozen, but the shock of the final hill has begun to take its toll on less-strong contenders. At the bottom of the incline, they clutch their hamstrings, their faces contorting as they pull up, hobbled by a bolt of searing pain. A middle-aged athlete with the beginnings of a belly executes a sharp about-face and, shameless, takes mincing steps up the hill backward.

The crowd applauds. Whistles.

As the big clock ticks on at the finish line, we still haven't seen David. He'd hoped to run the marathon in under four hours, but he had trained alone all those months and never wore a watch, so who could say where he might be and in what condition? But I'm not going to worry today, because one thing life with David has taught me: worrying never makes much difference in the way things turn out.

Three and a half hours into the race, my wrists are purple

from all the clapping. While the elite runners are already kicking back and enjoying their post-race beer, the crowd has really come alive to urge on the everyday runners. We imagine we can feel their pain. We think maybe next year we'll give it a try. That's when I notice the soldier from mile sixteen, the dark-skinned hand-crank wheelchair racer in the BE ALL YOU CAN BE T-shirt, approaching the incline.

I tug on Bruce's arm. "That's the guy who was keeping pace with David. I bet he'll be coming in right behind him. Keep an eye out."

But the drama right before us is too compelling. We zero in on the vet as he begins to push his racer up the 45° climb. His pace slows to a measured crawl and the crowd can't make itself look away as, muscles quivering, the wounded soldier's strength starts to fade. A ruddy-faced young marine manning the race course drops down beside him on the sideline and shouts into his face, "One hundred yards, Army—you got it, you know you got it!"

But Army's shoulders have drooped and his racer rolls back a foot. He squeezes the hand crank again, the crowd whistling and clapping, rooting for him in knee-bent unison with a grunted "Ar-MEE! Ar-MEE!"

Army's biceps shimmy as he presses his gloved hands into the crank. Unsteady now, he climbs one agonizing inch at a time while dozens of able-bodied runners sidestep him, giving him a wide berth as they press on toward the finish line. But Army has lost ground. His entire body trembling on the verge of defeat, he fights to hold steady at this angle. For a moment, the only things that seem to be moving on this course are the digital taunts of the big clock.

Suddenly the field of runners parts to make way for another hand-crank racer who's barreling straight into Army with a full-throated rebel yell. This gray-headed fellow picks up ramming speed and pounds into the back of Army's racer, notching it forward a couple of feet. And then here he comes again. He's leading with his chin this time, bearing down on Army for a second pounding—full force and "Yee-haw!"

With a warrior's reserve of strength, Army braces for a direct hit that knocks him up the incline another foot or so. "Thank you, sir!" Army shouts, straining to hold his new position on the hill.

The older marine keeps it coming at the soldier, repeating the hit with the young army vet cranking and holding steady, and it's the two of them now—*BANG!*—"Thank you, sir!"—*BANG!*—"Thank you, sir!"—*BANG!*—all the way to the top of the hill.

The two vets pump across the finish line side by side and the crowd around the Iwo Jima statue lets loose like it's V-J Day and the Super Bowl all in one. When the whiplash of emotion dies down a bit, I look over at Bruce wiping his eyes with his shirt.

And then, at three hours and fifty-two minutes into the race, here comes Our Dave—loping toward the end like a skinny wolf. As he glides by us, there is a wonderfully raw sense of aliveness to the upward thrust of his jaw.

At the finish line, we push past hundreds of sweaty

shoulders wrapped in aluminum thermal blankets. We hope to pick David out of the sea of silver blankets, but we have lost sight of him altogether.

"Oh, Bruce," I say, slipping my arm through his. "We'll never hear him say how he made it up that hill."

"What's to know?" he says. "He made it."

By chance, an hour later I spot David in the middle of the street festival spawned by the post-race. A heavy silver medallion hangs from the blue ribbon around his neck. He seems stiff but not quite limping. I'd put money on it that he is the only first-time finisher to skip the free-massage tent.

The Navy jazz band has started up a tune, so I have to yell over a feisty clarinet to get his attention. "Dave! David! Over here!" David turns at the sound of my voice, but a juggler weaves through the crowd and makes off with his attention like a pickpocket. Still, I race toward him. Part of me wants to grab the boy in my arms and twirl him around in a wide, wide circle with his big feet flying. But that will no longer do. A trombone swooshes directly across my path, nearly knocking my teeth out, and for a heartbeat I catch the edge of Dave's smile.

So he has seen me after all. Pulling up next to him, I fight to rein in how happy I am for this young man I will never really know.

"Congratulations!" I reach up to hug him, and when he jerks away, the stubble of his beard grazes my arm. "God, you must be tired! Knees okay? How'd you feel on that last hill?"

"Good," he says, no longer offering me his eyes. The window into his puzzling world already slamming shut. "Good" is all he has to say about what it means to run alone for years in the dark, to train solo in the rain and cold, to get lost and to find himself, and to end up on this day with a medal around his neck. But David owns his life now, and the small hand that once reached up to us for balance has a compass of its own.

So, here in the middle of a street festival that is positively giddy with post-race excitement, a lone competitor stands in silent triumph. Once again he has left me bewildered over how he's transformed his life into something to be proud of. My mind reels back in time to the therapist who plopped one-year-old David into a mesh swing that hung from the ceiling. She wound it up tight and released it, free-spinning his little body into the outside world. "Step back and let him go," she insisted. "He'll be all right on his own. . . ."

Perhaps so, and maybe not. Unknowability will always surround this lanky young man, and that will have to do. All I know for certain is this: my duty now is the same as it was back then:

To step back and let him go.

And so today I shake his hand. A big old handshake with a wide-open grip that starts high in the air and, while I can still hold his hand in mine, we seesaw back and forth, back and forth.

Back and forth.

ONE YEAR LATER

It's the last Saturday in September. The end of David's second season with the Nats is coming to a close. The Metro is already hopping with activity when he and I get to the Clarendon station. We descend the steep escalator into the tunnel and squeeze onto the packed train just as the doors close. This morning we have separate plans. I will soon fade into the throngs at an end-of-summer festival on the Mall while he'll head over to the baseball stadium by the river. Since my stop comes first, we'll soon split off and go our separate ways.

I take the only empty seat I can find and swivel around to look for Dave. He stands alone near the doors, angling an elbow around the pole. He doesn't seem to want to touch it, but when the train accelerates he grabs on.

I turn away from him to stare at his reflection in the dark glass. It must be his usher's uniform and the Nationals name badge that give him an official look, because two subway riders approach him for directions. He tells them which station is coming up and when to exit. The doors open and they send him a casual nod. He looks them in the eyes and salutes them with a two-finger tap to his ball cap.

But there is something else going on here. Somehow in the last year David has evolved from boy to man. He is as stress-free as I've ever seen him. His body is nearly at peace, the tics relegated to a nearly imperceptible head tilt. Here, underground, David seems at ease among the riders who fill the seats and hug the walls as thick as bats. With a steady rumbling beneath his feet, he is just an average guy.

As the train slides over the rails deeper into the darkness, it strikes me once again how cavelike it is down here, a sheltering place whose maps hold order and promise for him. But there is also mystery in these dark passages. Attention must be paid.

And now I've done it again. I've lost track of where I am. I rise from my seat and wend my way through to David along the crowded aisle.

"When do I hop off?" I whisper it because, after all, I should know this by now.

His eyes sweep over me and keep on moving. He raises a cool finger and points to the map plastered to the wall behind him. Mine is the next stop.

Saved again by David.

When the doors open, I step out onto the station platform, pausing for a moment as the crowd surges past. On the dimly lit walls, signs point the way aboveground to the festival, already in full swing. The crowd files up the escalator in a huge wave, keen to break out into the sunshine, the dust, and the noise that stretches blocks and blocks along Independence Avenue.

This is where I must get off. But I am in no hurry.

The Metro doors slide shut and I pause on the deserted platform. Here, deep down below the busy avenue, it is cool and quiet. And I realize: David has gotten it absolutely right. Indeed, the next stop turns out to be mine.

As the train pulls away, I catch a last glimpse of a young man standing in the middle of the aisle, focused and unescorted, looking into the darkness for his place in the world.

AFTERWORD

In writing this book, I sat down with each member of my family to record and include their deepest memories of David. The goal was to build a bridge to connect him to us with our stories and, through them, perhaps connect David to the world at large. Of course, my take on David's world is only a single view, and the obvious voice missing in these pages is his own. Yet how could it be otherwise?

Bruce's sensible ground rule was that David's physical strengths be acknowledged. That sole observation led to a much deeper, more reliable portrait of this young man's inner landscape.

From the outset, both of his brothers were concerned that the retelling should not make David's life any more difficult. "Don't embarrass him," Eric insisted, still protective.

So, in these pages, we as a family have tried our best to

be honest in our unriddling of David, and somewhere inside our perceptions a memory collage has created its own truth.

What has surprised me most is the wide circle of support David has created for himself, by himself. A close look into David's quiet life has given me a glimpse of those who share an openness to the many different ways of being human. The funny thing is, I suspect many of these people know very little about autism. People like Harry the service station owner, Brian the spelunker, Max's old history teacher on Election Day, and Isaac the very good cop. Although they may be unfamiliar with terms like "mind-blindness" and "static encephalopathy," they know plenty about human decency. The world could use more like them.

Over time Bruce and I will become only two more people among the many others in David's story. Despite our persistent efforts to help him manage his life, he will be the one to determine how he will live it. He is now a grown man who has earned the dignity of risk and the decisions he will make for himself are the ones that will see him through. As we prepare to step off the stage and make way for David to begin to tell his own story, it is clear that he will not escape the pummeling of ignorance or malice in this world, but he will experience it on his own terms and he will know his victories in ways mysterious to the rest of us.

Ultimately, I hope this story will build an even broader bridge toward understanding autism—one that encourages increased empathy for a growing population whose universal calling card is the very absence of this achingly human emotion. In the long run, I believe all of our lives will be better for it.

And wouldn't that be something else?

ACKNOWLEDGMENTS

First I would like to thank *Washington Post Magazine* editor David Rowell, a most careful listener who insisted I write about my son and who has been there for me at every turn. I am also grateful for the big-hearted encouragement of freelance writer Tamara Jones, the stranger who set this story on its course. From there on, I was in the good hands of superagent Richard Abate. It was Richard who landed on the idea for this book and he has my unending gratitude for his conscientious work ethic and continued enthusiasm. Over the next year and a half, my remarkably clear-thinking editor and publisher, Amy Einhorn, provided me with the room to grow and the support she knew it would take to complete this project. Amy's eagle-eyed crew at Putnam—Halli Melnitsky, Elizabeth Stein, and David Chesanow—helped make the arduous task of copyediting a rewarding challenge to return to, day after day.

Early on, in order to picture how this book should look and

ACKNOWLEDGMENTS

sound, I leaned heavily on the knowledge of others. Shannon O'Neill at the Writers Center guided me along in the professional design of a book proposal. Pentagon Police Sgt. Isaac Ho'opi'i and webmaster Derek Wilson were both patient with my questions and generous with their expertise. Kynneth Sutton, Larry Dinger, and Martha and Rick Neave of the Washington Nationals baseball organization provided me with hours of hospitality and individual insight. The story began to take real shape when the good folks at the Virginia Center for the Creative Arts in the Blue Ridge Mountains offered me a quiet room to write in, while just outside my window a hard winter pasture transformed itself into a bright spring meadow.

When it came time for fresh eyes to see the pages, Amina Hafiz Sarraf, Alex MacLennan, Janet Auten, Alice Powers, Jim McManus, David Mills, and Steve Cheng stepped in as smart, tough, but generous critics—exactly what you need from good writers and trusted friends. For their encouragement of my work, I thank Nickie Athanason, Lisa Solod, Jeannette Hektoen, Linda Richardson, Neill Slaughter, and Dick Traum. I am also indebted to authors Richard McCann, Jack McDevitt, Denise Orenstein, Andrew Holleran, Robert Bausch, Keith Leonard, Myra Sklarew, Chico Harlan, Phyllis Theroux, Roy Blount, Jr., and Ellen Herbert.

As a final point, it's often said that the remarkable thing about writing a family memoir is that the people closest to you will claim it's all lies, but if you call it fiction, they'll holler it's all too true— and nobody's happy either way. So I have to give it up here to my older sons Max and Eric for allowing me to sculpt parts of this story from what I've come to realize is their unique perspective as David's brothers. I am also grateful for David's own inimitable cooperation, the young man who gave us this story and the one who will determine how it plays out.

And through it all, after the cat's inside and the doors are locked each night, still waiting for me at the top of the stairs is my straight arrow Bruce, whom I will always turn to for the gift of his light and tender heart.

READERS GUIDE FOR

NEXT STOP

BY GLEN FINLAND

A CONVERSATION WITH
GLEN FINLAND,
AUTHOR OF *NEXT STOP*

Your youngest son is at the center of your family memoir, *Next Stop*. What is the book about?

Next Stop is the story of the summer I spent teaching my twenty-one-year-old son, David, who is tall, dark, and autistic, to ride the Washington, D.C., Metro by himself. In the process, he taught me how to let him go. His farecard turns out to be the best investment we ever made—his own set of wheels that will take him to a job, an apartment, and a shot at a real life he can call his own. But the story of a child with autism is also the story of the family who loves him, because autism affects everybody in the family, out there winging it every day. At various times while they were growing up, David's two older brothers were conflicted by feelings of loyalty, love, and embarrassment. And that was a crucial element to include in the story.

What surprised me most is the love story that came to light through the prism of our youngest child's autism. For the first time in our long marriage, I really tried to look at life through my husband's eyes. What I saw there was not how but *why* fathers of children with hidden disabilities often struggle with denial. After two sons, the rules of the game as my husband, Bruce, knew it changed completely when David was born. My husband is the first to admit he's not a very patient man, but he taught himself how to be another kind of father. No small task, because the job has no endpoint. It takes an enormous amount of maturity to parent a special-needs child, yet rather than try to change David, Bruce came up with ways to support a different kind of boy. Along the way he and I made a mountain of mistakes, but Bruce was absolutely determined to stick it out. "I'm not giving up on him," he told me a thousand times, "and neither are you."

How has "letting go" of David proven different from letting go of your older sons?

Young adults with autism are entitled to private lives just like their neurotypical siblings, but reaching independence involves the dignity of risk. I have found that risking failure has been humbling and empowering for both David and me. Especially when it comes with a do-over. Often, I close my eyes and watch him jump off a figurative cliff—I'm hoping for the best, but not expecting it. Like the first time I watched him hop on that subway train and disappear into the tunnel. I honestly wasn't certain I'd ever see him again. It's enough to make you crazy, but I've learned there's no whining in autism. Mostly because it's such a private thing between you and your child without a lot of folks around who *get* it. Who among us parents doesn't want to be able to say to our adult children, "Go lead your own life"? Roots and wings—the natural order of things. Whether it's protecting himself from an unscrupulous predator or fighting for competitive wages, the choices David makes going forward will create the map to a life he will one day call his own.

David's is a story of autism and special needs, but are there universal lessons any parent can take away from *Next Stop*?

Absolutely. All parents can relate to the image of giving their kids roots and wings. It's nature's way. But there's something else going on here. After I've done a reading, folks often come up to tell me their own stories—not just about autism, but also about personal struggles with substance abuse, depression, grief, or domestic violence, anything that has left them feeling isolated or marginalized by a society that finds them easy to overlook. Even parents of neurotypical children often find themselves protecting their kids in an ongoing stealth battle against subtle slights. I think many readers delight in the little ways David has found to push back on those people who think they own the blueprint for what it means to be human. Because it takes all kinds.

How have your older sons reacted to *Next Stop*?

Too often during their childhood the spotlight was not on them when it should have shone most brightly. So before I began the book, I asked their permission to write about them as the neurotypical testosterone-soaked teenage boys they really were. And about what life with David has taught them. We sat down with a tape recorder one-on-one so I could capture their responses verbatim. Max said, "Don't embarrass him, Mom." And Eric said, "Don't make his life any more difficult than it already is." Good advice. Several chapters rip the scabs off old wounds and they still hurt each of us to revisit them, but the story wasn't believable when I whitewashed it, so we agreed to let history be history. The result is my looking you straight in the eye and saying, *This is what happened*. Max and Eric are out of the house and busy with productive lives of their own now, and they have earned my respect. They've also made it clear that they will step up to the plate when my husband and I are no longer there for David.

How has having a differently abled child affected your relationship with your husband?

Oh, I could write a book about that. *Oh, wait—I did*. Seriously, it is a daunting task, no matter how you decide to make it work; the stress will fray the edges of even the strongest marriage. All parenting is hard, but the stressors for parenting a child with special needs are different. It is the sheer eternalness of it—24/7, 365 days a year for the rest of your life. Studies show that marriages of couples with autistic kids hold together pretty well until the kids are about age eight. It's when those kids become older teens and college-age adults that parents start to question their commitment to each other and what the financial arrangement will be for the rest of the child's life. So you have to find a way to be kind to each other. Sounds simple? It isn't. You have to figure out how to salt away something for yourselves, to make your own life as a couple rich and whole. Here's one thing we did: Many years ago my husband and I made a pact. Once a year, I would take a separate vacation, by myself. I wouldn't need to ask permission from anyone. I would simply step outside my box as the mother of an autistic boy and two older sons and go be anonymous *me* somewhere. A refresher course. "Just go," Bruce always said. So one year I went fishing. Another, a weeklong bike ride. I spent the night in a hotel near our house once just to drink a cup of coffee at breakfast uninterrupted.

Selfish, you say? Yes, completely and without reservation. And probably the best thing I ever did for my family, because when mama's not happy, *nobody's* happy. Just knowing I could open the window onto my old self and still—*still!*—want to return to my quirky family life made the difference.

You look back into your own family for some clue about where David's autism may originate. Do you think there is a connection to the past?

That's a loaded question. There is plenty of guilt in parenting a *typical* child—let alone one who struggles—and the issue of blame is fraught. But what causes autism? We've come a long way from the legacy of Dr. Bruno Bettelheim, who blamed "refrigerator mothers" who didn't show their children enough love. The answer is . . . we don't know. The latest research suggests a strong biological/neurological connection. Environmental toxins in the food we eat and the air we breathe are also suspect. On the other hand, current clinical evidence does not support a link between the MMR vaccine and autism. I think the answers lie somewhere between the brain and the gut, mixed together with each individual's genetic blueprint.

Explain the saying "If you've met one autistic child, you've met one autistic child."

When you think of people who have autism, think *snowflakes*, because each individual is neurologically unique. There is no one-size-fits-all poster child for autism, because the spectrum is so broad. An autistic individual doesn't look, talk, or walk any certain way. And that's why our stories are important: we families live the reality that researchers are digging ever deeper to comprehend. While we may not understand it, we *get* it, and other healing agents will come out of telling our stories. The word "autistic" is not the latest model of the mean-spirited R-word, used for decades to diminish people with intellectual disabilities. Rather, it's sort of a diagnostic catchall, and I'm not willing to turn it into a weapon to be used against autistic people when autism awareness is what we're trying to get across to the public. Using the word freely should help break down the *Rainman* stereotype people seem stuck on. Consider: If we embrace the word—just bust it wide open and use it as a learning tool—it might encourage people to start paying attention to the wide range of autistic individuals, in all their rich variations.

What have been the largest hurdles in David's quest for independence? The biggest triumphs?

The biggest triumph, the kickiest agent of change in my son's life, came the first day he bought a subway ticket and took off solo—his own set of wheels. Freedom! Imagine what that means to any young man. From that moment on, David mastered more complex ways to be independent, and it gave him the chance to be what he really wants to be: a regular guy. On the downside, the largest hurdle for him continues to be mind-blindness, the poor social skills that isolate him and make him appear to be unaware of others' feelings. Here's the thing: When David's older brothers leave the nest, their circle of support will broaden naturally with new friends and lovers and business associates. When David leaves the nest for good, his circle of support will shrink. Some things can't be sugarcoated, and this is one of them.

How has writing this book helped you personally to better understand David's reality?

It's turned me into an accidental noticer. It's often said that Outsiders see, Insiders know. I see people differently now. When I began the book, I thought it would be about letting go of David as he matured into an adult, but the deeper story is about accepting parts of a young man I will never fully understand and then stepping out of his way to let him make his own choices. I'd also like to think I have pulled a few readers into a different world and given them a connection they'll want to keep to better understand individuals with cognitive disabilities. For example, one reader told me she is less judgmental about the people around her on the Metro these days. Another told me he looks for David every time he heads to the ballpark.

It would be nice to think that the image of David as a regular guy might linger awhile. Maybe then we could start to change the conversation about autism, to move away from causes and cures, blessings and blame. But first we need to stop seeing people with autism as targets for pity or therapy and make room for a different kind of employee heading into the workforce with the legal rights he or she deserves. The real lives of autistic young adults are very nuanced, just like yours and mine. And these kids will grow up to face real-world problems just like ours—they'll need jobs and affordable housing, which will lead to meaningful and independent lives.

Where is David now?

David continues to work for the Washington Nationals during baseball season. The rest of the year he works with a supported employment service provider, doing various jobs. He prefers to be outside, even in rain, snow, sleet—he's out there and he likes it. He runs long-distance races, training solo for DC's Marine Corps Marathon and the New York City Marathon. That's when he is happiest and feeling the most independent. Recently, I've noticed a real maturity in David's decision-making abilities. He even carries himself with more confidence and an undeniable athletic grace. He's still aiming for that apartment of his own, and he'll get there one day. It's something we can all agree on.

DISCUSSION QUESTIONS

1. Rather than telling the story chronologically, Glen jumps back and forth in time, and sometimes there are no dates at all. Why do you think she chose this tactic? How does it help her to tell the story?

2. A portion of the book addresses how Glen feels guilty that she wasn't able to dedicate as much time to Max and Eric. How did Glen's limited attention to her older sons impact their development, both negatively and positively? Did Bruce struggle with a similar divide of attention?

3. The Metro plays a significant part in the story, acting as a supporting character; David gains independence when he learns how to take it alone. What else does the Metro symbolize for David? What about for Glen?

4. A major theme in *Next Stop* is time and how David's past and future is his present. "He couldn't know how devastating it was to lose time in a life where there was no extra time" (87). Why do you think Glen chooses to focus on this as she tells David's story?

5. When David is in Florida, Glen feels liberated, saying, "I did not feel guilty, but the new freedom struck me as flirting with danger, like driving down a dark country road with the headlights off" (10). Do you think her feelings are justified? How would you react if you were in her shoes?

6. When David expresses himself, he says exactly as he means, and his view of what is important is dramatically different from those around him. How does that change the family dynamic?

7. Discuss David's relationship with animals. He shares a genuine connection with all species—why do you think that is?

8. When David gains the right to vote, some very clear examples of the kind and unkind reactions from people in his everyday life are brought to light. What are some other examples? Since David physically fits in, what do you think makes people react to him the way they do?

9. Ultimately this is a story about a family. Which family member did you most identify with? Do you share traits with all of them?

10. In the afterword Glen writes, "So in these pages, we as a family have tried our best to be honest in our unriddling of David." Do you think they accomplished their goal?

11. Kynny's "purple" world view is an interesting concept, and David greatly benefits from it. Do you know anyone in your life who embodies that? Do you think it's practical? Why or why not?

12. What do you think started Sug's ritual of throwing eggs to release tension? What is your version of throwing eggs?

13. Sports and music both play a very strong role in the family dynamic. How much does David participate? Do you think this impacted his development, and how?

14. After David runs his marathon, Glen says, "Once again he has left me bewildered over how he's transformed his life into something to be proud of" (291). What are some of David's achievements that particularly resonated for you?

ABOUT THE AUTHOR

Glen Finland lives in the Washington, D.C., area. A former reporter, she received her MFA from American University, where she has taught writing. She is the 2012 recipient of the University of Georgia Henry Grady College of Journalism and Mass Communication's Medal of Excellence in Communication for *Next Stop.*

Visit the author's website at www.glenfinland.com.